The Nibelung's Ring

Peter Bassett has been an advocate of *The Ring* ever since hearing radio broadcasts of the Bayreuth Festival as a teenager. As a professional diplomat for more than twenty years, he was able to pursue his passion for opera – and Wagner's works in particular – in many parts of the world. He is now a recognised authority on the subject and is Dramaturg and Artistic Administrator for the 2004 Adelaide *Ring* – the first completely Australian production of this great work.   PHOTO: FAIE DAVIS

Wakefield
Press

The Nibelung's Ring

A GUIDE TO WAGNER'S DER RING DES NIBELUNGEN

PETER BASSETT

Wakefield Press
1 The Parade West
Kent Town
South Australia 5067
www.wakefieldpress.com.au

First published 2003

Cover and book designed by designBITE, Adelaide
Typeset by Michael Deves, Adelaide
Printed and bound by Hyde Park Press, Adelaide

National Library of Australia
Cataloguing-in-Publication entry

Bassett, Peter.
The Nibelung's Ring: a guide to Wagner's Der Ring des Nibelungen.

Bibliography.
Includes index.
ISBN 1 86254 624 X.

1. Wagner, Richard, 1813–1883. Der Ring des Nibelungen.
2. Wagner, Richard, 1813–1883 – Criticism and interpretation.
I. Title.

782.1

CONTENTS

NOTE ON THE ARTIST

HUGO L. BRAUNE, painter, lithographer and illustrator, was born on 1 February 1872 in Frankenhausen am Kyffhäuser in Thuringia. He studied at the School of Applied Arts in Leipzig and at the Academy of Fine Arts in Weimar under Th. Hagen and L. von Kalckreuth. He also studied in Munich, was active in Berlin in 1908, and was a war artist during the First World War. In Stuttgart he worked on a painted ceiling in the Königin-Olga-Bau (later destroyed). *Richard Wagner's Stageworks* was published in 1924, although the *Götterdämmerung* lithographs seem to have been prepared some years earlier. Other works include illustrations on the saga of Dietrich von Bern, and myths and folk tales. The date and circumstances of Hugo Braune's death are unknown. He may have died during the Second World War.

References
K.G. Saur, *Allgemeines Künstler-Lexikon*, 1996; Marcus Osterwalder, *Dictionnaire des illustrateurs*, 1989; Ulrich Thieme & Felix Becker, *Allgemeines Lexikon der bildenden Künstler*, 1910; *Dresslers Kunstjahrbuch*, 1909; W. Schäfer, *Steinzeichnungen deutscher Meister*, 1904/5.

ACKNOWLEDGEMENTS

I thank once again those whose names are recorded in the first edition of this book. To their number I gratefully add my sister-in-law, Dr Sherylee Bassett, for her expert advice on aspects of classical mythology and drama, and Dr Christine Rothauser, who has so generously allowed me to reproduce a complete set of the fine *Ring* illustrations of Hugo Braune, from her personal collection.

Peter Bassett, Canberra, 2003

PREFACE

In 1998 I gave a series of talks in connection with the production of *Der Ring des Nibelungen* in Adelaide. Those talks formed the basis of a book that I called *A Ring for the Millennium*. The study of Wagner's great work is a lifetime's adventure, and this revised version of the original book reflects the current state of my thinking. It has been published in preparation for a new production of *The Ring* by the State Opera of South Australia in 2004. This edition includes two new appendices – one is a prose version of Wagner's text, and the other some of the principal musical themes in *The Ring*.

Why a prose version of Wagner's poem? There are of course a number of excellent English verse translations available, including those by Peggie Cochrane, William Mann and Andrew Porter, all of which have been of assistance to me. However, it seems to me that a prose version is much easier to read, and there is no reason why it cannot preserve the detail and dramatic sense of the original. Librettos are intended to be sung, or at least to be read as if they were being sung. Liberties with meaning are often taken in translation in order to preserve structure, sound equivalents, rhythm and even appearance on the page. No such problems arise with a prose translation. I hope that mine will add to the appreciation by English-speaking audiences of Wagner's rich poetic lode.

Richard Wagner might well have achieved fame and fortune earlier in life if he had chosen the path of writing popular *bel canto* operas in the style of Bellini and Donizetti, or romantic spectacles in the style of Meyerbeer and Halévy. That he could have done either was never in doubt. In Paris in the early 1840s, he wrote a bass aria for Bellini's *Norma* (and convincing pseudo-Bellini it is too), and his first operatic success, *Rienzi*, was described by Hans von Bülow as Meyerbeer's finest work! Instead – and to the exasperation of his first wife, Minna – Wagner deliberately chose another, far more difficult path, and spent his life following it.

In the three operas that followed *Rienzi* – *Der fliegende Holländer*, *Tannhäuser* and *Lohengrin* – Wagner moved further and further into unchartered territory. After writing *Lohengrin*, which was performed in 1850, there was a pause of singular importance. For five years he wrote practically no music: then he composed *Das Rheingold*. Western music would never be the same again. After *Rheingold* came *Die Walküre*, two-thirds of *Siegfried* and *Tristan und Isolde*, but none of these ground-breaking works was seen or heard on stage until *Tristan* was performed in 1865, followed by *Die Meistersinger von Nürnberg* in 1868. Only in 1869 did *Rheingold* receive its first performance, fifteen years after its composition, and then at the insistence of King Ludwig II and against the wishes of the composer. Wagner wanted to wait until *The Ring* could be performed in its entirety. *Die Walküre* followed to the stage in 1870, again at Ludwig's insistence and despite Wagner's opposition. *Siegfried* and *Götterdämmerung* were not performed until 1876, on the completion of the Bayreuth theatre. That any artist could remain true to his goals and to himself over such a long time and in such testing circumstances is, in itself, a cause for admiration and wonder.

My own enthusiasm for *The Ring* is unabated after nearly forty years of discovery. I can still recall my delight on first hearing this remarkable music, and I am glad to say that, even after repeated hearings, it is still possible to re-awaken some of those original feelings, and to go on finding new beauties in the score and new perspectives on the drama.

SYNOPSIS

Der Ring des Nibelungen

(THE RING OF THE NIBELUNG)

A Stage Festival Play for Three Days and a Preliminary Evening

Das Rheingold (The Rhinegold) –
The Preliminary Evening

Deep in the River Rhine, three Rhinedaughters watch over their gold. Alberich (the Nibelung of the title) lusts after them. He learns that whoever renounces love and fashions a powerful ring from the gold can rule the world. In frustration, he renounces love and snatches the gold.

High on a mountain top, the god Wotan and his wife Fricka contemplate a gleaming fortress – Valhalla, an abode for gods and heroes, built by the giants Fasolt and Fafner. The giants had been promised the goddess Freia, keeper of the golden apples of eternal youth, as payment. But Wotan is reluctant to part with Freia since, without her apples, the gods will wither and grow old. Loge, god of fire and an accomplished trickster, provides a solution when he tells of Alberich's theft of the gold and manufacture of the ring.

Wotan and Loge climb down through a rocky cleft to Nibelheim, where Alberich's brother Mime and the other Nibelungs are enslaved, mining gold and working metals. Through Loge's trickery, Wotan takes Alberich prisoner and they all return to the surface. Wotan seizes the ring.

A bitter Alberich curses the ring and all who possess it. Instead of Freia, the giants agree to accept the Nibelung treasure, the ring and the Tarnhelm – a magic helmet of transformation and invisibility. Reluctantly, Wotan is persuaded to give up the ring by the earth goddess Erda, who warns him that the end of the gods is at hand. Almost at once, the giants quarrel over their prize and Fafner kills his brother. So Alberich's curse claims its first victim. The god Donner calls up the mists and Froh conjures up a rainbow bridge to Valhalla. As Wotan devises a plan to recover the ring and Loge looks on disdainfully, the gods pass into Valhalla triumphantly, insensitive to the lament of the Rhinedaughters below.

Die Walküre (The Valkyrie) – The First Day
ACT I

A man is being pursued through the forest during a stormy night and unwittingly takes refuge in the house of an enemy. Hunding, the owner, is absent but his wife takes pity on the stranger, and a bond starts to grow between them. Hunding returns and guesses the identity of his guest, who recounts the story of his childhood, the murder of his mother, the abduction of his twin sister and separation from his father, Wolf. The laws of hospitality protect the guest for the night but Hunding challenges him to combat the following day, and then retires with a drink in which his wife has put a sleeping draught. The stranger recalls his father's promise to provide him with a sword in his direst need. The woman draws attention to a sword buried in the trunk of an ash tree which grows through the centre of the house. She says that the sword had been put there by a one-eyed stranger during her wedding to Hunding, and no-one had been able to draw it out.

Passionate feelings grow between the guest and the woman and eventually she realises that he is the Volsung for whom the sword was intended. She names him Siegmund. He pulls the sword from the tree with a mighty wrench and calls it *Notung* – Needful. She tells him that she is his twin sister Sieglinde and they embrace ecstatically.

ACT II

While Siegmund and Sieglinde flee from Hunding, Wotan instructs his favourite Valkyrie daughter, Brünnhilde, to give victory to Siegmund in the impending fight against Hunding. Fricka, who is the guardian of marriage, is outraged, denounces the incestuous couple and castigates the promiscuous Wotan for not upholding divine law. Reluctantly, he agrees to give victory to Hunding. Wotan reveals to Brünnhilde his despair in the face of a declining, imprisoning destiny. He explains to her why they are bound to act against his own son, and demands her obedience.

Brünnhilde appears to Siegmund and tells him to prepare for death and a place in Valhalla – without Sieglinde. Moved by Siegmund's defiant response, Brünnhilde in turn decides to defy Wotan and to let Siegmund win. However, Wotan intervenes in the battle, Siegmund's sword is broken on Wotan's spear and Hunding plunges his spear into the unarmed man's chest. Bitterly, Wotan strikes Hunding dead with a wave of his hand. Brünnhilde flees Wotan's wrath, taking with her the pregnant Sieglinde and the broken pieces of the sword.

ACT III

On a wild mountain summit, Brünnhilde seeks refuge with her eight Valkyrie sisters. She tells Sieglinde to flee into the forest, gives her the pieces of the sword and informs her that she will bear the noblest hero, who will be named Siegfried. Wotan catches up with Brünnhilde and condemns her to mortality, to be left asleep and vulnerable to the first man who finds her. However, he is moved by her plea that she knew that he loved Siegmund and was only doing what he himself wanted in his heart. With great emotion, he bids her farewell and encircles her with magic fire through which only one who does not fear the point of his spear will be able to pass.

Siegfried – The Second Day
ACT I
Sieglinde has died giving birth to Siegfried. The boy has been raised in a remote part of the forest by the Nibelung Mime. Beyond Mime's forge in the forest, Fafner, in the guise of a dragon, guards his hoard and the ring. Siegfried has observed that all of the creatures of the forest resemble their parents and scoffs at the idea that Mime could be his father. Eventually, he is told the truth about his birth. Mime despairs of repairing the shattered sword *Notung*, with which he hopes Siegfried will recover the ring. Mime learns from the Wanderer (Wotan) that the sword can be restored only by one who does not know fear. Siegfried reforges *Notung*.

ACT II
Mime leads Siegfried to Fafner's cave. Resting under the green canopy of the forest, Siegfried wonders what his parents were like and if all human mothers die giving birth. He longs for congenial company and tries to communicate even with the birds of the forest. He awakens Fafner and, in the ensuing fight, kills him. Mime and Alberich squabble over who should get the treasure. When Siegfried involuntarily tastes Fafner's blood, he is able to understand the Woodbird's song and also Mime's murderous intentions. He kills Mime and then sets off towards the place where, the bird tells him, he will find a companion – Brünnhilde – who lies asleep.

ACT III

The Wanderer summons Erda, demanding of her whether his destiny can be changed. She is evasive and he accepts – indeed welcomes – the end of the gods. He recognises that the future now belongs to Siegfried. The young man arrives and the Wanderer stands in his way, seeing for himself that Siegfried is independent and fearless. Wotan's spear yields to the sword it had once shattered. After passing through the circle of fire, Siegfried awakens Brünnhilde with a kiss. At his first sight of a woman, he is alarmed and confused, but love stirs within them both. Siegfried and the now mortal Brünnhilde declare their love in terms of the utmost rapture.

Götterdämmerung (Twilight of the Gods) – The Third Day
Prologue and ACT I

The three Norns have spun the rope of world knowledge which binds past, present and future. They tell each other why they can no longer spin. The rope breaks in a premonition of the end of the existing order. Siegfried gives Brünnhilde the ring as a token of his love and sets off towards the Rhine, in search of adventure.

At a hall on the banks of the Rhine live the Gibichung rulers, Gunther and Gutrune, and their half-brother Hagen, the son of Alberich. Hagen urges Gunther and Gutrune to find partners and proposes Siegfried for Gutrune and Brünnhilde for Gunther. Siegfried arrives and is given a potion which blocks out the memory of Brünnhilde. Meanwhile, Brünnhilde rejects the pleas of her sister, the Valkyrie Waltraute, to free the gods from their impending doom by returning the cursed ring to the Rhinedaughters. To Brünnhilde, the ring symbolises Siegfried's love for her. Siegfried disguises himself as Gunther by means of the Tarnhelm, penetrates the circle of fire, seizes the ring and abducts Brünnhilde to be Gunther's bride.

ACT II

Hagen, slumbering on watch as he awaits the return of Siegfried and Gunther, is visited by his father Alberich who urges him to win back the ring. When, at the Gibichung court, Brünnhilde sees the ring in Siegfried's possession, she concludes that he has betrayed her. Misunderstanding her accusation, he swears on the point of Hagen's spear that he has not betrayed Gunther's trust and offers his body to the spear if he is lying. In turn, Brünnhilde, roused to fury, dedicates the blade to his downfall. Hagen plots Siegfried's death which will be made to look like a hunting accident. Brünnhilde and Gunther demand vengeance and Hagen invokes the spirit of his father Alberich, whose curse is about to claim another victim.

ACT III

During the hunt, Siegfried strays from the rest of the party to the river, where the Rhinedaughters try to persuade him to return the ring. He rebuffs them and rejoins the hunting party. He recounts the story of Mime, *Notung*, Fafner and the Woodbird. Hagen drops an antidote into Siegfried's drink and, gradually, as he speaks, his memory returns. When he recalls how he passed through the fire to Brünnhilde and embraced her, Gunther is shocked by this revelation. Hagen plunges his spear into Siegfried's back. Siegfried dies with the name of his beloved Brünnhilde on his lips, and is carried back to the hall of the Gibichungs.

Hagen kills Gunther in a fight over the ring. Brünnhilde interrupts the mourning. She understands Wotan's wish to end the rule of the gods and extinguish the curse which has now claimed her innocent lover. She directs the building of a funeral pyre and, taking the ring, joins Siegfried in the flames. The Rhine overflows its banks and, in the heavens, Valhalla itself is seen consumed by fire. The Rhinedaughters swim on the flood to reclaim the ring and, as Hagen tries to seize it, they drag him down into the depths. Thus the old order passes away. In its place is a new vision of human existence, revealed to Brünnhilde through her suffering and love.

The Rhinedaughters watch over the Rhinegold

AN INTRODUCTION TO

Der Ring des Nibelungen

R ichard Wagner wrote the text and music of *The Ring* between 1848 and 1874. Although he composed other masterpieces that had a profound effect on the direction of western art, it was *The Ring* that dominated the second half of his working life. He called it a 'stage festival play' and it comprises four operas: *Das Rheingold* (The Rhinegold), which is the preliminary evening, *Die Walküre* (The Valkyrie), *Siegfried* and *Götterdämmerung* (Twilight of the Gods).

The Ring is a drama of ideas. It belongs to no particular period but makes timeless statements about the destructive consequences of man's ruthless lust for power and greedy exploitation of nature.

Wagner was the most intellectual of composers and one of the great minds of the nineteenth century. For *The Ring* he drew on Greek tragedy, Germanic and Norse mythology, the writings of nineteenth-century philosophers and his own experiences in the social uprisings that swept Europe in the 1840s. As a result, *The Ring* can be interpreted from many political and sociological perspectives. Wagner originally intended it as a political allegory of his own century. However, over time, he became more concerned with questions of human nature and motivation, anticipating ideas that would later interest Freud and Jung.

What motivated Wagner to write this gigantic work? In a word – politics. He had been born in Saxony in 1813 during the Napoleonic wars and within twenty years of the French Revolution. As a young radical, he was convinced that the basic goodness of human beings had been subverted by the property-owning classes and the selfish interests of the state. Even though he became court conductor in Dresden at the age of twenty-nine and had notable successes with his operas *Rienzi*, *Der fliegende Holländer* (The Flying Dutchman) and *Tannhäuser*, he sympathised with reform movements that swept Europe in the wake of the industrial revolution.

1848, the year in which he first sketched out his ideas on the Nibelung myth, was also the year in which revolutions broke out in many European capitals, and Marx and Engels published their *Manifesto of the Communist Party*. Wagner sided with the revolutionaries and was involved in writing pamphlets, ordering munitions and reporting on troop movements. The Dresden uprising was suppressed and a warrant was issued for his arrest for treason. With the help of Franz Liszt, he managed to escape into Switzerland and exile.

Richard Wagner was an impassioned artist, not a political theorist, and his revolutionary leanings were motivated primarily by his artistic frustrations. He railed against shallow attitudes towards art, and against a soul-less and materialistic society that perpetuated such shallowness.

The Ring, as first conceived, was intended as a political allegory. The ruling class (represented in the story by the giants, used to simple-minded inactivity and ease) was succumbing to the greedy capitalism of the industrial revolution (represented by Alberich the Nibelung), while the Saxon king and his family (represented by Wotan and the other gods) were pragmatically trying to manipulate events and preserve their position. Wagner believed that, eventually, a new and more humane society would arise, characterised by the legendary Siegfried, a man who, in a loveless world, 'never ceases to love'. During the course of the intended opera – then called *Siegfrieds Tod* (Siegfried's Death) – the hero would confront the gods, Brünnhilde would purge their guilt by an act of self-immolation and a reformed Wotan would continue to reign in splendour. The lovers would share a glorious after-life together. Meanwhile, in the political arena, Wagner was publicly expounding the notion that the aristocratic/plutocratic regime should be swept away while the reformed Saxon king would remain, like Wotan, father of his people and head of a crowned republic. Thus, life would imitate art.

This was soon to change. By mid-life, Wagner had become a very different person. His breath-taking idealism had gone and he no longer looked to politics for solutions to society's problems. He was profoundly cynical of all forms of government and the mechanisms of production, distribution and exchange. He had reached the conclusion that there was no remedy for humanity's ills, at least by way of collective action. In October 1854 he wrote to Liszt: 'Let us treat the world only with contempt; for it deserves no better; but let no hope be placed in it, that our hearts be not deluded! It is evil, evil, *fundamentally evil* ... It belongs to Alberich: no one else! Away with it!'[1]

So, during the last three decades of his life, Wagner was more concerned with metaphysical issues than with political ones. In his greatest works – those written after the mid-1850s – he looked inwards at human nature, rather than outwards at human society. We can see this happening in *The Ring* from the second act of *Die Walküre* onwards. It certainly happens in *Tristan und Isolde*, where the lovers' goal is to escape from the harsh glare of separate existences. Scratch the surface of *Die Meistersinger von Nürnberg* and we find metaphysics even there. And, of course, we find it in *Parsifal*, Wagner's most mystical work, which is shot through with transcendental notions such as the denial of the will and rejection of the world. Wagner himself said that *Parsifal* owed its conception to his flight from the world and from a soul-less age of unfeeling utilitarianism. This is an idea that burns brightly in the dramatic closing pages of *The Ring*.

The scale and scope of *The Ring* was certainly unprecedented, and it is often said (mainly, I think, to frighten new-comers to the work) that a continuous performance of all four dramas would last around fifteen hours. However, if length were *The Ring's* only claim to fame, it might not have survived beyond the nineteenth century.

So, why does *The Ring* continue to exercise such a powerful fascination a century-and-a-quarter after its first performance? Firstly, because of its music. Most people know the popular excerpts which get regular airing in the concert hall, on recordings and in films – the Ride of the Valkyries, Siegmund's Spring Song, Siegfried's Funeral Music and so on. But the music of *The Ring* is exceptional for reasons other than big tunes or exotic instrumentation. It is unusually expressive and conveys ideas and emotions in what might be called a stream of consciousness. One critic from *The Times* who attended the first complete performance in 1876 likened the music to 'a wind that is always blowing, or a stream that is always flowing'; a rather nice analogy. Generally, the music follows the words, amplifying and illustrating them, but in many instances it functions quite independently of the words, commenting on them and drawing attention to unspoken ideas and implications. It even contradicts them when this is required by the drama, say, to express differences between what is being thought and what is being said. So, it is not sufficient to rely on the libretto or surtitles in order to know what is going on.

The orchestra in *The Ring* pours out information unceasingly, even when the action is static and the singers are completely mute. This phenomenon reaches its ultimate sophistication in *Götterdämmerung* where, in Ernest Newman's words, 'the course of the drama is told with absolute clearness in the orchestra itself'. When, in Act Two of *Siegfried*, the adolescent hero hears the Woodbird and tries to communicate with it, he is unable to understand its meaning until he has tasted the dragon's blood. Understanding *The Ring* is all about 'tasting the dragon's blood'; that is, being able to 'tune in' to Wagner's highly expressive musical language.

The second reason for *The Ring's* drawing power is, I suspect, the fact that it is a drama of ideas. The mythological narrative draws on archetypes that are recognisable in most cultures, even if their outward manifestations vary. And so, *The Ring* is about us all.

As a young man, Wagner had been highly critical of what he regarded as the degeneration of opera during the early nineteenth century into mere entertainment and triviality. 'When today we talk of opera music, in any strict sense,' he said, 'we no longer speak of an art, but of a mere article of fashion.' He was scathing about contemporary audiences who were only interested in amusement. 'Part of this amusement,' he said,

> was formed by the music sung upon the stage, to which one listened from time to time in pauses of the conversation. During the conversation and visits paid from box to box the music still went on, and with the same purpose as one assigns to table music at grand dinners, namely, to encourage by its noise the otherwise timid talk.[2]

Not surprisingly then, it is to Wagner that we owe the practice of darkening the theatre during a performance and directing everyone's eyes to the stage. The Wagnerian audience is expected to pay attention.

His aim in 1853 when composing *Das Rheingold* was to make the music serve the purpose of the drama; that is to say, not just to decorate some flimsy story line but to respond to the essence of what was being said or done on the stage. By the time he reached *Götterdämmerung*, twenty years later, the music of that tremendous work had itself become the principal vehicle for the drama.

Franz Liszt, who was two years older than Wagner, was one of his most perceptive champions. They first met in Paris in 1840, when Liszt was already a great virtuoso, sought after by elegant society and extremely wealthy. The twenty-seven-year-old Wagner on the other hand was struggling to keep himself from starvation by doing musical hackwork. After an initial flirtation with the popular genre of contemporary grand opera he decided, with characteristic egocentricity, that if the world did not appreciate what he was trying to do, then it was the world that would have to change. Liszt admired both his conviction and his music and, in 1850, took charge of the first production of *Lohengrin* in Weimar, when Wagner was in exile in Switzerland. 'Right from his first operas, but especially in *Lohengrin*,' said Liszt,

> Wagner has always mixed a different palette for each of his main characters. The more attentively you study this latest score, the more you realise what an interdependence he has created between his text and his orchestra. Not only has he personified in his melodies the feelings and passions which he has set in train ... it was also his wish that their basic features should be underlined by a corresponding orchestral colouring, and as he creates rhythms and melodies to fit the character of the people he portrays, so also he chooses the right kinds of sound to go with them.[3]

Lohengrin was a very progressive work for its time, but it had not entirely thrown off established operatic conventions. That step came with *Das Rheingold*, which was a watershed in Wagner's compositional output and in the history of music in general. In short, it was revolutionary. Any opera-lover coming to it for the first time can sense this, and getting to know it is an exciting experience.

To demonstrate how Wagner developed further the techniques that Liszt so admired, let us look at the way in which he dealt with three different groups of lesser characters in *The Ring*. They are all female, so their voices are similar, but the musical handling of each group is utterly distinctive, as their different natures demand.

Firstly, consider the three Rhinedaughters, naïve watery beings often (and somewhat misleadingly) called Rhinemaidens in English. Let us imagine ourselves in the theatre's darkness. Out of the silence comes the wondrous prelude to *Das Rheingold* evoking the depths of the River Rhine in 136 bars of increasingly fluid figurations of the chord of E flat major. The first voice that we hear is that of the Rhinedaughter Woglinde, but the melody that she sings does not continue the E flat tonality to which our ear has grown accustomed, but moves to that of A flat. The effect created by this abrupt harmonic change and the sudden withdrawal of the surging orchestral sound is that Woglinde is weightless and floating; which indeed she is supposed to be.

The Rhinedaughters' liquid and beguiling music contrasts with that of the nine Valkyries, who appear *en masse* in the third Act of *Die Walküre*. Their music is loud and violent and rather hysterical, epithets which fit precisely the Valkyries of Norse legend who were demons of death attended by storms. They scoured the battlefields gathering up dead heroes. Wagner gave them his own names, but in mythology they bore names such as 'Shrieking', 'Screaming' and 'Raging'. Listening to this music we know exactly why. It is, incidentally, a good example of Wagner the contrapuntist: at times, it combines simultaneously eight individual vocal lines.

Different again from the Rhinedaughters and the Valkyries are the three Norns, who appear in the prologue to *Götterdämmerung*. They are like the fates of Greek legend, old and wise, spinning the thread of world knowledge that binds past, present and future. They belong to all time and no time, and their music does too.

Nothing even remotely like *The Ring* had existed previously in the European operatic tradition, and yet, paradoxically, it drew from some of the deepest well-springs of European culture. One of these is ancient Greek tragedy. Even as a schoolboy learning Greek, Wagner had been fascinated by the ancient world and, in later years, he studied the works of Aeschylus, Sophocles and Euripides in translation. The form of *The Ring* owes much to his view of these works, especially the *Oresteia* and *Prometheus Bound* of Aeschylus. There are some telling points in common between the classical tragedies and *The Ring*, and an awareness of them helps to explain Wagner's motivations.

The subjects of Greek tragedy were almost always taken from legend and legendary history, as was the subject of *The Ring*. The usual format offered was a tetralogy of three tragedies and a lighter 'satyric' drama. In the works of Aeschylus, the four plays dealt with different stages of the same story, just like *The Ring*. The purpose of Greek tragedy was not the frivolous one of mere enter-tainment and spectacle. Its emphasis was civic, that is, it dealt with issues that had vital implications for the state or society as a whole, as does *The Ring*. In classical drama, the family was often the focus for tragic action, as it certainly is in *The Ring*, and the extreme passions of love, hatred, matricide, patricide, fratricide, adultery, jealousy and even incest, to be found in the ancient plays, all resonate powerfully in *The Ring*.

Although the classical narrative was concerned with great issues and mythological happenings, invariably the Greek dramatists also dealt with the psychological forces which shape human behaviour, and the ways in which men and women cope with events beyond their control – again prominent themes in *The Ring*.

The Greek chorus commented, reflected and made forecasts. Sometimes it was used to sound the *leitmotiv*, or recurrent theme, of the play. If, for instance, the story involved the working of an inherited trait which brought ruin on the members of a family, that motif is sounded by the chorus at appropriate points in the drama as a reminder; just as the motif of Alberich's curse, for example, is used to colour the music of *The Ring*. We can see therefore, that *The Ring* orchestra, which comments on the action, weaving 'motifs of reminiscence' as Wagner called them and providing transitional interludes, has a distant ancestor in the Greek chorus.

Wagner's detailed stage directions are often dismissed as impractical or old-fashioned, and therefore to be treated as if they were never written. This misses the point. The scenery and props of the Athenian theatre were of the simplest kind, but that did not deter Aeschylus from specifying that Prometheus be shackled to a peak in the Caucasus while conversing with the priestess Io, who had been turned into a cow! The drama was an enactment of a well-known story and the audience understood the setting even if this was only suggested by conventional scenic devices. Similarly, in much later European dramas, such as medieval miracle plays, the poet had no hesitation in setting a scene (with the most rudimentary props) in Heaven or Hell or on the deck of Noah's Ark supposedly crowded with every kind of beast. The miracle play *Noah's Flood* begins with the stage direction: '*And first in some high place, or in the clouds if it may be, God speaketh unto Noah standing without the Ark with all his family.*' Compare this with Wagner's directions for the second scene of *Das Rheingold*: '*When the mist has completely vanished aloft in gentle little clouds, in the dawning light an open space on a mountain height becomes visible. The daybreak illuminates with increasing brightness a castle with gleaming battlements …*'

Of course, in *Das Rheingold*, Wagner seems to be asking rather a lot of the production designer, requiring the action to be first on the bed of a river, then on a mountain top, then deep in the bowels of the earth, back to the mountain top and finally on a rainbow. Some demands of the other *Ring* dramas seem equally

DAS LICHT LOESCH ICH EUCH AUS;
DAS GOLD ENTREISS ICH DEM RIFF,
SCHMIEDE DEN RAECHENDEN RING!

2

Alberich resolves to steal the gold and fashion the ring.

impossible, notably in the final scene of *Götterdämmerung* where the heroine is required to ride a horse into a funeral pyre, to be followed by conflagrations in heaven and earth, collapsing buildings and an overflowing Rhine! But it seems to me that these fantastic directions are essentially no different from those of the classical and medieval dramatists or, indeed, of Shakespeare, whom Wagner idolised. Shakespeare did not think twice about locating his scenes in the midst of battle, on ships at sea and in fairy-filled forests when, in fact, Elizabethan audiences expected to see nothing more tangible than the actors in contemporary dress and a few props on a bare stage. Audiences in earlier centuries were quite used to seeing with their mind's eye and, indeed, to drawing parallels between events in the drama and events in their own time. Today we, who are less practised in these skills, partly because of the impact of cinematic literalism, call that sort of treatment 'minimalist'. I do think that, when it comes to staging *The Ring*, less is more, so that the music can work its magic in an unencumbered way.

After being greatly dissatisfied with the first complete production of *The Ring*, which he had personally supervised to the smallest detail, Wagner himself sensed that an audience might come closest to an ideal understanding of his intentions if they were willing to see with their ears, so to speak. Indeed, he joked that having invented the invisible orchestra (a reference to the sunken orchestra pit at Bayreuth) he wished he could invent the invisible theatre! It was left to Adolphe Appia and Wagner's grandson, Wieland, to demonstrate that the music uses so expressive a language that any attempt to duplicate its inner visions for the eye risks diminishing them. Most modern directors now accept this view as axiomatic.

Richard Wagner believed that music could go beyond the power of the spoken word to stir emotions, unlock subconscious feelings and repressed desires, appeal to widely-shared sensibilities, and convey a sense of character and even the physical environment. It was the dramatist's ultimate mode of expression.

Where did this idea come from? From a number of sources, but in particular from his response as a teenager to the music of Beethoven. He was especially taken by the mysterious opening of the *Ninth Symphony*, in which Beethoven seems to be assembling the building blocks of the cosmos and bringing order out of chaos. Wagner and Beethoven were contemporaries, although they never met. Wagner was fourteen when Beethoven died. The young Richard had been drawn to music at an early age and was particularly enamoured of the works of Carl Maria von Weber, especially *Der Freischütz*. But it was his exposure to Beethoven's music that made the greatest impression on him. Later, he characterised this exposure as 'shattering'. He drew particular significance from the fact that, in the last movement of the *Ninth Symphony* the 'absolute' music had taken voice, and he saw in this an anticipation of his own objectives in the realm of music drama.

Wagner records that in Leipzig, where he lived, the *Ninth Symphony* was regarded by many as the raving of a semi-madman. Nevertheless, Wagner at the age of seventeen was so taken by it that he carefully transcribed the full score and then made a piano arrangement which he tried, unsuccessfully, to sell to the music publisher Schott. He did not actually hear a performance of the *Symphony* until the following year but it was the one work, apart from his own, with which he was most closely involved throughout his life. He conducted it many times including, symbolically, after the laying of the cornerstone of his own theatre in Bayreuth in 1872.

After finishing *Lohengrin* when he was thirty-five, Wagner did not write any music for five years. All this time he was brooding on how best to handle a subject which had long been at the back of his mind: the story of the German legendary figure, Siegfried, also known as Sigurd in Norse mythology. It was a story that was extremely popular at the time, and even Mendelssohn toyed with the idea of setting it to music. Another composer, Heinrich Dorn, actually wrote a five-act opera called *Die Nibelungen* (*The Nibelungs*), which was produced by Liszt in 1854 with Wagner's niece, Johanna, as Brünnhilde. In 1848, Wagner wrote a prose sketch setting out his ideas, then a prose scenario and then a three-act poetic drama – *Siegfrieds Tod* – which would eventually be the basis of *Götterdämmerung*.

It was Wagner's practice to gather friends and acquaintances together and read his dramatic texts to them. This was partly to awaken interest in his work but it also gave him audience feedback at an early stage on the structure and dramatic impact of his ideas, before he moved on to the music. After one of these readings of the prose sketch of *Siegfrieds Tod*, a remark by the actor Eduard Devrient led him to add what is now the prologue to *Götterdämmerung*, during which the Norns recount, from their perspective, the story of events up to that point.

The repeated re-telling of the story from various perspectives is an often-criticised feature of *The Ring*. It occurs in one form or another in each of the dramas and, to a modern listener impatient for action, this can seem an unnecessary hold-up. However, the practice of repetition has a respectable lineage in oral story-telling and epic poetry, where it is used as an *aide-mémoire*. Although the four parts of *The Ring* are aspects of a great whole, they are performed over an extended period and can be staged as entirely separate dramas. Consequently, each work needs to have some narrative overlap with the others. Repetition has another use as well. In our own time, we are familiar with the convention in detective stories that allows different individuals to describe the same events through the lens of their own recollection or self-interest. The recapitulations in *The Ring* are of interest not so much for their story content as for the light that they throw on the character of each narrator. From the composer's perspective, they also provide an opportunity to draw attention to musical themes and to reinforce these in our minds, just as the teller of an epic poem might use repeated verbal imagery to reinforce the qualities of a character or place. This is an important feature in both the *Iliad* and the *Odyssey* for example.

In May 1851, Wagner wrote to a friend:

> All through last Winter I was plagued by an idea which lately has taken possession of me to such an extent that I must bring it to fruition. Did I not once write to you with regard to a lively subject? It was that of the youth who sets out to 'learn what fear is' and is so stupid that he never manages to learn. Imagine how startled I was when I realised that this youth is no other than – the young Siegfried, who wins the Hoard and awakes Brünnhilde! The plan is now ready. I am gathering my strength together to write next month the poem of The Young Siegfried.

This work, he decided, would enable him to put visibly before his audience, and develop musically, many more details of the struggle for power than would have been possible in only one drama. What's more, *Der junge Siegfried* (*The Young Siegfried*), which we know simply as *Siegfried*, would provide an exuberant foil to the tragic atmosphere of *Siegfrieds Tod*.

Late in 1851 Wagner came to the conclusion that the wealth of mythological material explaining events leading to Siegfried's birth was so great that it could only be dealt with satisfactorily by writing yet another full-scale work and a 'big prelude', to use his own description. The new work he at first called *Siegmund and Sieglinde: The Punishment of the Valkyrie*. His dramatic sense soon told him that this title was far too long so he renamed it *The Valkyrie*. The 'big prelude' he called *The Theft of the Rhinegold* (its title reminiscent of the satyr play *Prometheus the Fire-kindler*, by

Aeschylus, about the theft of fire), simplifying this in due course to *The Rhinegold*. And so it happened that the plots of the four *Ring* dramas were created more or less in reverse order. Wagner then set about composing the music in the correct order. The text underwent numerous revisions as the entire *Ring* unfolded.

AUF BERGES GIPFEL
DIE GOETTER-BURG.

PRVNKVOLL PRAHLT
DER PRANGENDE BAV

Hugo L. Braune

Wotan and Fricka survey the mighty fortress, Valhalla.

Das Rheingold

———◆———

The beginning of *Das Rheingold*, like that of Beethoven's *Ninth Symphony*, suggests a darkness over the face of the deep; a primal state of creation. But whereas Beethoven seems to be assembling his universe from discrete musical molecules, Wagner's creation grows organically out of a single cell, a sustained deep E flat on the double-basses. After what seems a long time, this cell begins to divide into the components of that most basic entity in music, the major triad. Spread out melodically as an arpeggio by the horns, this forms what might be called the basic motif of Nature. As it continues to grow, a gently undulating theme appears in the strings, and then the whole motif begins to travel at twice the speed, acquiring the unmistakable motion of flowing water – the River Rhine, in whose depths the whole drama begins.

The prelude to *Das Rheingold* lasts about four-and-a-quarter minutes, and the listener is gradually overtaken by a sense of time-lessness. Only the startling sound of a Rhinedaughter's voice breaks the spell and brings us abruptly into a more recognisable world. The transition, as Warren Darcy has noted,[4] is from time-lessness to measured time, from indistinct musical shapes to dis-tinct shapes, from simple forms of nature to human consciousness. In one sense therefore, *The Ring* might be seen as a parable about the tragic consequences of humanity losing touch with its natural origins; a topical subject for our time.

The most important feature of *The Ring* from a musical point of view is Wagner's use of so-called *leitmotivs*, a word usually trans-lated as 'leading motifs'. This was not Wagner's term: he used

The giants Fasolt and Fafner.

other descriptions, including 'chief motifs', 'ground themes', 'motifs of reminiscence' and even 'melodic moments of feeling'. Whatever name we give them, they are themes associated with characters, objects, events and emotions. They are usually quite short and, in essence, melodic, and they are capable of the most subtle manipulation. They can be used in their basic form, which is how we first encounter them, or they can be modified or hybridised through a kind of musical genetic engineering, to reflect particular developments in the drama. They can be superimposed one upon another or turned upside down to imply their opposite. Sometimes it is sufficient to hint at them by using just their rhythms, their general shape, or an associated harmony or instrumental colour. In the continuous flow of the music (the so-called endless melody, unbroken by conventional arias, recitative, ensembles and the like) even the most fleeting reference can be sufficient to reveal some point or consideration relevant to the story. As well as reminding us of things past, the leitmotivs can also be used to foreshadow things to come, preparing our emotions for some action or visual image.

Consider one or two straightforward examples of the way in which Wagner manipulates his musical themes. Water and earth are both manifestations of nature and so one would expect to find some thematic connection between them. Sure enough, the motif of Erda, the all-wise earth spirit, is clearly derived from the 'nature' motif, but in the process it has moved from a major to a minor mode and from flowing 6/8 time to the solid 4/4 of terra firma. In Das Rheingold, Erda is roused from eternal slumbers to warn Wotan and the other gods that the ring will seal their fate and that everything they represent has been compromised and is coming to an end. The antithesis of creation is destruction, so the 'nature' motif, which has already been transformed in connection with Erda, is turned upside down as she warns of the end of the gods.

The motifs of the 'gold' and the 'ring' are, obviously, of central importance. The 'gold' motif is derived from the 'nature' motif, as is the motif of the 'ring'. But whereas the motifs of 'nature' and 'the gold' use benign major chords, the notes of the 'ring' motif make up a chromatic dissonance in the minor key. The life-giving gold has become a death-dealing ring.

To discover how Wagner's motifs mutate in the context of the drama, it is useful to look at what happens to, say, the 'ring' motif in different circumstances. At the beginning of *Siegfried* for example, we are made aware musically of Mime's scheming, even before the curtain rises, and we can tell just from the harmonies, which are those of the 'ring' motif, what this scheming is all about. Through the music we read Mime's mind. By the time we get to *Götterdämmerung*, the motif has evolved further in relation to Hagen. The dissonance that we hear at the beginning of this transformed motif permeates *Götterdämmerung*, suggesting a state of progressive decline.

One could go on in a similar vein pointing out connections and derivations of this kind in relation to a whole host of motifs. In some cases, one motif acts upon another, producing an independent musical offspring. In a letter of 1854, Wagner observed that *Das Rheingold* had become a close-knit unity. 'There is scarcely a bar in the orchestra,' he said, 'that does not develop out of preceding motifs'.[5] Other thematic families have been identified and given labels, such as those of Wotan's spear, love, heroic humanity, the sword, the inspiring power of women, magic and mystery, and so on. The total number of motifs has varied in different calculations from 82 to as many as 367. It is interesting to play 'spot the connection' and people have been doing this ever since Hans von Wolzogen produced a guide book on the subject in the late nineteenth century. Ultimately though, the names of the motifs are just convenient labels. They were not used by Wagner and they do him a disservice if they lead people to think that the *leitmotiv* is only a musical signpost, introduced at appropriate times to assist with comprehension of the drama.

Undoubtedly, the musical ideas – those 'melodic moments of feeling' – which Wagner devised were intended to have a dramatic and narrative function. However, they were far from arbitrary and he did not set them out in advance like pieces of coloured fabric ready to be assembled into a patchwork quilt. Indeed, many of his ideas seem to have evolved during the process of composition.

During the course of a performance, it is hardly practicable to try to pick out and name various motifs as they appear, evolve and disappear in the musical stream, any more than one would consciously name the changing moods of a companion or the passing features of a landscape. We register such things intuitively and absorb them unconsciously. However, familiarity makes us more aware of them, and so it is with the music of *The Ring*.

Wagner's particular skill as a composer was two-fold. Firstly, he exploited his rich thematic material with consummate mastery. He was proud, and rightly so, of the subtlety with which his themes were interwoven and developed 'symphonically' in order to give expression to dramatic action. Secondly, he was able to create themes that not only seemed appropriate to their subject but had a powerful effect on the listener's own sense of recollection. His 'melodic moments of feeling' make an impression, not because we hear them once and so recognise them again, but because they seem familiar even when we hear them for the first time. The most obvious examples are the melodic representations of nature – the Rhine, the woodbird, the forest and so on – which strike us immediately as utterly recognisable. However, we can also identify instinctively with the musical representations of a whole range of emotions and moods.

This amalgam of the musical and the extra-musical is a potent and essential part of the Wagnerian magic, although it was anathema to Igor Stravinsky and his followers as they struggled to

Wotan and Loge in Nibelheim.

escape the long shadow cast by Wagner over late nineteenth- and early twentieth-century music. However, its legacy is still with us today in many forms, both popular and serious.

In *The Ring*, one particularly long shadow is cast by Alberich, the Nibelung of the title, whom we first encounter in *Das Rheingold* clambering out of an underwater cleft to watch the three Rhinedaughters disporting themselves in the pristine waters of the Rhine. (This is mythology remember!) Alberich is not exactly what you would call a good catch. With his fellow Nibelungs he inhabits Nibelheim, a place of gloomy caverns and fissures beneath the earth's surface, and he smelts and smiths hard metals. Alberich is everything the Rhinedaughters are not. They are beautiful and agile; he is ugly and awkward. They are naive and playful; he is calculating and lustful. All of this is apparent from the music, as well as from the text.

Wagner's texts combine archaic and modern language and even words of his own invention, because he saw words and music as two sides of the one dramatic coin. One feeds from the other. In *The Ring*, unlike his earlier works, the lines are short and declamatory and use alliteration rather than end rhyme. All of these features are immediately apparent from the very first words that we hear in *Rheingold*: *Weia! Waga! Woge, du Welle!* The use of alliteration, known as *Stabreim*, is frequently found in old German poetry, and in old English and Latin poetry too. It allows for flexible musical treatment and it contributes to an impression of a mythological time frame.

The *Ring* exercises inexhaustible fascination as a drama of ideas, largely because of its diverse sources and influences. Greek tragedy, Germanic and Norse mythology, the writings of nineteenth-century philosophers such as Feuerbach and Schopenhauer, the 1849 Dresden uprising and its brutal suppression, were all fuel for the restless and inventive mind of Richard Wagner. Consequently, it has been possible to interpret *The Ring* from just

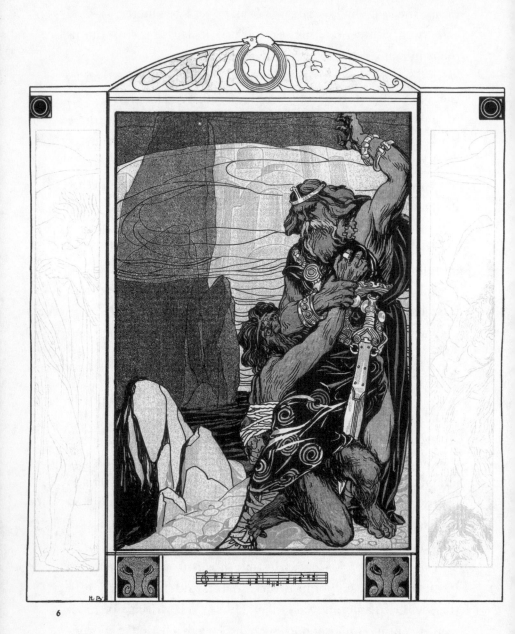

Wotan steals the ring from Alberich.

about any political or sociological perspective, a fact which stage directors have found particularly useful.

Alberich personifies an all-too-human craving for wealth and influence at any cost. You will notice how easily he renounces love when the Rhinedaughters let slip that by doing so he can have world dominion. The important motif of the renunciation of love reappears many times in different forms throughout *The Ring*, with telling effect.

Some might say that Alberich is just getting his priorities right, subscribing to the modern notion that power is the ultimate aphrodisiac. He manages to beget an ungodly son, Hagen, by buying a human partner, and that will ultimately lead back to the Rhine, to the murder of Siegfried and the return of the ring to the Rhinedaughters. So things come full circle, but at a price. It is worth listening closely to the way in which Wagner describes the rape of the gold, the frenzied despair of the Rhinedaughters and the atmosphere of foreboding which descends on an unsuspecting world.

Das Rheingold was written to be performed without intervals or even the closing of the curtain. To effect his scene-changes, Wagner wrote transitional passages which were masterpieces of musical description. From the depths of the Rhine, plunged into darkness by the theft of the gold, he takes us up into less watery realms, up, with occasional echoes of grief through mists and fogs, to the bright sun-lit atmosphere of a very high place where the chief god Wotan and his consort Fricka are slumbering on a flowery bank. The towers of Valhalla, built by the giants Fasolt and Fafner at Wotan's behest, gleam in the rays of the rising sun, and the hymnlike 'Valhalla' motif, implying the majesty of the gods, resounds in the brass. This motif will be used from here on to refer to the gods and, in particular, to Wotan.

But all is not sweetness and light. The liquid, plaintive music of the Rhinedaughters and the slippery, pungent music of Alberich have given way to a brittle mood of marital stress and strain. Wotan and Fricka are definitely in need of some marriage guidance counselling. We cannot really blame Fricka of course. Her husband is a notorious philanderer, like Zeus in Greek mythology. As payment for building Valhalla, he has even promised to hand over her sister Freia, the goddess of youth and love, to the brutish giants. In a sense then, Wotan too has renounced love by offering Freia as the price for Valhalla. In Norse mythology, the giants were implacable enemies of the gods. Fricka goes on and on about foolish schemes and about men making decisions without consulting the women. For his part, Wotan's preoccupation is with grand plans and ambitions and the challenge of ruling the world. Wagner's own experiences with his first wife Minna must have seemed all too relevant when he was writing Scene Two of *Das Rheingold*. In a letter written during the composition of *Das Rheingold*, Wagner observed:

> Alberich and his ring could not have harmed the gods unless the latter had already been susceptible to evil. Where, then, is the germ of this evil to be found? Look at the scene between Wotan and Fricka ... The firm bond which binds them both ... constrains them both to the mutual torment of a loveless union. [6]

His implication is clear: lovelessness, either deliberately chosen, as in the case of Alberich, or the product of circumstance, as in the case of Wotan and Fricka, carries the seeds of destruction. The corollary is that an act of love – especially love to the point of self-sacrifice – carries the seeds of life. In Wagner's dramas, self-sacrificing love is frequently (though not exclusively) offered by a woman, in a redeeming and life-affirming role.

Apart from Wotan and Fricka, the gods in *Das Rheingold* are rather sketchily drawn, with the exception of the demigod Loge whose element is fire. He is the most interesting character in the drama because he is clever and mercurial, and he stands apart from the others. He does their bidding and solves their problems, but he is never accepted as 'one of them' – consequently, he despises them. In dramatic terms he stands between the gods and the audience, letting us see what is going through his mind. His Scandinavian prototype, Loki (whose father was a giant) has six rather contradictory functions. He is a free agent, unrelated to the other gods; a mischief-maker who gets the other gods into trouble and out of it again; an uncompromising teller of unpalatable truths; a mocker of the other gods; a 'blood-brother' and favourite of Wotan, distrusted as such by the other gods; and the god of fire. The last attribute has only a dubious basis in mythology, although it came to be given prominence by Wagner as he worked on *The Ring*. The connection seems to have arisen through a play on Loki's name and its similarity to words such as the archaic *Lohe*, meaning 'flame' or 'blaze'. Wagner indulges in all sorts of word play with Loge's name, including drawing comparisons with *Lüge*, meaning 'lie' or 'falsehood'.

We learn more of Loge's shifty character as events unfold. For example, it is Loge who, in the magnificent final scene of *Das Rheingold*, declares in a voice that only we can hear: 'They are hastening to their end, those who think they are so great … I'm tempted to change into flames and burn them all up … I must consider. Who knows what I shall do.' But, for all his talk, he is just an opportunist. As the gods process into Valhalla, he tells the mournful Rhinedaughters to stop their wailing. 'You might have lost your gold,' he says to them, 'but the gods' new golden splendour will shine on you instead.' Everyone laughs, except the Rhinedaughters. Loge's ethics are as shifting and insubstantial as the flickering, flame-like motif that accompanies him.

There is an interesting example in Scene Two of *Rheingold* of the subtlety of Wagner's technique in using leitmotivs to refer to a character by implication, without needing a verbal reference. At

WEICHE, WOTAN, WEICHE!

FLIEH' DES RINGES FLUCH!

7

Erda warns Wotan to give up the cursed ring.

one point Wotan and the giants, Fasolt and Fafner, are discussing the contract for the building of Valhalla. Wotan is reneging on the deal to give the giants the goddess Freia and tells them to ask for some other fee. Fafner accuses his brother of having been taken in by Wotan's tricks. However, we know that the 'fine print', so to speak, in the contract was not Wotan's doing but Loge's, for it is he who personifies trickery and manipulation. It was Loge who encouraged the deal on the basis that he would find a ransom for Freia. So, when Fafner speaks of Wotan's trickery we hear, in the soft flickering music of the violas, not a reference to Wotan but one to Loge, reminding us of who was the real architect of the loophole.

When Loge appears with the much-awaited news of a means of ransoming Freia, he admits that he has searched in vain for a ransom that would compensate for the power of love. But he does say that he has heard about Alberich's renunciation of love, the theft of the Rhinegold and manufacture of the ring. The ring is referred to ten times in the orchestra during Loge's account, and Wotan becomes mesmerised by the idea of getting his hands on it. The giants decide that they would settle for Alberich's gold if this could be obtained for them.

Loge enjoys one special advantage in being an outsider. He has avoided the gods' addiction to Freia's golden apples of youth. When Freia is carried off by the giants as security for the promised gold, the other gods suffer withdrawal symptoms and begin to feel their age – which, if you are a god, is not inconsiderable! Loge observes their discomfort rather smugly. The music of this passage provides another example of Wagner's skill in evoking intangible things. How many other composers would have dared to set the ageing process to music?

One of the most exciting passages in *Das Rheingold* is that known as the descent to Nibelheim. Determined to obtain the ring and the golden hoard and wriggle out of his commitment to

Fafner clubs Fasolt to death, and the curse claims its first victim.

give Freia to the giants, Wotan decides to go with Loge down through a fissure in the rock to the subterranean caverns where Alberich has enslaved the rest of his race. It is not just a geographical journey that we undertake, although that seems real enough with its downward rush and sulphurous chromaticism. There is a psychological journey too. The motifs which drive the orchestral sound are those of 'Alberich forswearing the love of woman', 'the gold' and 'the ring', 'the spurning of Alberich by the Rhinedaughters' (the latter theme transforming itself into the hellish and unforgettable hammering of anvils), and once again, pervading everything, the sinister harmonies of 'the ring'.

What happens next is a black comedy with overtones of Hieronymus Bosch. We hear the tormented shrieks of the terrified Mime and the other Nibelungs as they are whipped by the all-powerful and invisible Alberich. *Nibelheim* is literally 'the home of mist'. Could there be a more apt name for the smoggy and polluted mines and factories of a nineteenth-century industrial city? Into a world of bountiful nature has come the lust for power, with which love can never coexist. We are plunged into moral darkness as Alberich sets about enslaving his people – even his own brother. Industrial man has chosen wealth and power above all else.

We see (or at least imagine with the help of the music) Alberich being tricked by Loge into transforming himself firstly into a monstrous dragon and then into a tiny toad, whereupon Wotan and Loge pounce on him. (Incidentally, this latter detail is reminiscent of the fairy-tale of *Puss in Boots* in which the ogre is goaded into turning himself into a lion and then into a mouse, enabling the cat to pounce and devour him.) The gods return to the surface with Alberich bound and bitter.

Wagner's orchestration is nowhere more varied and brilliant than in this scene in Nibelheim, nor his vocal line more lively and to the point. It is a striking manifestation of his theories about *Gesamtkunstwerk*, the fusion of text, music, scene and action in the service of the drama. All of the considerable dramatic detail – the contest of wits between Loge and Alberich, Alberich's plan to rule the world, Loge's taunting of Alberich, the latter's transformations and the capture of the Nibelung – are ingeniously arranged, as Warren Darcy points out, as a nine-part rondo in which a recurrent musical refrain – the rondo theme – alternates with four contrasting episodes. The refrain recurs each time in the controlling key of A major, while the episodes explore different tonalities and thematic material. In such a way, Wagner controls the varied forces that are at work in this extended scene. Here, as in many other instances in *The Ring*, the apparently free form of the work belies its carefully organised structure. This structure is disguised by the large scale of the work and the narrative function of the themes.

In the midst of all this activity, there is one rather haunting motif which is worth special mention. It is associated with the Tarnhelm or magic helmet which renders Alberich invisible and allows him to change his form at will. Metamorphosis plays a part in *The Ring*, as it does in the myths of the Greeks and Romans. We are left in no doubt as to the Tarnhelm's supernatural qualities by Wagner's use of pianissimo muted horns and unworldly harmonies. This simple but very effective motif will appear in various guises throughout *The Ring* whenever magic, which is to say deceit, is afoot. It is related in form to the motif of Loge, though played much more slowly. The logic in this, of course, is that magic, deceit and trickery are all related concepts.

Back on the surface, events are about to take a disastrous turn. Not satisfied with the golden treasure that is dragged up by the enslaved Nibelungs to ransom Alberich, Wotan demands the ring as well. The motif of his 'spear', symbol of his will and lawful authority, blares out on the trombones before he commits the violent and unlawful act of wrenching the ring from Alberich's finger. Thus the law-maker turns law-breaker. The 'spear' motif is another of those primal themes that seem to mirror the physical shape of the objects they represent. It is a strong descending line of notes, like a straight shaft, uncompromising in its force and sense of authority. It is also associated with agreements, treaties and laws generally.

Then, in one of the most vitriolic passages in all music, Alberich damns his tormentors, cursing the ring and whoever possesses it. It is amazing to think that this shocking music was written nearly a century-and-a-half ago, at the time when Verdi was writing the three great works of his middle period – *Rigoletto*, *Il trovatore* and *La traviata* – and five years before Gounod wrote *Faust*. Masterly as these works are, *Das Rheingold*, by comparison, comes from quite another world.

The sinister motif of 'Alberich's curse' begins with the notes of the 'ring' motif turned upside down. The implication? That the power of the ring will be negative rather than positive, destructive rather than creative.

With the return of the giants and Freia, the gods regain their youthful appearance. As ransom for Freia, the giants demand sufficient gold to obscure her from head to toe. The gold is piled up but the goddess's hair remains visible. Loge, with great reluctance, yields the Tarnhelm to obscure it. Fasolt checks for any other gaps and catches a glint from Freia's eyes. The music suddenly takes on a soulful quality, for the uncouth giant has quite fallen for Freia and bitterly regrets having to give her up. Only the blocking out of her gaze will persuade him to depart without her. Fafner points to the ring on Wotan's finger and insists that it be handed over to fill the gap. Loge interjects that he had promised to return the ring to the Rhinedaughters but Wotan tells him to think again; he took the ring for himself and won't give it to anyone. The giants conclude that, if this is Wotan's last word, they will take Freia after all.

Amidst the pleading and confusion that follows, the all-

Donner summons the mists and creates a thunderstorm.

knowing earth goddess Erda appears and tells Wotan to give up the ring. Her music looks back to the world's beginning, and forward to the end of the gods in *Götterdämmerung*. Wretchedness, doom and disaster lie in the ring, she warns. After much thought and prompting by the others, Wotan heeds her advice, and so the cursed ring passes to the giants. Almost at once it claims its first victim when Fafner slays his brother Fasolt in an argument over who should keep it. The orchestra reminds us of Alberich's curse.

The giants are a bit of a challenge for stage directors. In Wagner's original concept, they represented the ruling classes in early nineteenth-century Europe, simple-minded and used to a life of inactivity and ease. They were no match for the aggressive, wealth-seeking capitalists and plutocrats of the industrial age. They have been variously depicted as Neanderthal blockheads, rude mechanicals in the Shakespearian sense, pieces of heavy machinery, and even astronauts. In the Sydney production of the 1980s they resembled shaggy muppets. In the centenary production at Bayreuth, Patrice Chéreau put his singers on the shoulders of strong men, all draped in oversize costumes. They are often depicted as being gigantic in size compared with the gods – but how tall is a god? Perhaps it makes more sense to emphasise their brutishness and complete lack of culture. Wagner's own solution in 1876 was to use men of large (but not abnormal) stature, primitively dressed in furs from head to foot. Their roughly hewed staves, still with the remnants of branches attached, contrasted with the elegantly engineered spears of the gods.

The giants' music is seismic and unsubtle in the extreme. Well, no one expects them to be scintillating conversationalists and ballroom dancers, and the music gives us a fairly uncompromising picture of just what they are like, mentally and physically. They go to great trouble to win the gold, the ring and the Tarnhelm, but when the surviving giant, Fafner, gets his hands on all of these things he can think of nothing more productive to do than to

The gods pass across the rainbow bridge to Valhalla.

transform himself into a dragon and guard them. If Alberich demonstrates the destructive consequences of craving wealth and misusing power, Fafner personifies the pointlessness of hoarding wealth and squandering power. *The Ring* is, amongst other things, an allegory of personal, social and political behaviour, and its messages would not have been lost on Wagner's contemporaries.

In 1848, the year of the first prose sketch for *The Ring*, there were popular revolts and uprisings in Paris, Vienna, Berlin, Frankfurt and Prague. Revolution was in the air and Wagner wrote to a friend that he had become so depressed with his position in Dresden where, although he was Court Conductor, he could get none of his artistic reforms approved, he had become a revolutionary – 'in thought if not in deed'. He delivered a speech to a left-wing political association in which he demanded one-man-one-vote, the abolition of inherited wealth and power, and the surrender by the aristocracy of its position of privilege. He joined the revolutionary Popular Front and was an associate of the anarchist Mikhail Bakunin. In 1849 the King of Saxony dissolved the Chambers of Deputies and soldiers opened fire on protesting Dresdeners. The government appealed for Prussian troops to assist in suppressing the revolt. Wagner had leaflets printed and distributed amongst the King's soldiers asking 'Are you on our side and against foreign troops?' and he took his post in a church tower reporting on troop movements. The revolt was brutally suppressed, a warrant was issued for Wagner's arrest and he went into exile in Switzerland. The whole experience made a lasting impression on him.

There is no doubt that the reform of society, in a fairly general sense, was a subject close to his heart, and this is certainly reflected in *The Ring*. Indeed, in 1852 he told his friend Theodor Uhlig that composition of *The Ring* would have to wait until 'after the revolution', for only then would the world understand the revolutionary content of the work.[4]

Wagner does not mention Karl Marx in his writings, but Marx certainly mentions him. Nearly thirty years later, Marx was to complain 'No matter where one goes, one is plagued with the question "What do you think of Wagner?" '

There have been several notable Marxist interpretations of *The Ring* and, in 1963, the Soviet Union issued a special postage stamp to commemorate the 150th anniversary of Wagner's birth. But before we conclude that Wagner was a proto-communist, as directors in the old Eastern Europe were prone to do, or a proto-Nazi as Adolf Hitler and his friends decreed, we need to remember that *The Ring* is singularly accommodating of just about any political and social gloss that one wishes to give it. There have been *Rings* of the left, the right and the centre, *Rings* of the industrial revolution, fairytale *Rings* and environmental *Rings*. There have been *Rings* set in outer space and *Rings* with laser beams, *Rings* of a post-nuclear catastrophe and *Rings* with motor cars and rubbish bins on stage and Brünnhilde with her head in a paper bag. In short, the stagings have changed according to generation and the notions of individual directors, but the work itself, like John Brown's soul, still goes marching on.

Each of the gods reacts in a different and revealing way to the murder of Fasolt and the loss of the ring. Loge, ever the courtier, puts a favourable complexion on the events. You are well rid of the ring, he tells Wotan. See how your enemies are now murdering each other for the gold that you let go. Fricka turns her attention to a comfortable domestic future in her new home, the gleaming Valhalla. Gone for the moment is the nagging goddess of marriage vows; instead we see Fricka the helpmate, caressing and cajoling, urging her lord to lead her through the splendid portals. However, Wotan is not to be soothed, and responds gloomily that an evil wage has paid for their home. He frets about losing the ring and is already agonising over how he might retrieve it.

Donner, the god of thunder, decides it is time to clear the air.

In purely musical terms, this means a transmutation of the B flat minor tonality associated with Alberich, and other musical elements identified with the Nibelungs, into a tonal environment more favourable to the gods. With one of those dramatic touches which reveal the composer's unerring sense of theatre, Donner whips up the clouds and creates a tremendous flash of lightning and clap of thunder. We share in the sudden release of tension. The clouds disperse and, in the evening light, a rainbow bridge stretches from the feet of Donner and his brother Froh, the god of Spring, across the Rhine gorge to Valhalla. Wotan's spirits are lifted by the glorious sight, and a 'great idea' suddenly occurs to him. The music tells us so, although we shall have to wait until *Die Walküre* to find out just what this idea is.

A procession is formed and the gods move grandly off across the rainbow bridge to happiness ever after. But their reverie is interrupted by mournful cries from the river below: 'Rhinegold! Rhinegold! Shining gold! ... For your true radiance we are mourning.' Wotan and Loge throw a few sarcastic words in the direction of the Rhinedaughters and, amidst laughter, the procession resumes with all its delusions of triumph. However, the Rhinedaughters, overwhelmed with longing for their gold, have the last word, just as they had the first: 'Goodness and truth dwell but in the waters,' they sing, 'false and base all those who dwell up above!' There speaks the authentic voice of the forty-year-old Richard Wagner, Wagner the revolutionary, for whom the artistic gods of the mid-nineteenth century were equally false and base. Those gods, like their cosmic counterparts, were much too pleased with themselves to listen; but that was about to change.

Hunding tells the stranger that his hearth and house are sacred.

Die Walküre

———◆———

If Richard Wagner had written *Die Walküre* in the 1980s instead of in the 1850s he might well have called it *Aspects of Love*, for love in its various forms is central to this most popular of the *Ring* dramas. 'Only love,' he wrote,

> the union of man and woman (physical and metaphysical), creates the human being. Fulfilment comes to us only through the enjoyment of love, that most eternal of all things. The world attains complete reality for me only through a loved one and through the appearance of the beloved. This may be a child or a friend but we can only love that child or friend wholly if we already have the capacity of love. That, a man learns only through a woman. [7]

When Wagner was composing the music for *Die Walküre* his first marriage was in tatters, but he was deliriously infatuated with Mathilde Wesendonck, the wife of a German business man who lived in Zurich. The Wesendoncks became generous supporters and ardent champions of his music. The beautiful Mathilde is best remembered as his muse for *Tristan und Isolde*, but the manuscript of Act One of *Die Walküre*, written several years earlier, already bears testimony to the composer's infatuation. The score contains various jottings in Wagner's hand referring secretly to Mathilde. These jottings are sometimes associated with particular musical phrases and take the form of cryptic sets of initials: *i.l.d.g.* meaning in German 'I love you infinitely', and *L.d.m.M?* 'do you love me

Mathilde?'. Others, once deciphered, spell out: 'Were it not for you, beloved', 'You are my all!', and 'Beloved, why have you left me?'. The delirium of love had made him rather childish and he admitted as much to Mathilde, but it also provided the catalyst for some of his greatest love music. Throughout his life, Wagner seems to have needed the strong stimuli of relationships and sensory experiences in order to conjure up his imaginary world of the emotions.

There is a common emotional thread linking Act One of *Die Walküre* and *Tristan*: a powerful sense of love and longing, made even more intense by illicit relationships. Sieglinde's offer to Siegmund of a drinking horn filled with mead in *Die Walküre*, has an obvious parallel in Isolde's offer to Tristan of the cup with its potion. While the immediate result in *Die Walküre* is less convulsive than it is in *Tristan*, the similarities are plain. Both couples drink from their respective cups. Siegmund's gaze, according to the stage directions, rests on Sieglinde with growing warmth, his expression betraying strong emotion. Tristan and Isolde gaze with deepest emotion and a growing longing into one another's eyes. And Siegmund, like Tristan, is destined for sorrow.

In the First Act of *Die Walküre* we experience intensely the joy of love's presence and the pain of love's absence. The twins, Siegmund and Sieglinde, separated in childhood, rediscover each other in a forest hut, although mutual recognition comes slowly. Siegmund arrives exhausted in the midst of a storm, fleeing from his enemies. The storm is both a natural phenomenon and a metaphor for the turmoil in his mind and soul. The hut in which Siegmund has sought refuge is built around the trunk of an ash tree and belongs to the grim and forbidding Hunding. We can tell exactly what type of man he is from the music associated with him.

We have already seen in connection with *Das Rheingold* that marriage and happiness were far from synonymous for Wagner. In the case of Wotan and Fricka, marriage is, as envisioned by Wagner, a bond that constrains them to the mutual torment of a loveless union. How much more then is this true for Sieglinde, who has been forced to marry Hunding against her will. She offers a drink of water to the exhausted man, and a solitary cello mirrors the gentleness of her action with music of extraordinary beauty.

Then Hunding enters. His suspicions of the stranger are confirmed when Siegmund recounts the story of his flight and the sufferings of his family. When he was a boy, Siegmund says, he and his father, Wolf, returned one day from hunting to find their home burned to the ground. He refers to his home as the 'wolf's lair'. This and other wolfish references derive from the ancient myths from which Wagner drew much of his raw material. Siegmund had found his mother dead and his twin sister abducted and, eventually, he was separated from his father. A wolf's skin lay in the woods but his father was nowhere to be found. The 'Valhalla' motif is heard in the orchestra, and we realise, even if the young man does not, that his father is the god Wotan. Siegmund continues with his narrative. He wandered as an outcast, attracting ill luck wherever he went. What he thought right others thought wrong. What he held base others considered fair. He longed for loved ones but found only enemies. Finally he was involved in a skirmish during which he killed other men. Pursued and alone, he had taken the name *Wehwalt* – Woeful.

Hearing this, Hunding knows beyond doubt that they are mortal enemies, for the men killed by Siegmund were his kinsmen. Custom requires that the stranger be given sanctuary for the night, but on the morrow, Hunding insists, it will be necessary for them to settle their differences in combat.

Wagner's use of the orchestra throughout this scene is full of subtlety and revelations. The thematic structure which he had established so effectively in *Das Rheingold* now shows its great flexibility, and he is able to manipulate it with growing confidence.

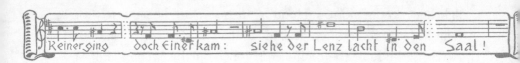

Keiner ging doch Einer kam: siehe der Lenz lacht in den Saal!

2

Spring smiles into the room.

For example, the relationship between Hunding and those killed in battle is foreshadowed simply by use of the rhythm of Hunding's motif while Siegmund is telling his story. Again, when Hunding notices a physical resemblance between Siegmund and Sieglinde, his remarks are accompanied by an orchestral reference to the spear motif, symbol of Wotan's authority and will. Why? Because Wotan was their father and the twins, unwittingly, are the instruments of his will.

Siegmund's arrival on that stormy night had stirred deep feelings within Sieglinde (although she does not know why) and her initial reaction of sympathy grows into something stronger. Wagner gives Siegmund a theme derived from the spear motif, implying that he is far from being a free agent. As the feelings of the twins towards each other begin to grow, this is reflected by an intertwining of musical themes associated with them.

Hunding retires and Sieglinde gives him a drink laced with a sleeping draught. Siegmund, left alone by the fire, recalls his father's promise to provide a sword for him in his hour of need. In his desperation he now calls out to his father for help. From the orchestra we hear the sword motif, first heard when it blazed forth at the end of *Rheingold* when Wotan had had his 'great idea'.

While Siegmund is preoccupied with his thoughts, firelight glints on a sword buried to its hilt in the trunk of the ash tree. We can guess its significance: Wotan's 'great idea' had been to use his mortal offspring to regain Alberich's ring. Siegmund, armed with the sword, would do what the god, enmeshed in his treaties and laws, could not.

When Sieglinde returns, she explains how the sword was left in the tree by a stranger who appeared at her wedding feast. No-one could draw it out, although many had tried. We can tell from the orchestra that the stranger was Wotan, and from Sieglinde's account that the sword was intended for a hero. Brother and sister grow more ardent in their exchanges and begin to use the ecstatic,

hojo-to-ho! — hojo-to-ho! —

Wotan's favourite daughter, the Valkyrie Brünnhilde, with her horse, Grane.

compressed language which later would be taken to such extremes in *Tristan und Isolde*. Suddenly a gust of wind blows open the great door of the hut and moonlight floods into the room. 'Ah, who went there?' she cries. 'No one went, but one has come,' he answers. Siegmund describes the passing of the winter storms and the arrival of spring in music of great lyrical beauty, and Sieglinde tells her brother that *he* is the spring. In Wagner's music, love and lyricism are inseparable.

For the first time, in the moonlight, brother and sister are able to see each other clearly: they comment on their likenesses – the way they look, the way they sound – and they probe relentlessly at each other's identity. When the young man calls his father by another name, Wälse, and acknowledges his race as the Volsungs, Sieglinde tells him joyously that the sword is intended for him. She names him *Siegmund*, which means 'guardian of victory', and with a mighty effort, he pulls the sword from the tree, calling it *Notung* – 'Needful'. She reveals herself as his sister Sieglinde. Passionately he draws her to him and with music of the greatest excitement, they embrace as the curtain falls. The First Act of *Die Walküre* has few equals in its emotional appeal and dramatic construction.

There is a striking contrast between Act One of *Die Walküre* and the cosmic 'morality play' of *Das Rheingold*, where we were confronted not so much with characters as with characterisations. Instead of Wotan, Loge, Fafner and Woglinde, these *dramatis personae* of *The Ring's* Preliminary Evening might equally have been named 'Power', 'Trickery', 'Brute Force' and 'Naivety', just as in medieval morality plays one would find characters called 'Good Deeds', 'Knowledge', 'Strength' and 'Beauty'. In *Rheingold*, Love is spoken about and even renounced, but is never apparent on stage. Now in *Die Walküre*, human beings, real characters, make their appearance for the first time, and so too does human love. Even the immortals, Wotan and Fricka, who reappear on this First Day of Wagner's Festival Play (to use his terminology), are more rounded and complex characters than they had been in *Rheingold*. Of course, events have moved on. Forces have been unleashed from which neither gods nor humans can remain aloof.

In the whole scheme of *The Ring*, it might seem strange that the little domestic drama which is played out in Hunding's hut warrants a whole Act to itself. But this very fact is an indication that we are now truly in the world of men and women (albeit of divine origin), and such is the expressive power of the music that any reservations are quickly dispelled.

If a composer in our own time wrote an opera in which one of the most sympathetically handled characters drugged her husband so that she could commit adultery and incest with her brother, this would attract more than passing interest from those concerned with public morals and the corruption of minors. But that is precisely the subject of *Die Walküre*, written nearly a century-and-a-half ago and performed countless times ever since. Indeed, this work has unquestionably become the most popular of the *Ring* dramas and is often performed independently of the others. It wasn't always so. Critics at the first complete performance at Bayreuth in 1876 liked *Siegfried* best, and the Viennese critic Eduard Hanslick thought that the whole of *Walküre* should be dropped. Nevertheless, before long Wagner was complaining that this work was being promoted more than the others by touring companies.

Wilhelm Mohr, another critic present in 1876, described the brother-sister relationship as 'overpoweringly repulsive to the healthy sensibility', and *The Times* critic of the day reported that the 'matter was so objectionable to modern thought' that the very survival of *The Ring* was unlikely. He also took exception to Siegfried's marriage to the eldest of his aunts – long before Anna Russell did!

Incest: what can one say about this controversial aspect of the work? The first thing, I suppose, is that we are not talking about incest in the ordinary sense, despite the very human qualities exhibited by the sibling lovers. We are talking about mythological incest involving the children of a god, and that is a very different kettle of fish. Consider some parallels in a variety of religious traditions. The Book of Genesis provides an account of the creation of the first humans, Adam and Eve, and goes on to identify their children and grandchildren. Taking the story at face value, one can only assume that the grandchildren were the fruit of inter-marriage by Adam and Eve's children. In Egyptian mythology, Osiris and Isis, brother and sister, became the parents of Horus. In Mesopotamian mythology the god Shamash was the husband and brother of Ishtar, goddess of love and fertility. Niörd, the Scandinavian spirit of water and air married his sister Nerthus. In Greek mythology, Kronos married his sister Rhea and fathered Zeus, who in turn married his own sister Hera. Elsewhere in Norse mythology, the fertility god Frey, whom Wagner calls Froh, had an incestuous relationship with his sister Freya (Freia), also a fertility figure. Unlike the taboo against literal incest which has applied in most cultures from time immemorial, incest amongst mythical beings, often to explain natural phenomena, has been given the highest sanctity.

However, mythology aside, the feelings between Siegmund and Sieglinde are convincing and command our sympathy, not because Wagner is endorsing an incestuous relationship (in fact the relationship leads to the death of both parties) but because he is describing a loving one. It is the musical expression of their love which is irresistible. In an essay written in Paris when he was twenty-eight, Wagner had this to say:

> What music expresses is eternal, infinite and ideal. It does not express the passion, love or longing of this or that individual in this or that situation, but passion, love, or longing in itself; and this it

„Lass' von dem Waelsung!"

4

Fricka tells a dejected Wotan to abandon Siegmund.

presents in that unlimited variety of motivations which is the exclu-
sive and particular characteristic of music, foreign and inexpressible
in any other language.

Some of Wagner's critics found in the relationship between
Siegmund and Sieglinde yet another example of morally repre-
hensible and socially corrupting tendencies in Wagner's music,
tendencies which, in their view, continued scandalously in *Tristan*
and culminated morbidly in *Parsifal*. Friedrich Nietzsche, after he
had turned against Wagner in the 1870s, declared: 'Is Wagner
human at all? Is he not rather a disease? Whatever he touches he
infects. He has made music sick ...' An English critic writing in
1882 said: 'We cannot refrain from making a protest against the
worship of animal passion which is so striking a feature in the later
works of Wagner ... The passion is unholy in itself and its representation is impure ...' So, decadence and immorality were high
on the list of objections to Wagner in the late nineteenth century.

During the mid-twentieth century, when Fascism and
Communism were at their most prominent and anti-Semitism at
its most appalling, the works were shamelessly exploited by the
Nazis (with the active collaboration of the widow of Siegfried
Wagner), and Hitler's regime depicted them as anti-Semitic and
anti-Bolshevist. The opponents of Nazism then damned them
precisely on these grounds, swallowing Hitler's propaganda whole.

And what are the objections during our own age? As recently
as 1982, one writer, Hartmut Zelinsky, maintained that Wagner
had used music as a drug, as an intoxicant, as a philosophy of life.
'This,' he went on, 'is a phenomenon unknown before his time in
the history of music and culture. Its consequences were fatal.'

If we accept all of these views, we must conclude that Wagner's
music is intoxicating and philosophically unsound as well as
unhealthy, immoral, anti-Semitic and anti-Communist. Frankly,
this is absurd, and such claims only serve to attract people who, in

the past, might have believed that Paganini was in league with the devil and that Lord Byron was 'mad, bad and dangerous to know'.

The reality, of course, is that music, of itself, can be neither moral nor immoral. But it can have a powerful, even disturbing, effect, because it can by-pass our faculty of reason and tap directly into our emotions and subconscious mind. Wagner was the supreme exponent of using music to do just that. People who prefer their emotions to remain firmly under the control of their reason are often uncomfortable with Wagner's music, although they might not realise why. Ironically, this can result in apparently rational individuals indulging in the quite irrational objections and associations to which I have referred.

The waters of Wagnerian musical appreciation have, at least in the popular mind, been muddied by the phenomenal amount of (often trivial) material available on his personal life, and on his views on subjects as diverse as vivisection, vegetarianism, hydropathy, institutionalised religion, philosophy, Buddhism, the cultural life of European Jewry, literature, social reform, and nineteenth-century European politics. Towards the end of his life, in despair of developments in Bismarck's Germany, he even contemplated a new life in the United States of America (Minnesota to be precise), comparing its society to that of ancient Athens.[1] His comments and opinions on everything under the sun flew like chips of marble from the sculptor's block. Many were ludicrous; some were insightful. They were often contradictory. Wagner was not alone in exhibiting personal foibles, and in his voluminous correspondence and other writings he certainly did not attempt to hide them. But no other composer, perhaps no other artist of any kind, has shared his thoughts – wise and foolish, generous and self-centred, open-minded and prejudiced – as he did.

Like other great dramatists – Shakespeare for instance in *King Lear*, or Sophocles in *Oedipus the King* – he was concerned to express as powerfully as possible human emotions, strengths, weaknesses and relationships. However, his primary focus was not on the outer world of events, but on the inner world of emotions, because this was, in his view, what music could best express. That he was very aware of the distinction is clear in an essay of 1851 entitled *A Communication to My Friends*, in which he wrote: 'The artist addresses himself to Feeling, and not to Understanding. If he is answered in terms of Understanding, then it is quite clear that he has not been understood.'

What about the subjects he chose? What was his intention there? He had something to say about this himself. In 1844, while at work on *Tannhäuser*, he wrote:

It is not my practice to choose a subject at random, to versify it then think of suitable music to write for it; – if I were to proceed in that way I would be exposed to the difficulty of having to work myself up to a pitch of enthusiasm on two separate occasions, something which is impossible. No, my method of production is different from that: – in the first place I am attracted only by those subjects that reveal themselves to me not only as poetically but, at the same time, as musically significant. And so, even before I set about writing a single line of the text or drafting a scene, I am already thoroughly immersed in the musical aura of my new creation. [8]

In other words, his principal creative stimuli were the emotions prompted by a subject and, in particular, the musical ambience that he associated with those emotions.

Wagner's main source for the story in Act One of *Die Walküre* was the Icelandic *Völsungasaga* (*The Saga of the Volsungs*). He modified and compressed some of the detail but the essentials were retained: Siegmund is descended from Wotan as Volsung was descended from Odin. In both stories the house is built around a tree. The heroine (called Signy in one and Sieglinde in the other) is married against her will, and at her wedding feast an old, one-eyed stranger enters the hall and plunges a sword into the tree trunk, bequeathing it to him who can extract it. Many try to draw the sword from the tree but, in both stories, only Siegmund succeeds. In the *Völsungasaga*, Signy bears her brother's son, as does Sieglinde in *Die Walküre*. The basic plot, therefore, is not really Wagner's at all. He adapted and dramatised an ancient legend, turned it into poetic form and, through music of unprecedented power and beauty, made it interesting to audiences of his time and ours.

If the music of Act One of *Die Walküre* drew inspiration from Wagner's infatuation with Mathilde Wesendonck, Act Two was influenced by a muse of a very different stripe: the philosopher Arthur Schopenhauer. The composition of Act One was finished before the end of August 1854 and, in September that year, Wagner encountered a book which became vastly important to him. It was Schopenhauer's *The World as Will and Representation*. He had, hitherto, been moved philosophically by what he described as the 'cheerful' Greek view of the world, but Schopenhauer's thesis offered the annihilation of the will and complete self-abnegation as the only true means of redemption. Schopenhauer's writings fitted his own mood like a glove and gave him an intellectual framework for the remainder of his life's work. At the heart of Schopenhauer's thesis is the idea that willing, wanting, longing, craving are not just things that we do: they are things that we are. They are the source of our unhappiness and all the evil and strife in the world. We can only avoid this destructive element in our nature by achieving a state of detachment, a condition not unlike the Buddhist notion of *Nirvana*, which is literally the 'blowing out' of the fires of greed, hatred and delusion.

Schopenhauer also took the view that music had a privileged place amongst the arts and that it was in music that the 'inner side' of man and also the world in general, found its most profound and complete artistic expression. What music gives us, Schopenhauer had said, is nothing less than the 'secret history of our will', and in melody the constant digressions from and return to the keynote reflects the eternal nature of the human will, which strives, is satisfied, and ever strives anew. Wagner recognised that, instinctively, he had been moving towards a similar conclusion in respect of music. He also saw the relevance of Schopenhauer's view of the world to his Nibelung dramas and, in particular, to the character of Wotan. This then was the springboard from which he continued with the composition of *Die Walküre* late in 1854.

Act Two opens boisterously in a wild, rocky place, inhabited by Wotan and Brünnhilde, the Valkyrie after whom the drama is named. She is his eldest and favourite daughter by the earth goddess Erda. It is a matter of some dispute as to whether the other Valkyries are also daughters of Erda. Wagner's text offers no particular information on the subject and, in mythology, the Valkyries had no identified parents at all. However, since Brünnhilde and her sisters share characteristics and functions, it is logical to conclude that they also share parents. That is usually the way mythology works.

The introduction to the Act is filled with agitation. The theme that we last heard associated with the love of Siegmund and Sieglinde is now burdened with distress. The two lovers are fleeing from Hunding, and Sieglinde in particular is exhausted and overcome with guilt and remorse. Why does she feel such guilt and remorse? It is not because of her adulterous and incestuous relationship with Siegmund – which is what we might assume to be the case – but because of her long humiliation and abuse at the hands of Hunding. It was Hunding and his loveless marriage that had made her feel unclean and unworthy of the loving man with whom she now flees.

In his earliest drafts for what, at the time, was called *Siegfrieds*

SIEGMUND! — SIEH' AUF MICH!
ICH — BIN'S, DER BALD DU FOLGST.

The annunciation of Siegmund's death.

Tod and *Der junge Siegfried*, Wagner had intended to make the young legendary hero the central character of his dramas. However, as his story evolved and *Die Walküre* and *Das Rheingold* were added, it became clear that the central character was really Wotan. All that happens in *The Ring* can, in a sense, be linked to Wotan's needs, his ambitions, his weaknesses and, eventually, his willingness to accept his own end. In a sense, he represents the current, flawed state of humanity, which is why Wagner referred to him as 'the sum of the intelligence of the present'. If human intelligence is to progress to a more enlightened stage, Wotan cannot survive. The twilight of the gods must come to pass.

Act Two of *Die Walküre* lies at the very heart of *Der Ring des Nibelungen*. It is the fulcrum about which the whole drama turns. It is an Act that requires all of the audience's concentration, because, not only does it place a particular emphasis on the text, but it also contains not one, but two, dramatic high points: the tormented soliloquy of Wotan as he reveals his innermost anxieties, and the great scene which commences with the annunciation of death by Brünnhilde to Siegmund and ends with her disobedience and fall from grace. These are passages of biblical gravity, and Wagner found their writing a harrowing experience. In November 1854 he wrote to the Princess Sayen-Wittgenstein: 'The subject of the *Valkyrie* affects me far too painfully. There is no grief in the whole world that is not here expressed, most agonisingly. I have been quite ill over it'. In a letter to Liszt in October 1855, he wrote:

> I am worried about the weighty second act: it contains two catastrophes, each so significant and so strong that they really provide content enough for two acts. But the one is so dependent on the other and they follow each other so directly that it was quite impossible to separate them.

When the curtain rises, things are going well for Wotan. He is relishing the idea of the coming battle between Siegmund and Hunding, in which his son is to be victorious. Brünnhilde is instructed to ensure that Siegmund will win and Hunding will die. She launches into her war-cry, a sound so elemental and self-confident that, once heard, it is never forgotten.

Brünnhilde warns Wotan that his wife Fricka is approaching, and his heart sinks: 'The usual storm,' he says gloomily, 'the usual strife'. When Wagner and his second-wife-to-be, Cosima, lived at Tribschen on Lake Lucerne in the 1860s, they kept, amongst other creatures, two peacocks called Wotan and Fricka. No doubt the incessant screeching of these birds reminded them daily of the turbulent married life of the chief of the gods and his consort.

Fricka takes her responsibilities as guardian of marriage very seriously. Her particular crusade on this occasion relates to Wotan's adulterous and incestuous children, and her support for the wronged husband, Hunding. In her view, even a loveless and degrading marriage is to be defended, whereas a loving relationship that flouts convention must be crushed. Wotan, rather disingenuously, in view of his involvement in the whole affair, feigns surprise that anyone could take exception to the natural consequences of spring. In his view, the greater crime is a marriage in which there is no love. The parallel with Wagner's own circumstances is obvious.

Wotan urges Fricka to keep an open mind, but she is not to be put off with that sort of talk, and she brings up the subject of Wotan's many infidelities. He ignores these barbs and explains that the gods need a free hero who can achieve their objectives without their intervention, and without even realising that he is assisting them. Fricka argues that, far from being free, Siegmund is merely Wotan himself acting vicariously. Wotan protests that he has not lifted a godly finger to help Siegmund throughout his sad life, to which Fricka replies with devastating logic: 'Then do not help him now! Take back the sword.' She demands that, in the battle which is to come, Brünnhilde should protect the wronged husband and let Siegmund die. Wotan is unable to answer these arguments and, in the words of Wagner's stage directions, from this point onwards his whole demeanour expresses an ever-increasing uneasy, profound dejection. A motif that might be labelled 'Wotan's frustration' figures prominently in the orchestra. It derives from the 'spear motif', symbol of Wotan's authority and will, but it is turned back upon itself with obvious significance. This motif evolves through several other forms as the drama dictates. After Fricka's exit it becomes what might be called the motif of 'Wotan's revolt', an extreme expression of his frustration. In Götterdämmerung, the motif of 'Wotan's frustration' appears in many guises, especially in connection with Hagen's plotting to destroy Siegfried – the ultimate negation of Wotan's will.

Needless to say, Brünnhilde, on her return, is more than a little surprised to discover that her father has changed his mind. However, she is not at all surprised to learn who changed it for him. Eventually he confides in her (indeed he seems to be think-ing aloud) that he now despairs of ever freeing himself of the entanglements and treaties which, in the pursuit of power, have been of his own making. For all his hard-heartedness and sup-pressed emotion, Wotan undergoes a strange and moving process of self-revelation. Trapped in a political and moral quagmire, he begins to accept the inevitability of his demise and the end of the gods. He puts himself on the psychoanalyst's couch. At first he hesitates, not wanting to lower his guard, too frightened to con-front his inner self. Only when Brünnhilde convinces him that she really is his *alter ego* does he let go, and everything comes pouring out. This scene, with its graphic raising of Wotan's sub-conscious mind to consciousness, was completed in 1854, two years before the birth of Sigmund Freud.

Wotan recounts, quietly at first, the story of the theft of the

TRIFF'IHN, SIEGMUND! —   ZURÜCK VOR DEM SPEER!
TRAUE DEM SIEGSCHWERT!   IN STÜCKEN DAS SCHWERT!

Wotan intervenes and Siegmund is doomed.

gold and the making of Alberich's ring, his own cunning theft of the ring with Loge's help, Erda's warning, the loss of the ring to Fafner, the birth of Brünnhilde and her eight Valkyrie sisters, the need for a free man to win back the ring, and the threat foretold by Erda of a son born to Alberich. Finally, and bitterly, he instructs Brünnhilde to give victory to Hunding and let Siegmund die. His favourite daughter, who knows him well, cannot believe that he really means this, for he has loved Siegmund. Furiously, and in his frustration, Wotan threatens Brünnhilde with punishment if she disobeys him, and at last she agrees to do what he asks.

This long scene is demanding for an audience, but Wagner considered it the most important scene in the whole *Ring*. Why? because it depicts a complete reversal in Wotan's fortunes and a profound development in his character. By the time it is finished, he has reached the startling conclusion that all he really wants is an end to everything. Wagner, in a letter to August Röckel in 1854, explained what was happening in these terms:

> The course of the drama thus shows the necessity of accepting and giving way to the changeableness, the diversity, the multiplicity, the eternal newness of reality and of life. Wotan rises to the tragic height of willing his own downfall. This is everything that we have to learn from the history of mankind: to will the inevitable and to carry it out oneself.

No wonder that Wagner was so drawn to the philosophy of Schopenhauer when he read *The World as Will and Representation* later that same year.

Wotan storms off, leaving Brünnhilde to direct the course of the battle between Siegmund and Hunding. In the scene that follows, the lovers pause, exhausted in flight, while Hunding's dogs and hunting horns pursue them relentlessly. Sieglinde hallucinates, imagining all kinds of disasters befalling Siegmund and, at last, she drifts into unconsciousness. Then begins the remarkable passage known as the Annunciation of Death.

The music of the doomed lovers is interwoven with that of the destiny to which all human beings must, in the end, yield. Wagner the magician begins casting his spells, which carry us into a sort of waking sleep in which the Valkyrie Brünnhilde appears to Siegmund and tells him of his fate. 'Siegmund,' she says, 'look on me'. Since only those heroes who are about to fall in battle actually see the Valkyries, it is clear that Siegmund's time has come. Siegmund replies that he will gladly go with Brünnhilde as long as Sieglinde can go with him. However, this cannot be. Brünnhilde implores him to give Sieglinde and her unborn child into her care. Defiantly, he refuses to leave his sister-bride and even threatens to slay her while she sleeps if they are to be separated. As Siegmund prepares to kill Sieglinde and himself, the sword motif is heard in the minor key but then transforms itself loudly into an embryonic version of the motif of the unborn Siegfried, reminding us that even more is at stake here than the hapless pair who now await their fate.

Brünnhilde is overcome with compassion for the lovers. She resolves to give victory to Siegmund after all and to risk her father's wrath, knowing that, in doing so, she is carrying out his innermost wish. Sieglinde, in her delirium, relives the destruction of her family home and the murder of her mother. Hunding's voice is heard, battle is joined and Brünnhilde is seen protecting Siegmund. Suddenly Wotan intervenes and extends his spear, on which Siegmund's sword shatters. Hunding drives his spear home and Siegmund falls. No man may continue to live once he has seen a Valkyrie.

Brünnhilde, with fine presence of mind, collects up the broken pieces of the sword, places Sieglinde on her horse and flees the scene. Wotan tells Hunding to inform Fricka that her shame has now been avenged and, with a contemptuous wave of the hand, strikes him dead. Beside himself with rage – and not a little humiliation – Wotan sets out in pursuit of the defiant Valkyrie amidst thunder and lightning. So ends Act Two.

I would hazard a guess that the two pieces of operatic music best known in the world today are both by Wagner. They are the Bridal Chorus from *Lohengrin*, played each week in countless marriage ceremonies from Alaska to Zanzibar, and the Ride of the Valkyries which opens Act Three of *Die Walküre*.

There could hardly be a greater contrast in musical character-isations. In one case, we are in the bridal chamber of the demure and noble Elsa and the shining knight of the unknown name. The music is transparent, gentle and coy. In the other case we are on a wind-swept peak where the wild daughters of Wotan, bearing the corpses of dead warriors, drop from the clouds to rest and regroup *en route* to Valhalla. The Valkyries call to each other, their horses snort and neigh, the wind howls and all the forces of nature are unleashed. The Ride is not subtle, but then neither was the chaos of northern battlefields where the Valkyries appeared, terrifyingly, to dying warriors. It is a *tour de force* of scene-setting and, after the emotionally draining second act, offers a tremendous sense of release and physical excitement. Its theatrical value in this sense is not appreciated when it is torn from its context and played in isolation.

In early Norse mythology, the Valkyries were dark angels of death. It seems that originally, they determined who would live and who would die on the battlefield and in stormy seas. They gathered up chosen heroes to bear them to Odin's glittering hall of those slain on the battlefield – *Walhall* – Valhalla. ('Die Wal', is an archaism, meaning battlefield.) In later mythology, the Valkyries were romanticised as virginal maidens who waited on the heroes, serving them meat and drink as they prepared for the last great battle, called *Ragnarok*, between the gods and the giants; a kind of Armageddon, a twilight of the gods.

Wagner's names for the nine Valkyries have particular meanings.

Brünnhilde, or Brynhild in Norse mythology, means roughly 'she of the burnished armour'. *Gerhilde* means 'armed with a spear', *Helmwige* 'warrior with a helmet', *Waltraute* 'mighty on the battle-field', *Schwertleite* 'sword wielder', *Ortlinde* 'she whose sword has a flashing point', and *Siegrune* 'she who knows the runes of victory'. Other Valkyries are *Rossweisse* 'riding on a shining horse', and *Grimgerde* 'protected by a helmet'.

What are the warrior maidens calling to each other as they arrive in ones and twos on the rocky peak? To begin with, it is all rather trivial. They are talking about their horses; where to tether them, whether the mares should be next to the stallions, and how to stop them kicking at each other. They exchange information about the dead heroes on their saddles, and blame these former enemies for the unruly behaviour of their mounts. In mythology, the steeds of the Valkyries had probably been suggested by wind-swept rain clouds, and their soaking manes were thought to spray the earth with frost and dew. At last, Brünnhilde arrives in a state of high emotion. Her horse, Grane, has been ridden to exhaustion, and her sisters are astonished to see that she has a woman over her saddle. 'That is no hero!' says Helmwige, foreshadowing Siegfried's startled observation in the last act of *Siegfried*: 'That is no man!' when he uncovers the sleeping Brünnhilde.

In their anxiety to learn more of Brünnhilde's plight, her sisters all speak at once, as people do in such circumstances. This gives Wagner an opportunity to display his mastery of ensemble writing, of which there has been practically none so far in *The Ring*. Four and then eight vocal lines are handled simultaneously to create an effect of agitation and concern. These examples of polyphonic writing remind us that, even though Wagner was a great champion of new developments in music (his oft-quoted injunction to others was 'create something new!'), he was a master of old forms as well.

We saw in *Das Rheingold* how he put new wine in old bottles, so to speak, in the scene in Nibelheim, where a complicated series of events was given unity and form along the lines of an extended rondo. In *Die Meistersinger von Nürnberg*, that sublime comedy of his maturity (which was written, along with *Tristan*, during a twelve-year break between Acts Two and Three of *Siegfried*), he showed what could still be done with the chorale and the fugue. But, in all of these cases, the old forms were harnessed for particular dramatic purposes. So, for example, the chorale gives us an image of the worthy citizens of post-Reformation Nuremberg, and the fugue gives musical expression to a street brawl.

In his adult life, Wagner came to revere J.S. Bach. Wagner had been born in Leipzig and was baptised in the Thomaskirche, at which Bach had been Cantor. Bach had spent the latter half of his life in Leipzig until his death in 1750, and Wagner spent his early life there, including a short and colourful time at the University. Theodor Weinlig was one of Bach's successors at St Thomas's, and Wagner became Weinlig's pupil at the age of eighteen, in 1831. After a nearly disastrous beginning to their relationship, the months that they spent together as pupil and master became one of the happiest periods in Wagner's life. He drew on his memories of it in *Die Meistersinger*, in which Hans Sachs advises the impetuous young Walther not to reject the old in his rush to embrace the new. Most importantly, it was from Weinlig that the young Richard learnt the art of the fugue. In his autobiography, *Mein Leben*, he describes what happened in the following way:

> The joint work on fugues became the basis for the most productive affection between me and my genial teacher, for we both enjoyed such tasks immensely. I was amazed to see how quickly the time flew. In eight weeks I had not only gone through a number of the most intricate fugues but had also waded quickly through the most difficult contrapuntal exercises, when one day, after I had handed him an extremely elaborate double fugue, he took my breath away by telling

7

Wotan rides in pursuit of Brünnhilde.

me I should have the piece framed because he had nothing more to teach me … One of the most important results of his influence on me was the satisfaction I now found in clarity and fluidity, which he had taught me to value by his own example. Even when he gave me that first fugal exercise, I had had to write proper vocal parts for it with the words written in below the stave; my feeling for vocal writing had been awakened in this manner.

According to Cosima's diaries, Wagner considered the 48 Preludes and Fugues of *The Well-tempered Clavier* and the Motets the most consummate of Bach's works. There are many references in the diaries to the Preludes and Fugues, to Wagner's playing of them and his comments on this one or that. For example: in December 1877, he says of one:

That gave me my direction. It is incredible how many things in music passed me by without leaving any impression, but that made me what I am. It is immortal! No one else has ever done anything like it!

Again, in 1878:

In him [Bach] you find all the seeds which later flourished in so fertile a soil as Beethoven's imagination; much of what Bach wrote down was done unconsciously, as if in a dream; my 'unending melody' is predestined in it.

If you think it strange to speak of Bach's *Well-tempered Clavier*, and Wotan's hysterical daughters in the same breath, then consider this. Bach's compositions, quite frequently, utilised extra-musical ideas derived from textural references. Albert Schweitzer catalogued many examples which, by their form, rhythm, or harmonic structure described actions such as walking or falling, natural phenomena such as waves or clouds, and emotions such as terror, grief and joy. So for example, in the aria 'Come, healing cross' in the St Matthew Passion, the viola da gamba obbligato, with its quadruple stopping and dotted rhythm, provides a pictorial representation of the effort involved in lifting and dragging a heavy cross. In one Cantata, which uses Christ's words 'It is expedient for you that I go away. For if I go not away, the Comforter will not come unto you', Bach gives to the basses a 'walking' motif, while, to use Schweitzer's words, the noble arabesque of the oboe above it expresses sublime consolation.

Keep this in mind when you listen to the scene in Act Three of Die Walküre, in which the eight Valkyries express their dismay at Wotan's decision to punish Brünnhilde. The punishment, which has just been announced, is that Brünnhilde will be put to sleep on the rock where they are standing. She will be left as a mortal woman, to be claimed by the first man who comes along and awakens her. The Valkyries plead with their father not to enforce such a punishment, and lament the shame of Brünnhilde's having to submit to the will of a man. We hear the eight pleading voices in counterpoint and then, as if to describe the object of their fears, the orchestra projects over the vocal parts a striking vision of a stranger joyfully encountering the sleeping Brünnhilde and claiming her for his own. All of this is accomplished in just half a minute, but it fits seamlessly into the dramatic context and is a good example of Wagner's contrapuntal technique, first acquired under the guiding hand of Master Weinlig of the Thomaskirche in Leipzig.

But we are getting ahead of ourselves. Before Wotan arrives in search of Brünnhilde, a highly charged scene has been taking place involving Sieglinde. She has arrived with Brünnhilde, traumatised and exhausted by her flight from Hunding and shocked by the sudden death of Siegmund. Brünnhilde herself has just witnessed the fearsome anger of her father and has fled in

INTRODUCTION - DIE WALKÜRE

panic. She pleads with her sisters to lend her a fresh horse but they tell her it would be of no use. There can be no escape from Wotan. Sieglinde overhears the various exchanges and says that she should have been left to die at the side of Siegmund. However, when Brünnhilde urges her to live for the sake of the Volsung who grows in her womb, Sieglinde is at first terrified but then becomes elated with the thought that she is carrying Siegmund's child. Now she asks the Valkyries to save her unborn child and to shelter them both.

Only Brünnhilde is willing, once more, to put herself at risk. She will stand and face Wotan's wrath while Sieglinde escapes on foot to the east. In the east, her sisters report, there is a great forest in which Fafner, now in the form of a dragon, guards the Nibelung hoard and Alberich's ring. Wotan avoids going there. In German mythology, the east often carries a connotation of being mysterious and forbidding, a place of magic and danger. Brünnhilde urges Sieglinde to endure the hard life which will be her lot, for the sake of the noblest of heroes whom she carries within her. She gives Sieglinde the fragments of the sword that was shattered on Wotan's spear. Your son shall forge it anew, says Brünnhilde, and he shall be called Siegfried – which means 'peace through victory'.

If Brünnhilde's appearance to the doomed Siegmund in Act Two was an annunciation of death, her message to Sieglinde in Act Three must surely be an annunciation of life. There is an obvious parallel with the angel's annunciation to the Virgin Mary that she will bear a son and shall call him Jesus. This is hardly a coincidence. Siegfried will be a hero in a legendary sense because he will be fearless, kill the dragon and win the ring. But he is already a hero or, if you like, a deliverer, in a philosophical sense, in that he symbolises hope and life amidst hopelessness and decay. Just as Mary fled into Egypt to protect the infant Jesus from the wrath of Herod, so Sieglinde flees into the forest to protect the unborn Siegfried from the wrath of Wotan. The Christ/Siegfried

Wotan searches for the disobedient Brünnhilde.

parallel was referred to by Wagner in his essay *Die Wibelungen* of 1848, as was a conceptual link between the Nibelung hoard and the Holy Grail. And incidentally, in 1849, one year after writing his prose sketch for a Nibelung drama, Wagner sketched out a five act tragedy called *Jesus of Nazareth*. Nothing came of this, but it is not too fanciful to see how aspects of the Gospel story might have fertilised his poetic treatment of the story of Siegfried. The poem (as he called the libretto) of *Die Walküre* was written only a couple of years later.

At the mention of her son's name, Sieglinde's spirits soar ecstatically. *O hehrstes Wunder!* – O sublime miracle! – she sings, and proceeds with her own Magnificat, praising Brünnhilde for being the bearer of such news, and vowing to save the infant 'for him whom we loved', that is, for Siegmund. The motif which expresses the words *O hehrstes Wunder!* is sometimes known by the title 'redemption through love'. Wagner called it 'the glorification of Brünnhilde' and 'the theme in praise of Brünnhilde'. We hear this motif for the first time with Sieglinde's words, and we shall hear it only once more, in the closing bars of *Götterdämmerung*. It will become the very last musical idea of *The Ring*. Whatever *The Ring's* ultimate message is to be, there can be no doubt that Brünnhilde will have a central role in proclaiming it.

Apart from its highly effective dramatic qualities, which are heightened because it is used so sparingly, the *'hehrstes Wunder'* motif is interesting in that the vocal line uses a melodic phrase of six notes for just two syllables, which is unusual for Wagner. The idea of mangling a word to fit a pre-determined musical phrase, (*à la* Handel, for example) was anathema to him. However, once again, Wagner was prepared to break his own rules and hark back to earlier practices in the interests of the drama. This happens again in the final scene of *Siegfried* when Brünnhilde rhapsodises with the unusually extended melody that is also heard at the beginning of the *Siegfried Idyll*. Ecstasy, rhapsody, delirium: all seem to warrant this kind of treatment in Wagner's mind. Heard in isolation, Sieglinde's music is glorious enough, but in the context of all that has gone before – anxiety and despair, death and hopelessness – it is positively electrifying.

Sieglinde has left the scene by the time Wotan arrives, bristling with anger. We sense that Brünnhilde's disobedience is only part of the reason for his black mood. Below the surface he is also angry at having opened himself to humiliation by Fricka. He knows all too well that his favourite daughter was doing what he really wanted to do, but failed to do. In lashing out at Brünnhilde therefore, he is also punishing himself. Again, Brünnhilde is a manifestation of his own ego. And what punishment he metes out! He lists the ways in which he had depended on her before her disobedience, and he says that never again will he ask her to do anything for him. She will be a Valkyrie no more. He condemns her to mortality and to the ignominy of being claimed by the first man who chances by. Again, We have not heard anything like this since Alberich's curse in the fourth scene of *Das Rheingold*.

After her initial shock at the extent of her father's rejection, Brünnhilde begins a quiet appeal to the feelings of love and compassion which she knows are still buried deep inside him. She is on strong ground in reminding him of what was really in his heart: his feelings of love for his son. He acknowledges that, in his words, cruel fate had forbidden what he had longed to do. Brünnhilde tells him that she would rather he strike her dead with his spear than have to submit to his intended punishment. But if she must be locked in sleep, she says, if she must become a mortal woman and succumb to the first man who finds her, then let that man be fearless and free. 'At your command,' she adds, 'a flame can be kindled, a fiery guardian girding the rock, which will lick with its tongues and tear with its teeth any craven who dares to approach'. As Wotan's rage subsides and compassion returns to his heart, he finally agrees. 'Farewell, my valiant, glorious child!' he says. 'You were the holiest pride of my heart. Farewell! Farewell!'

Then begins one of the most moving and wonderful parts of the whole *Ring*. Wotan promises to encircle the Valkyrie's rock with fire: 'one alone wins you as bride,' he says, 'one freer than I, the god.' Page after page of words and music is filled with tender expressions of paternal love. Gone is the wrathful god; in his place now is a protecting father. He kisses her gently on the eyes, and slumber gradually overtakes her. He lays her on a mossy bank, closes her helmet and covers her with her shield. The orchestra passes through successive veils of chromaticism and we feel the magic of sleep descending and enveloping the whole scene. The 'slumber' motif gently rises and falls, like the rise and fall of breathing in the midst of sleep. Wotan says nothing for quite a long time, the orchestra expressing feelings which are too deep for words.

The 'slumber' motif is one of those miraculous themes which Wagner was able to produce on cue to convey the essence of the drama. It depends for its effect both on its particular shape and on its tempo, which needs to be broad and peaceful.

Wagner was one of the fathers of modern conducting, and he attached the greatest importance to correct tempo. This was not tempo determined in a mechanical and inflexible way, but tempo which came naturally out of what he called the *melos*, the melodic soul of a scene, a movement, a section, a phrase, even an individual bar. Time and again he lamented the fact that few conductors of his day could appreciate why one tempo was right and another was wrong. His comments on finding the right tempo are quite illuminating and they are still a useful guide for conductors, whether in the concert hall or the opera house.

In an essay on conducting written in 1869, he said:

I furnished my earlier operas ... with eloquent directions for tempo, and fixed them past mistaking (so I thought) by metronomic ciphers.

Wotan the wrathful father and Brünnhilde a pleading daughter.

But whenever I heard a foolish tempo in a performance of my *Tannhäuser*, for instance, my recriminations were always parried by the plea that my metronomic marks had been followed most scrupulously. So I saw how uncertain must be the value of mathematics in music, and thenceforth dispensed with the metronome; contenting myself with quite general indications for the principal time measure and devoting all my forethought to its modifications, since our conductors know as good as nothing of the latter.

He quoted Mendelssohn who, he said, had told him that 'a too slow tempo was the devil, and for choice he would rather things were taken too fast'. Mendelssohn had suggested that 'a really good rendering was a rarity at any time; with a little care, however, one might gloss things over; and this could best be done by never dawdling, but covering the ground at a good stiff pace'. During a visit to London in 1855, to conduct concerts for the Philharmonic Society, Wagner discovered that this Mendelssohnian dictum had been raised to the status of a tradition.

In fact it so well suited the customs and peculiarities of this Society's concerts that it almost seemed as if Mendelssohn had derived his mode of rendering from them. A huge amount of music was consumed at those concerts, but only one rehearsal allowed for each performance ... The thing flowed on like water from a public fountain; to attempt to check it was out of the question, and every allegro ended as an indisputable presto. [9]

Soon after the final performance of *The Ring* in 1876, Wagner wrote to a friend:

I simply do not know any conductor I could trust to perform my music in the right way, or any actor-singer of whom I could expect a proper realisation of my dramatic sense unless I myself had taught him everything, measure by measure, phrase by phrase. The German

WER MEINES SPEERES   DURCHSCHREITE DAS
SPITZE FÜRCHTET   FEUER NIE! ∞

No-one who fears the point of Wotan's spear will pass through the fire.

capacity for bungling in every sphere of art is unique: it reduces me to the condition in which you found me after the last *Götter-dämmerung*. What horrified me was the discovery that my conductor, Hans Richter, whom nevertheless I regard as the best I know, often could not maintain the right tempo even when he had found it, simply because he was incapable of understanding why it should be thus and not otherwise.

The final scene of *Die Walküre* is filled with a serenity and inevitability which sets it apart from everything else in *The Ring*. It also creates a mood of suspended animation. We have reached an end point, but it is not *the* end. More will happen, but nothing will be the same again. Wotan's reverie is broken by his sudden realisation that he must summon Loge, or at least his element, to encircle Brünnhilde with a fiery moat. This will be his last positive act and will fix irrevocably his own destiny. The stern, descending spear motif, symbol of his authority, signals his resolve. Three times he strikes a rock with his spear, in a gesture which is reminiscent of Moses striking a rock in the desert to bring forth water for the children of Israel.

What happens next is best left for the music alone to describe, and for our mind's eye to imagine. As Wagner's grandson, Wieland, put it, it is well-nigh impossible to duplicate for the eye what the orchestra is conveying so triumphantly to our ears. A flame leaps from the rock and gradually increases to an ever-brightening fiery glow. Flickering flames appear and bright shooting flames surround Wotan. With his spear, he directs the sea of fire to encircle the rock, from where it spreads to enclose the whole mountain. 'Whoever fears my spear-point' he says 'will never through this sea of flame!', and the motif of the unborn Siegfried makes its presence felt in the orchestra. With one last, sorrowful look back at the sleeping Brünnhilde, Wotan disappears through the fire.

After his separation from Brünnhilde, Wotan is no more than a departed spirit. Now he can only accept things; let things happen as they must. It is left to Siegfried – the man of free will, who knows that death is preferable to living in fear – to brave Wotan's spear point and pass through the fire. But these are matters for the future. For the moment, we are conscious only of the glorious music of the magic fire and Brünnhilde's sleep and, surprisingly, of a passing reference to the annunciation of death. Brünnhilde will still live, but now she is as dead to Wotan as is the hapless Siegmund.

When the fire music takes hold of the orchestra completely, the curtain falls.

Siegfried

'He is small and bent, somewhat deformed and hobbling. His head is abnormally large, his face a dark ashen colour and wrinkled, his eyes small and piercing, with red rims, his grey beard long and scrubby, his head is bald and covered with a red cap. He wears a dark grey smock with a broad belt about his loins: feet bare, with thick coarse soles underneath.' No, this is not Siegfried! It is Mime, the Nibelung, whom we last saw in *Das Rheingold*, howling pitifully at the bullying of his brother Alberich. This description appears in the original stage directions of *Der junge Siegfried* which Wagner had written in 1851 as a lighter prologue to the tragedy of *Siegfrieds Tod*.

The description is not retained in the final version of the work, but it is reflected in what Siegfried himself has to say in the first scene: 'I only have to look at you to see that you're evil in all that you do. When I watch you standing about, shuffling and nodding, twitching and slinking and blinking your eyes, I'd like to seize you by your nodding neck and put an end to your loathsome blinking!' Hardly a kindly attitude towards a guardian one might think, but then, Mime harbours similar feelings towards Siegfried, although he keeps these very much to himself. 'From the sap of plants,' thinks Mime, 'I'll make a potent brew. If he tastes just one drop he'll fall asleep. I'll seize the sword and dispatch him easily; then the ring and the gold will be mine.'

Where else would one find such vivid statements of greed and mutual mistrust, such devious scheming and bloodthirsty intent,

DAS GAB MIR DEINE MUTTER: —
SIEH' HER, EIN ZERBROCHENES SCHWERT

Mime gives Siegfried the broken pieces of sword,
passed to Mime by Siegfried's mother.

such an association of evil with the strange and the ugly? The answer, quite plainly, is in children's fairy-tales and, especially, the tales collected by the brothers Grimm.

Grimms' *Fairy-Tales* or, more correctly, *Children's and Household Tales* by Wilhelm and Jakob Grimm, as well as Wilhelm Grimm's *German Book of Heroes*, held a great fascination for Wagner. Indeed, in the late 1840s, he told a friend that he would write no more grand operas but only fairy tales.[10] I referred earlier to his inspiration in 1851 to combine the legend of Siegfried, derived from *Das Nibelungenlied* and the earlier *Poetic Edda*, with the *Story of the Youth Who Went Forth to Learn What Fear Was*. Acts One and Two of *Siegfried* are pure fairy-tale. Consider the ingredients. The location is a dark forest. We see, in turn, an evil dwarf, a handsome youth who does not know fear, a bear, an ominous stranger who calls himself the Wanderer, a second evil dwarf who is the brother of the first, a talking dragon and a talking bird. In Act Three there is also a beautiful maiden who is awakened from a long sleep by a kiss from the handsome youth who passes through a wall of fire to reach her.

Fairy-tales, as works of art, serve the purpose of informing us that life involves dangerous struggles, and that only by mastering crises and confronting fears can we eventually find our true selves. That is why frightening and unpleasant things often happen in them. Furthermore, the image of a man in a dark, impenetrable forest is an ancient literary symbol for the search for self-knowledge, for the resolution of a moral crisis or the overcoming of some obstacle to self-confidence. Dante, for example, uses such an image at the beginning of *The Divine Comedy*. The darkness of the forest is a projection of a darkness within the character himself. By overcoming these obstacles the character wins a moral victory over his own weaknesses.

One of the best known of the Grimms' fairy-tales, that of *Hänsel und Gretel*, illustrates the role of negative characters in helping the positive characters to grow in self-knowledge and self-reliance. Consider this passage, which seems particularly relevant to Act One of *Siegfried*:

> The old woman had only pretended to be kind, but she was in reality a wicked witch, who lay in wait for children and had only built a house of bread in order to entice them there. When a child fell into her power, she killed it, cooked and ate it, and that was a feast day for her. Witches have red eyes, and cannot see far, but they have a keen sense of smell like the beasts, and know when human beings draw near. [11]

We know that Gretel saved her brother by pushing the witch into her own oven. Because the children were able to gain control of their nightmare – made tangible in the form of the witch – they gained confidence in their own abilities to defeat evil and rescue themselves. So it is with Siegfried, although he is in such a state of ignorance or, if you like, innocence, that he does not even realise that he should be afraid of the dangers which confront him.

We have moved into a dramatic world that is very different from what has gone before. I have described *Das Rheingold* as a kind of morality play, in which the world's innocence is lost to greed and a lust for power and wealth. Different again is *Die Walküre*, the first day of Wagner's Festival Drama, which is full of human warmth and introspection, illuminated by occasional flashes of passion and tragedy. In it we witness the rapid decline of Wotan from a position of power and confidence to one of impotence and dejection. We also witness the growth of Brünnhilde from a devoted daughter to a noble individual, motivated by love and compassion. Then comes the fairy-tale of *Siegfried*. Like *Rheingold*, it is an allegory of the human condition, but the focus this time is not on venality but on vulnerability – both male and female.

Because Wagner wrote the poems of the four dramas in reverse order, he had to revisit the earlier texts and make adjustments to accommodate events which, although written later, occurred earlier in the narrative. He described this process in his auto-biography.

I wrote the poem of *Das Rheingold* in October and November of that year [that is 1852], whereby I brought the whole cycle of my Nibelung dramas to completion in reverse order. At the same time I revised *Der junge Siegfried* and especially *Siegfrieds Tod* in such a way that they now related correctly to the whole, and this last work in particular was considerably expanded to reflect the palpable signifi-cance of the entire drama. Accordingly, I had to give this final drama in the cycle a new title that would correspond to this altered relationship. I called it *Götterdämmerung*, while I changed *Der junge Siegfried*, inasmuch as this work no longer represented merely an isolated episode in the life of its hero but rather showed him in relationship to the other principal characters of the dramas, simply to *Siegfried*.

The young hero is an innocent abroad in a very dangerous and unsympathetic world. He is probably about seventeen when we first encounter him. After Sieglinde died giving birth, he was raised by Mime in the depths of the forest. Mime is a much weaker char-acter than his brother Alberich, and has to resort to wiles and stratagems to get his way. What amazing good fortune, he would have thought, to have come across a scion of the Volsung race in the form of a frail, orphaned baby. Now, at last, he would get even with his bullying brother. He would train Siegfried to win for him Alberich's ring and the golden hoard which Fafner, the giant turned dragon, guards in his forest lair. And after that? Well, Siegfried would have served his purpose. There would be no place for him in Mime's new world, a world in which Mime would be king!

The Wanderer leaves Mime's head forfeit to one who doesn't know fear.

But what of Siegfried's world? It is important to remember that Siegfried has not met, nor has he even seen, another person – male or female – other than Mime the Nibelung. All that he knows has been learnt from his evil guardian and from observing the forest creatures. He is, in every sense, a child of nature.

Consider this drama from Siegfried's perspective, a perspective dominated by physical experiences and by the corrupting tutelage, the bad influence, of Mime. To a large degree, Siegfried is a product of the forest and of his five senses. That is why he feels a kinship with his friend the bear, the birds of the air, the fish of the streams, and even the gentle doe which he associates instinctively with his unknown mother. Wagner draws attention to this sensory world through the 'texture' of instrumental sounds, the melodious evocations of nature, the clash and clang, heat and steam of Mime's forge, the taste of Fafner's blood, the flickering, menacing lights of the forest, the dazzling sunlight of the mountain top, even the 'warm, fragrant breath' of the sleeping Brünnhilde. However, nature is evoked not just for its own sake.

It seems to me that in this work, more than in any other, Wagner uses the physical environment as a metaphor for psychological influences and relationships. In true fairy-tale fashion, the physical ugliness of Mime is taken to be an outward and visible sign of his evil intentions. The benign aspect of the forest, with its rustling leaves and bird songs, is more of a real home to Siegfried than Mime's bleak cave, or anything else he knows. Little wonder then that, in Act Two, it is within the comforting embrace of a linden tree and the womb-like sounds of the Forest Murmurs, that his thoughts turn to the mother for whom he longs, and he wonders what she was like. 'Must every human mother die when a child is born?' he asks himself. How sad the world would be then.

Throughout this marvellous work, the orchestra paints not only the changing physical environment (which it does with unsurpassed eloquence) but also the changing moods and hidden feelings of the characters. We cross from the physical world to a metaphysical one when we hear the dragon and the Woodbird speaking. This doesn't happen in any of the other dramas. The rams that draw Fricka's chariot don't speak, nor does Brünnhilde's horse nor Wotan's ravens (which makes them easy to dispense with in modern productions).

The dragon and the bird speak in *Siegfried* because we are in the realm of sign and symbol, allegory and illusion. We even hear the secret thoughts of Mime, as he tries to mask his murderous intentions with hypocrisy and guile. Appearances conceal hidden meanings; symbolism is everywhere; nothing is what it seems. The shattering of Wotan's spear by the sword *Notung* in Act Three, reversing the order of events in *Die Walküre*, signifies Wotan's irrelevance and makes it plain that the future belongs to Siegfried. The fire through which Siegfried passes in order to awaken Brünnhilde symbolises the last of the trials he must undergo in order to fulfil his destiny.

There is an obvious parallel here with the Grimms' fairy-tale of *Briar-Rose*, better known to us as *The Sleeping Beauty*, in which the prince must pass through a wall of briars to awaken the princess with a kiss. There is also a similarity with Mozart's *Die Zauberflöte*, a work which Wagner admired greatly. In that opera, Tamino must undergo an ordeal by fire in order to overcome fear of death and enter the temple with Pamina. The awakening of Brünnhilde marks the point at which the adolescent Siegfried becomes a man. It is his initiation rite, for it is through his discovery of woman that he learns fear and passion at the same time. Thus, from Act Three of *Siegfried* onwards, both Siegfried and Brünnhilde are transformed. They begin new lives, both as individuals and together.

Wagner had several reasons for interrupting work on *The Ring* at the end of Act Two of *Siegfried*, but it was a logical point at which to leave behind the allegorical atmosphere of the forest with its implications of childish innocence, and begin a transition to the tremendous new sound world of *Götterdämmerung*. Before this could happen, he would write two utterly contrasting master-pieces, *Tristan und Isolde* and *Die Meistersinger von Nürnberg*.

Let us go back to the beginning of Act One. Before the curtain rises, we hear the soft and ominous roll of a kettledrum, to which is added an equally soft 'scheming' motif low on the bassoons. Somebody is pondering something, but who and what? Other motifs soon provide an answer. We hear the rhythmic sound of a smith's hammer on an anvil, familiar to us from the Nibelheim scene in *Das Rheingold*, and a curious 'limping' musical figure involving three grace notes and a falling note, suggestive of deviousness and malign intent. This motif is associated with the Nibelung, Mime. When the 'ring' motif is added shortly afterwards, we are left in no doubt as to the object of Mime's scheming. So, the picture is complete even before the stage is revealed to us.

When the curtain rises, sure enough, there is Mime tapping away at a sword blade, to which he is putting the finishing touches. He complains that every time he makes a sword, the insolent boy Siegfried just laughs and snaps it in half. Only the sword *Notung* would be strong enough to withstand this rough handling, but there is no way that he can weld its fragments together. In the course of his monologue he reveals that he intends to use Siegfried to kill Fafner and obtain the ring.

While Mime is still complaining to himself, Siegfried's bois-terous call is heard and he runs in, driving before him a great shambling forest bear. The double-basses growl in a bear-like man-ner as the beast heads towards the Nibelung. Mime is frightened out of his wits and hides behind the anvil until the laughing Siegfried has had enough of his childish pranks and drives the bear out into the forest again. This lively interlude is typical of teenage mischief, but it is more than that. It demonstrates, early in the piece, Siegfried's complete absence of fear, and his naivety.

After all, a fully grown bear is a dangerous creature which might just as easily turn on the boy as on Mime. It also points up Mime's extreme nervousness, and shows that although Siegfried is just a boy, his physical strength and exuberance make him more than a match for the dwarfish Mime, who has to resort to cunning in order to get his way.

Siegfried, as a character, has had rather a bad press in modern times, especially since the Second World War. The popular parody, which is usually conjured up by people who know nothing about *The Ring*, is of some Teutonic super-hero with nasty habits and more brawn than brain. The fact is that, despite all the references to heroic expectations, the only heroic thing that Siegfried does is to pass through the wall of fire that encircles Brünnhilde's rock. He saves no one from danger and changes nothing for the better, and even when he kills the dragon he uses a magic sword and is insensitive to any risk.

He does not understand what the fuss over the ring is all about and he certainly does not attempt to use the ring, other than as a token of his love for Brünnhilde. He is deceived, drugged, betrayed and eventually murdered. Some hero! No, in practice, Siegfried is just an innocent abroad, a symbol of hope in a hopeless world, who is caught up in machinations he does not comprehend, just as the innocent Prince Tamino was caught up in the machinations of the Queen of the Night and Sarastro. Siegfried becomes a tragic figure. The hope which is vested in him never bears fruit and he falls victim to an evil which he barely understands. That is why his funeral music is filled with such poignancy. So much promise is cut short and remains unfulfilled. We can identify with this even in our modern world. Every time we hear of a promising young life snuffed out by a senseless killing, a tragic accident or the brutality of war, we can appreciate what Siegfried really stands for in *Der Ring des Nibelungen*.

Wagner himself was appalled by thoughts of the waste of young life, so often associated with the collapse of an old political order. He was especially sensitive to this after the birth of his own son, whom he named Siegfried. He had personally witnessed the killing of students and other revolutionaries by the Saxon and Prussian authorities during the Dresden uprisings of 1849. He shared the strong folk memories of invasions, firstly by the armies of Louis XIV who had attacked the decaying Holy Roman Empire in the 1680s, then by French revolutionary armies who had annexed German cities west of the Rhine in 1792, and then by Napoleon's armies between 1804 and 1806, and again in 1813, also preying on the remains of the old Empire. Inevitably, it seemed, the passing of one era and the birth of another was attended by tragedy and the sacrifice of the young.

It is not easy to convey Siegfried's youthful vulnerability on the stage, because only singers of experience and stamina can do justice to this most demanding of roles; and they seldom resemble athletic teenage boys! It also takes a while to warm to Siegfried as a character. He is ill-mannered, breaks swords that have taken a long time to make, tips over food that has been prepared for him, and sets a wild animal on his guardian. His attitude towards Mime is one of unmitigated hostility.

For his part, the wizened dwarf whines on and on about how much he has done for the boy and the sacrifices he has made. He keeps this up while he is preparing a meal, and the orchestra follows his domestic activities with an entertaining commentary on cooking; violas and cellos using the wooden parts of their bows, and low clarinets bubbling their amusement. Despite Mime's best efforts to make Siegfried feel guilty for his ingratitude, the boy continues his torrent of abuse. He says that the only thing Mime hasn't been able to teach him is how not to loathe the sight of him! Indeed, he is so repelled by him that he doesn't know why he keeps returning to the cave. Mime suggests that this must be because, deep down, he is dear to Siegfried's heart. This makes the

Nothung!
Nothung! Neidliches Schwert! ==
jetzt haftest du wieder im Heft.

Siegfried reforges Notung, *the sword.*

boy laugh. 'Have you forgotten that I can't bear the sight of you?' he says. Mime replies that he must learn to tame his wild feelings. All creatures return to their parents because they love them. This invites the obvious question from Siegfried – then where is Mime's wife? Where is his own mother? Mime is rather embarrassed by this line of questioning and replies desperately that he is father and mother in one. Siegfried doesn't believe this for a moment. He has observed the creatures of the forest and has seen how the young resemble their parents. He knows from his own reflection in a stream that he does not resemble Mime any more than a silvery fish resembles a toad. 'And no fish had a toad for a father!' he says. Siegfried then realises why it is that he keeps returning to Mime: because Mime alone can tell him about his father and mother.

At first, the dwarf pretends that he doesn't understand what the boy is talking about. 'What father! What mother! Meaningless questions!' he exclaims. Siegfried then grabs him by the throat and shakes him until Mime gestures that he will tell him everything. And so he begins his account of how, in the woods, he found a woman who lay and wept. She gave birth, a birth cruel and painful. She died but Siegfried was born. 'My mother died because of me?' says Siegfried quietly. Mime reveals that her name was Sieglinde, but he pretends not to know the name of his father, revealing only that he fell in battle. The boy asks for proof that all of this is true, and Mime produces the shattered pieces of the sword *Notung*. Elated by the discovery of his father's sword, Siegfried instructs Mime to repair it as quickly as possible so that, at last, he can leave the miserable cave and roam freely through the world. He can barely contain his delight: 'As the fish swims through the waters, as the finch flies through the branches, so shall I fly far away with the wind through the woods; then Mime, I shall never see you again!' He rushes out into the forest with Mime shouting after him.

Mime is now faced with a dilemma. If Siegfried leaves him he will lose his opportunity to win the ring from the dragon Fafner. But he also knows that without *Notung*, Siegfried will not be equipped to confront Fafner. While Mime is pondering this predicament, crouching behind the anvil, Wotan in the guise of the Wanderer enters the cave from the forest.

The Wanderer greets Mime courteously: 'Hail, worthy smith!' He introduces himself as a weary traveller who would rest awhile by Mime's hearth. Mime is irritated by this interruption and his attitude is cool, to say the least. He suggests that the Wanderer might like to keep on wandering. The visitor asks if Mime would like to learn something from him and hints that ill fortune attends those who withhold their hospitality. He offers to wager his own head in trying to answer any three questions put to him.

Mime succumbs to the invitation and asks three simple questions about the roles of the Nibelungs, the giants and the gods in the cosmic order of things; all of which are easily answered. When the Wanderer speaks of the gods, his spear point touches the ground and distant thunder is heard, much to Mime's alarm. Then, to Mime's continuing distress, the Wanderer asks him three questions on forfeit of *his* head. He asks about the race whom Wotan loves above all others but has treated harshly – the Volsungs. He asks the name of the sword which Siegfried must use if he is to kill Fafner – *Notung*. So far so good for Mime.

The question-and-answer game serves to remind us of events in earlier dramas and to reinforce story lines and musical motifs. However, it also reveals how the narrator (in this case Wotan) views past events. One new piece of information emerges about Wotan's perceptions. He refers to Alberich as 'Black Alberich' and himself, Wotan, as 'Light Alberich'. In other words, he acknowledges that they are two of a kind, two sides of the one coin, two aspects of the one persona.

The Wanderer's last question is: who shall forge *Notung* anew?

This sends Mime into paroxysms of fear because, quite frankly, he doesn't know and foolishly had not used one of his questions to find out. The answer is revealed: 'One who has never learnt fear'. The Wanderer advises Mime to guard his head well and leaves it forfeit to him who does not know fear. He then departs as mysteriously as he came.

If Mime thought he was in trouble before, that was nothing compared to the mess in which he now finds himself. Put simply, if Siegfried learns about fear he is unlikely to confront Fafner. But if he remains ignorant of fear, then it will be to him that Mime's head will be forfeit. It is all too much for Mime and he begins to hallucinate. He sees flickering lights in the forest, hears strange noises and imagines the gaping maw of a monster about to devour him. It is Fafner! Fafner!

This fascinating outburst is a kind of waking nightmare, which the orchestra describes in graphic detail. The 'slumber' motif, which conveyed such peace and calm at the end of *Die Walküre*, is now twisted and distorted, its harmonies stretched out of recognition. The full descriptive palette of the Wagnerian orchestra is used to evoke the nightmarish vision which reduces Mime to a quivering heap behind his anvil.

The orchestral richness of *Siegfried* is one of its particular glories. In this work, Wagner uses instrumental tone colour as never before, to create and then change a mood with powerful effect. The late John Culshaw, producer of the celebrated Decca recording of the 1960s, observed that it takes time to play even a simple melody or to establish an harmonic progression; but a subtle, unexpected change in instrumental colour can alter a mood in an instant.

Wagner was very particular about the structure of his orchestra and the use to which its instruments were put. He was one of the greatest orchestrators of any period, as other composers have been quick to acknowledge. Richard Strauss, for example, recommended

DEN TARNHELM HAT
ER —
DOCH AUCH DEN RING

DA LIEG', NEIDISCHER KERL! —
NOTHUNG TRÄGST DU IM HERZEN.

MICH MAHNE DER TAND,
DASS ICH KÄMPFEND
FAFNER ERLEGT.

5

Siegfried kills the dragon, Fafner.

that the student of orchestration should compare Wagner's eleven scores with each other, and note how each has its own combination of instruments, its own orchestral style, and how each says what it wants to say in the simplest way, with moderation in the use of means.

Contrary to what many people believe, Wagner's use of the orchestra does exhibit great restraint and the most careful judgment. His orchestra was large, but this was to give him a wider variety of tonal colours and textures from which to draw, not to give a bigger sound overall, although that might at times be a consequence. Wagner's approach to the orchestra was reflected in his comment that it was 'no mere compost of washy tone ingredients but consisted of a rich association of instruments with unbounded power of adding to its numbers'. In his words, each instrument has a definite individuality and clothes the tone produced with an equally individual garment. Conductor Jeffrey Tate has commented that Wagner's very sparing use of his huge orchestra is astonishing, and he has described *The Ring* as a whole, as one of the most intensely beautiful creations of the European tradition.

With many composers it is possible to take, say, an aria or ensemble or orchestral interlude from one of their works and insert it, virtually unchanged, into another, without the average listener being any the wiser. Some quite famous composers made a regular practice of doing just that! Their approach was 'when you're on a good thing, repeat it'. But this would be quite impossible with Wagner's music, because each of his works exists in its own distinctive sound world. Almost every bar belongs to a unique emotional environment – the silvery, dream-like world of *Lohengrin*, the atonal eroticism of *Tristan*, the mellow confidence and good-humour of *Meistersinger*, and *Parsifal*, at once mystical and sensual, whose colours, said Debussy, seemed to be 'illuminated as from behind'.

And then, of course, there are the four parts of *The Ring*, each of which has as much in common with the others as it has differences in mood and purpose. Interestingly, Wagner does quote himself in one of his works, just as Mozart quotes *Figaro* in the last scene of *Don Giovanni*. In Act Three of *Die Meistersinger*, Hans Sachs refers in a few lines to the sad tale of *Tristan und Isolde*, and the orchestra, in an instant, takes on the distinctive harmonies and colouring of that tragic story of love and longing. There is no way that this insertion could pass unnoticed, even by those who did not understand a word of what was being sung.

Berlioz, who was a master of instrumentation and wrote a famous handbook on the subject, referred particularly to the extraordinary effects created by Wagner in unexpected ways. 'In order to represent the blazing flickering flames,' he observed, 'Wagner wrote a figure which is almost impossible for a first-rate soloist to play cleanly throughout. But when played by 16 to 32 violinists, the passage has such a marvellous, overwhelming effect that it is absolutely impossible to imagine a better representation of the blazing fire flickering in a thousand hues.'[12]

Rimsky-Korsakov, another master of instrumentation, remarked that 'Wagner's methods of orchestration struck Glazunov and me, and thenceforth his devices gradually came to form part of our orchestral tricks of the trade'. Bruckner, Mahler, Strauss, Debussy, Ravel, Scriabin, Dvorak, Schoenberg, Pfitzner, and many others down to our own day, have been inheritors of Wagner's innovations and, in turn, have influenced others.

His orchestra for *The Ring* was large compared with contemporary practice, and it is still large by modern standards. The original manuscript indicated a total of 107 instruments, which was increased to 119 for the premiere performance in 1876. For the second production at Bayreuth in 1896, the number was increased to 124. Compare this with the Dresden orchestra, one of the finest and largest in Europe, which had only forty players in 1783, and even in the late 1840s just sixty-six players. The Leipzig

Gewandhaus orchestra had thirty-five players in the 1840s. In 1838, when Wagner had been musical director in Riga, he conducted performances of six of Beethoven's symphonies with orchestras of just twenty-four musicians. Against such numbers, an orchestra of 119 players must have seemed a wanton extravagance – until people heard what it could do.

In *Siegfried*, the orchestral sound is extraordinarily descriptive. Viewing the work as a whole, we can recognise a general movement of tone and texture from darkness to light, from the hidden dangers of Mime's cave and the depths of the forest to the clarity and transparency of Brünnhilde's mountain top. The first and third scenes of Act One have a dark and ominous mood, emphasised by the use of violas, lower strings, bassoons and tubas. Against this dark background, the two tenor voices of Siegfried and Mime are thrown into high relief. The presence of Fafner, who is never far from Mime's mind, is made palpable by the tubas. The violas in particular, come into their own in the early part of *Siegfried*, for they are able to express, as nothing else can, the dark and scheming nature of Mime. The Wanderer, on the other hand, radiates dignity and a kind of grandeur, not only because of what he sings and the form in which he sings it, but also because of the musical aura which surrounds him. The changes in feeling and mood are clearly apparent during the exchanges between Mime and the Wanderer as they ask each other questions.

Just when the audience is beginning to wonder if all of the action is over, Wagner gives us one of the most energetic scenes in the musical theatre. Siegfried returns to collect his sword, only to find Mime still cowering behind his anvil. In the conversation which follows, Mime tries to explain to Siegfried what fear is all about. He describes the apparition which he had seen in the dark forest, and the orchestra again conjures up the flashing, flickering lights and murmuring noises. But to Siegfried, fear is still incomprehensible, and this is reflected in the orchestra which repeats

SCHWARZ-ALBERÍCH,
SCHWEÍFST DU HÍER?
HÜTEST DU FAFNER'S HAUS?

H.·BRAUNE

4

Old enemies, Wotan and Alberich, meet in the forest at night.

Mime's fevered imagery without the terror and anxiety. Mime then tells Siegfried about Fafner, and says that he will learn all about fear by confronting the dragon in its lair.

Siegfried is anxious to do just that, but since Mime is clearly unable to repair the sword *Notung*, Siegfried decides to do it himself. He piles charcoal on the hearth and fans the fire. He files the sword fragments into small pieces and puts them into a crucible which he then heats, using the bellows to raise the temperature of the flames. While Siegfried is engaged in smelting and toiling away at the bellows, Mime is equally busy mixing his poisonous brew. Their singing continues in deadly counterpoint.

The contents of the crucible are poured into a mould, which is then plunged into water with much hissing of steam. The orchestra works overtime to produce an amazing variety of sound effects. The mould is thrust back into the fire, then broken open, and the glowing steel is placed on the anvil. Siegfried sings his forging song as he strikes the blade with his hammer. Sparks fly and Mime savours the prospect of getting rid of this tiresome boy for ever.

When his work is finished, Siegfried hails the return of his father's sword and holds it aloft. He then brings it down violently on the anvil, which splits in half with a crash, causing Mime to fall to the ground with fright. The splitting of the anvil is not just a piece of theatricality. It has its origins both in a Norse saga of the thirteenth century, *Thidrekssaga* (Dietrich's saga), in which Sigurd shatters Mimir's anvil with a hammer, and in the tale of the youth who did not know fear, in which the boy shatters an anvil with an axe.

In his autobiography, *Mein Leben*, Wagner describes how, as a nine-year-old boy living in Leipzig, he had met the composer Carl Maria von Weber, who visited the family home on a number of occasions. He was impressed, he said, by Weber's 'refined, delicate and spiritual appearance' and by his enquiries as to the young Richard's ambitions. But most of all, wrote Wagner, he was

Siegfried hears a bird, singing in the forest canopy above,
and thinks of his mother.

impressed by the music of Weber's most famous opera, *Der Freischütz*, which had had its premiere the year before. Nothing, Wagner recalled, moved him more strongly than this music, even as a nine-year-old!

Der Freischütz was a milestone on the road to a recognisably German operatic genre and to the development of romantic opera in general. It is easy to find Weberian influences in Wagner's early works, but by the time of *The Ring*, these have all but disappeared, with one notable exception: in *Siegfried*. The spooky atmosphere of the wolf's glen in *Der Freischütz* finds a clear echo in the scene in the forest at night, during which firstly Alberich, then Wotan, and then Siegfried and Mime make their appearance at the entrance to Fafner's cave. In both cases, the tremolo strings and soft, ominous kettle drums create the unmistakable mood of the supernatural. It is Wagner's homage to his great predecessor. There is even, in *Der Freischütz*, an embryonic suggestion of the Forest Murmurs, which will feature a little later in Act Two of *Siegfried*.

The curtain rises on Alberich, keeping watch outside Fafner's cave. A bluish light in the forest heralds the appearance of the Wanderer. A tense conversation ensues, during which the Wanderer informs Alberich (and us) that a hero approaches who will free the golden hoard, that Mime is Alberich's rival for the gold, that Fafner will be killed and the ring pass to a new owner.

Eventually, the Wanderer awakens Fafner and warns him that he is in danger. He offers the dragon safety if he will give up the golden hoard, but Fafner declines the offer. Alberich then offers to take the ring off his hands whilst leaving the rest of the treasure intact. Again, Fafner declines and asks just to be left alone to sleep. He yawns. Yawning dragons? If anyone wonders about Wagner's sense of humour, Act Two of *Siegfried* provides plenty of examples.

The Wanderer laughs and departs, warning Alberich to beware

of his brother, Mime. As day begins to dawn, Alberich hides himself in a rocky cleft on one side of the cave, and the stage remains empty for some moments. Then Mime and Siegfried arrive.

What should we make of this dragon who is so reluctant to stir from his cave? From one perspective, Fafner represents the pointlessness of hoarding wealth. The treasure in his cave is the equivalent of money under the bed, talent not developed, resources left unused. But a dragon also symbolises the fears we all carry about within us – except Siegfried of course. Our own personal dragons are the things which we regard as frightening and intimidating, and which we must overcome if we are to grow as individuals.

Our irrational prejudices are dragons too. Siegfried has no quarrel with Fafner, but his mind has been moulded by Mime. He intends to destroy Fafner, just as Mime has told him to. Actually, the ring is perfectly harmless as long as Fafner has it, because he wishes only to guard it, not use it. If it is not to be returned to the Rhinedaughters, surely the next best thing is for it to remain in Fafner's possession. By killing the dragon and freeing the ring, Siegfried is only putting it back in the public domain where it can do more harm. Of course, it is not Siegfried of his own volition who wants to do this but Siegfried under the malign influence of Mime. Unfortunately, this is not the last occasion on which Siegfried will be manipulated in this way.

Mime provides the obligatory warnings about the Dragon's jaws, its corrosive saliva and its deadly tail. Siegfried promises to watch out for all of these dangers and ascertains that the beast's heart is in the usual place. Mime then goes off to cool himself in a stream and leaves the boy to rest in the shade of a linden tree. Siegfried muses on what his father must have been like – like him perhaps – and then he tries to imagine his mother. The music takes on a most delicate and tender quality and, for the first time, we feel sympathy for Siegfried, who is revealed as being desperately lonely. He will do anything for true companionship.

We hear the gentle rustling of the Forest Murmurs, and nature is evoked with the most exquisite orchestral writing. Years later, Cosima Wagner recorded in her diary her husband's comments during a performance of the *Siegfried Idyll*, which draws on the music of Acts Two and Three of *Siegfried*. She wrote: 'What a sound such a wind instrument makes!' Richard says. 'The strings are like a forest, and the woodwinds like the birds within it.' [13]

In his desire to communicate with a Woodbird that sings in the branches above him, Siegfried cuts a reed and fashions it into a simple pipe. His attempts to mimic the bird are woeful and, in the end, he gives up and just blows his horn instead. This wakens the dragon. In the fight that ensues, Fafner is mortally wounded but asks, before he dies, who the brave boy is who has finished him off. Siegfried cannot say who he is, other than that he is called Siegfried. Fafner, more giant than dragon at the moment of his death, tells him in a moving passage that the brothers Fasolt and Fafner are now both victims of the cursed gold, and he warns of Mime's murderous intentions. Then, repeating the young hero's name, he expires.

When Siegfried removes his sword from Fafner's heart, some of the dragon's blood gets smeared on his fingers. Involuntarily, he puts his fingers to his mouth and, when he tastes the blood, he finds that he can understand what the Woodbird is saying: 'Hei! Siegfried has won now the Nibelung hoard! Now let him find it within Fafner's cave! The Tarnhelm that's his will assist him with marvellous deeds. If he could discover the ring it would make him lord of the world.' Thus, prompted by the Woodbird, Siegfried enters the cave.

What should we make of this talkative Woodbird? When Siegfried encounters the Wanderer in the third Act, he says that a Woodbird had told him about a woman asleep on a rock, sur-rounded by fire. The Wanderer replies that a bird may chatter about all sorts of things but no human can understand it. Of

NOCH HÄLT MEINE HAND
    DER HERRSCHAFT HAFT,
        DAS SCHWERT DAS DU SCHWING'ST,
ZERSCHLUG EINST DIESER SCHAFT:
        NOCH EINMAL DENN
ZERSPRING' ES AM EWIGEN SPEER!

H.Braune

*Wotan's time is running out. Siegfried does not fear his spear-point and will,
briefly, inherit the future.*

course Siegfried, who has tasted the dragon's blood, can indeed understand the language of birds. Wagner took this detail from old sources such as the thirteenth-century *Thidrekssaga*, in which Siegfried is told what he needs to know by two woodbirds. Following this model, Wagner originally intended to use multiple birds. In myths and folk legends, birds are often used to symbolise the getting of self-knowledge. In the very fine Tyrolean Folk Museum in Innsbruck, for example, one can find several striking representations of 'The Bird of Self-knowledge'.

During Siegfried's reverie under the Linden tree he first hears the bird's song without understanding its meaning, and he says: 'it would surely tell me something – perhaps about my dear mother?' In the abandoned prose text for *The Young Siegfried* the boy exclaims: 'I think I hear my mother singing!', and in the verse text and composition text: 'I think my mother is singing to me!'. At the end of the music for the Woodbird's warning about Mime's treachery, we hear the '*Wälsung*' motif, always associated with Sieglinde and Siegmund. Wagner explained this in a note to King Ludwig: 'We hear, softly, softly, mother Sieglinde's loving concern for her son.' According to Hans von Wolzogen, Wagner called the Woodbird 'Sieglinde's maternal soul'.

So there is good reason to think that, for Siegfried, the Woodbird is the voice of his mother's love, warning her son of danger and leading him to Brünnhilde. In a narrow sense, his mother is Sieglinde but in a more general sense she is nature itself, for Siegfried is surely the quintessential child of nature. In a letter to his own mother in 1846, Wagner wrote: 'Nature lovingly reminds us that we are part of her, like trees. And when I feel myself as one with nature, I long for you.'

As Siegfried disappears into the cave, the unholy Nibelung brothers, Alberich and Mime, emerge from the rocky cleft and the forest, respectively, and start bickering about which of them should have the ring and the other treasures.

Wagner handles the scene which follows with consummate skill. The rivalry of the brothers takes the form of a scherzo, whose tricky rhythms and insistent phrases reveal all too clearly the essential natures of Alberich and Mime. Each claims the gold as his own, and bids the other to keep his greedy eyes and hands off it. 'It is mine by right,' claims Alberich, 'for who robbed the Rhine of its gold and who wrought the spell of the ring?' 'And who,' counters Mime, 'made the Tarnhelm for you?' So the petulant dialogue goes on, each taunting and attacking the other.

At last, Alberich wears Mime down and the latter suggests a compromise: Alberich can keep the ring if Mime can have the Tarnhelm. Alberich rejects this with a scornful laugh: would he ever be safe in his sleep if Mime had the Tarnhelm, which gives invisibility to its wearer? Beside himself with rage, Mime shrieks, 'Not the Tarnhelm? Do I get nothing then?' Alberich declares that he will not give him even a nail, to which Mime responds that he will call for support from Siegfried, who will avenge him with his sword on his 'dear brother'. In this amazing scene, the vocal lines are written in 6/8 time, while the orchestral parts are in 2/4 time.

Siegfried reappears from the cave with only two items – the Tarnhelm and the ring. He does not really understand what they are and has only taken them because the bird counselled him to do so. They are tokens of his triumph over Fafner. He thrusts the Tarnhelm into his belt and puts the ring on his finger. Once more the bird speaks to him, warning him of Mime's treachery and telling him that, having tasted the blood of the dragon, he will be able to see through the dwarf's words to the secret intentions of his heart. Mime slinks back on stage and, with oily hypocrisy, greets the young dragon-slayer.

Siegfried says that he regrets Fafner's death, especially when more evil figures still roam free, and adds that he hates him who provoked the fight more than he hated the dragon. Mime then imagines himself saying flattering and deceiving things to Siegfried, but the latter can now understand what the dwarf really intends, which is to murder Siegfried and take all that he has won. Mime becomes increasingly perplexed because Siegfried seems to know what is really in his mind as opposed to what he thinks he is saying. The orchestra conveys simulated affection and concern, while Mime's words reveal exactly the opposite. Dramatically, this is a most daring device and it works superbly.

As Mime tries, in honeyed tones, to give Siegfried a poisoned draught, he is all the while revealing that when the boy is unconscious he will hack off his head. Provoked beyond endurance, Siegfried raises his sword and, with a single blow, strikes Mime dead. Alberich's mocking laughter rings out from the cleft nearby. Siegfried drags Mime's body on to the golden hoard which he had so long desired and which can now be his for ever.

Now Siegfried is truly alone in the world. Once again the Woodbird comes to his aid and tells him of a glorious bride: Brünnhilde, who awaits him on a rocky height surrounded by a fierce flickering fire. Excited at the prospect of finding a companion, Siegfried sets off after the bird which, at first, teases him by flying around in circles and then going hither and thither, before heading off towards Brünnhilde's rock. At last, Siegfried will discover fear, not in the depths of the forest nor in a dragon's cave, but in the arms of a woman.

In June 1857 Wagner abandoned work on *Siegfried* to start on *Tristan und Isolde*. There is plenty of evidence that the world of *Tristan* was occupying more and more of his thoughts while he was working on *The Ring* and that, at last, he could contain himself no longer and had to do something about it. There are scraps of music foreshadowing what was to come, and there are letters on the subject which are most revealing. For example, he wrote to the Princess Marie Wittgenstein in August 1857: 'The second act is finished. Fafner is dead, and Siegfried has run after the

WAS STRAHLT MIR DORT ENTGEGEN ? —
WELCH GLÄNZENDES STAHLGESCHMEIDE!
BLENDET MIR NOCH
DIE LOHE DEN BLICK?

Siegfried passes through the fire surrounding the sleeping Brünnhilde.

Woodbird, but while working on *Siegfried*, *Tristan* has given me no peace. In fact, I have been working simultaneously on both.' He did a little more work on *Siegfried* in July of that year and completed the orchestral draft of Act Two in August but, after that, work on *The Ring* was left in abeyance for a full twelve years, until 1869. Inevitably, when he did resume work, he was able to bring to Act Three of *Siegfried* and to all of the scoring of *Götterdämmerung* the wealth of experience gained in writing *Tristan* and *Meistersinger*, each in its own way a pinnacle of Western art.

From the opening bars of Act Three of *Siegfried* we can only marvel at the new facility with which Wagner handles his complex musical forces and elaborate thematic structures. Wotan is riding to see Erda to find out what the future holds. No fewer than nine motifs are woven into the prelude to Act Three to describe the god's search for answers, the turbulent state of his mind, and the drastic consequences of events which are now out of control.

We are a long way, conceptually, from Siegfried's forest; closer perhaps to the spirit of *Die Walküre*. The issues are of cosmic significance, and although Wotan is still in the guise of the Wanderer, he is no longer the rather genial, if awe-inspiring figure who bantered with Mime in their game of Trivial Pursuit. He summons Erda from her sleep and pours out his troubled heart to her. He is desperate for her wisdom and advice. She tells him to consult her daughters, the Norns who spin the rope of world knowledge which binds past, present and future. This is not what the Wanderer wants to hear. Erda recalls that she once bore to Wotan a maiden, Brünnhilde, who is both brave and wise. Why doesn't he consult her? The Wanderer replies that Brünnhilde has been condemned to sleep and to mortality for her wilfulness. This astonishes Erda, for she knows that the very attributes that Wotan has condemned in their daughter characterise his own nature.

The world now seems upside down. Like Fafner, Erda just wants to return to her slumber. But the Wanderer won't let her go until she tells him how to deal with his worries. She replies unhelpfully that he is no longer what he purports to be and should not be disturbing her sleep. After a long silence, he brings himself to acknowledge the inevitability of change, the demise of the old moral order which he personifies, and the emergence of a new order to which the young Siegfried belongs. He bequeaths the future to the young Volsung who does not even know him but who is destined to awaken Brünnhilde. She, in turn, will set the world free.

This noble passage, in which the Wanderer accepts the inevitable, again demonstrates Wagner's ability to weave together many different motifs into a rich emotional fabric. Prominent amongst the motifs is a new and splendid one, usually referred to as 'the world's inheritance'. I doubt if Wagner could have written this scene before he had written Die Meistersinger. There is more than a touch of Hans Sachs in the Wanderer in this last Act of Siegfried.

Surprisingly perhaps, Buddhist influences are to be found in The Ring, notwithstanding its primary sources in the myths and legends of the north. In the mid 1850s, Wagner became very interested in Buddhism, particularly after his encounter with the writings of Schopenhauer. It was an interest that remained with him to the end of his life, and it also played a part in the creation of both Tristan und Isolde and Parsifal. In May 1856, after finishing Die Walküre but before taking up Siegfried, Wagner sketched out his proposed Buddhist music drama, Die Sieger, (The Victors). The title was inspired by the Jinas, Indian holy men whose name in Sanskrit means 'victors'. Their victory was over human passions. Die Sieger dealt with an event in the legendary life of the Buddha, one of whose titles was Jina – the Victor. For many years, Wagner intended to work on Die Sieger after he had finished Parsifal, and it was only in 1882 that a combination of exhaustion and realism led him to abandon the idea for good. He also felt that he would be duplicating much of what had been said in *Parsifal*. He had been attracted to the story for a number of reasons, not the least of which was its theme of reincarnation, which he saw as a vehicle for his compositional technique of Emotional Reminiscence. 'Only music' he said, 'can convey the mysteries of reincarnation'.[14]

How does this relate to *The Ring*? In July 1878, Cosima wrote the following in her diary: 'When I was looking through some papers with him yesterday, I came upon the original theme for *Sangst du nicht, dein Wissen*; I tell Richard that the present theme (meant at first for the Buddha) pleases me far more.'[15] What is this theme that was composed originally for the Buddha in *Die Sieger*? It first appears in Wotan's final scene with Erda in Act Three of *Siegfried*, and is used to express his new-found wisdom in accepting that he must 'will' the coming of a new order and the demise of the gods. Although the theme is usually referred to as 'the world's inheritance' or 'the world's heritage', as Hans von Wolzogen labelled it, it should, I suggest, be thought of as 'the getting of wisdom' or 'enlightenment'; hence the connection in Wagner's mind with that defining characteristic of the Buddha – 'the Enlightened One'.

In the scene in Act Three, after a long silence which is specifically indicated in the text and score, Wotan tells Erda that she is not wise, for he is no longer concerned about the inevitable end of the gods and, in fact, consciously wills it. What he once resolved in despair, he will now do gladly. At that point, we hear in the orchestra the majestic theme once intended for the Buddha. All the burdens of self-interest and denial are lifted from Wotan's shoulders, and we share with him a tremendous sense of release and relief. It is truly a moment of revelation. During the first rehearsals, Wagner said that this passage 'must sound like the proclamation of a new religion'.[16] Indeed it does.

The theme occurs again shortly afterwards when Wotan tells Erda: 'Brünnhild wakes to the hero. Then your child of wisdom

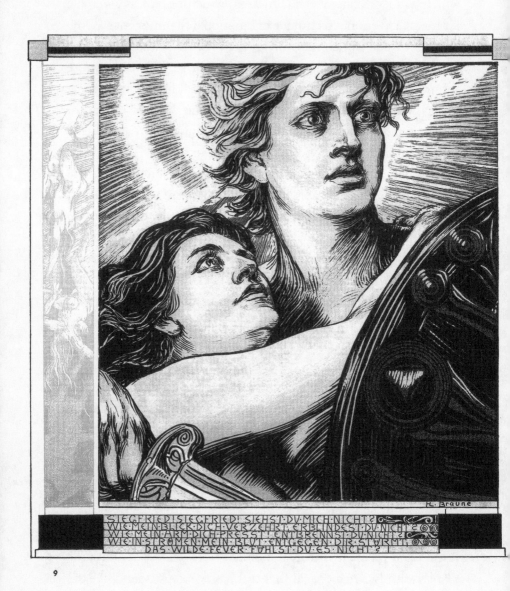

SIEGFRIED! SIEGFRIED! SIEHST DV MICH NICHT?
WIE MEIN BLICK DICH VERZEHRT ERBLINDEST DV NICHT?
WIE MEIN ARM DICH PRESST ENTBRENNST DV NICHT?
WIE IN STRÖMEN MEIN BLVT ENTGEGEN DIR STVRMT
DAS WILDE FEVER FVHLST DV ES NICHT?

9

Brünnhilde and Siegfried in each other's arms.

will accomplish a deed that will set the world free.' We now have the juxtaposition of Brünnhilde's wisdom, and the freeing of the world. The next significant entry of the theme comes after Brünnhilde's awakening, later in the third Act, when she tells Siegfried: 'What you would know, know it from me, for I am wise because I love you'. So, Brünnhilde's wisdom flows directly from her love for Siegfried. Finally, when Brünnhilde's fears overwhelm her and she says that her mind is in confusion, her reason is silent and her wisdom seems to be failing her, Siegfried offers reassurance: 'Didn't you tell me' he says, 'that all of your wisdom came by the light of your love for me?' This is the phrase to which Cosima had been referring. Brünnhilde therefore is 'made wise through love'; and isn't that suspiciously close to being 'made wise through compassion', the distinguishing attribute of Parsifal? Remember Wagner's words: 'It must sound like the proclamation of a new religion'.

This then, is the profound development brought about by Wotan in his final confrontation with Erda.

Erda descends once again into her timeless sleep, just as Siegfried appears in the distance. The Woodbird, which is leading him, takes one look at Wotan's ravens and flees in alarm. In the conversation that follows between the Wanderer and Siegfried, things go well enough for a while, but the Wanderer's probing questions begin to annoy Siegfried who comments rudely on the older man's appearance; he has lost one eye, and Siegfried threatens to put out his remaining one. The Wanderer replies enigmatically that with his missing eye, Siegfried is looking at the one that remains. The old man bars the way with his spear and, in doing so, discloses that Siegfried's sword had been broken once before on this spear. The boy thinks that he has at last discovered his father's foe (which is not far from the truth) and, with a single blow, he slices the spear in half. Thus Siegmund is avenged. The Wanderer collects the broken pieces of the spear and tells Siegfried to proceed. He can stop him no longer. Ironically, this incident, which seems so anti-climactic for Wotan, is exactly what the god had been hoping for. In Act Two of *Die Walküre*, Wotan confided in Brünnhilde that he needed a truly independent man, a free agent, who by defying him would be most dear to him. He wondered then how he could find such a man. Now at last he had found him.

In *Das Rheingold*, Wagner used some of his most descriptive writing in the transitional passages which link scenes: the movement from the River Rhine to the mountain top overlooking Valhalla, and the descent to and return from Nibelheim. Now he uses the same procedure to link the scene at the base of Brünnhilde's rock with that on the high place where she sleeps. However, what makes this extended musical interlude so interesting is that, as well as climbing upwards, Siegfried must pass through the sea of flames which surround the mountain.

The result is a dazzling picture in sound, drawing on a variety of motifs reviewing Siegfried's circumstances and state of mind while he presses on determinedly through the seething, flickering fire. The feeling of gradual ascent is conveyed by the movement of the orchestral texture from lower, darker, heavier sounds to higher, lighter, more transparent ones.

Finally, we leave the flames behind us and reach the brilliant sunlight and pure atmosphere of the mountain top where Brünnhilde sleeps. For the first time in several hours, we hear the orchestral sound of very high strings, woodwind chords, and the shimmering delicacy of the harp. The effect is magical.

The tenor playing Siegfried has been on stage for the best part of three hours before Brünnhilde is awakened. He is engaged in vigorous and demanding singing, has to act like a youngster less than half his age and undertake all kinds of energetic activity such as forging and fighting. The soprano playing Brünnhilde, on the other hand, has not sung a note in all this time and spends the first part of this final scene lying comfortably on some sort of bedding. One might assume therefore that, for Brünnhilde at least, this scene is a 'piece of cake'. Nothing could be further from the truth. Birgit Nilsson has commented that even if she sang as beautifully as ten angels, she could not compete with the incredibly vibrant 'awakening' music in the orchestra. Brünnhilde never seems to stop singing from the moment she is kissed until her last stratospheric high C.

Nellie Melba had a disastrous involvement with the *Siegfried* Brünnhilde, as she records in her autobiography.[17] She had long wanted to sing the role and had engaged a German language coach to train her. She secured a performance at the Metropolitan in 1896 (at the expense of her main artistic rival, Lillian Nordica, who was the resident Brünnhilde) but soon realised that she had made a great mistake. She said afterwards that she had felt as if she were struggling with something beyond her strength. She had had the sensation of suffocation, of battling with some immense monster – a very different feeling from the usual exaltation which she had experienced in other roles. When she returned to her dressing room, she sent for her manager and told him to tell the critics that she would never do that again, that it was beyond her and she had been a fool. For Melba, that was quite an admission.

When Siegfried reaches the summit of the mountain, he sees Brünnhilde's horse, Grane, also asleep. In fairy-tales and legends of this type, animals behave very much like the humans to whom they are attached. So, for example, in the tale of *Briar-Rose*, when the princess pricks her finger and falls asleep, the household and all of the animals in the castle yard fall asleep at the same moment. They then awaken at the same moment too. In a sense, Grane is an extension or aspect of Brünnhilde's own personality.

Siegfried is attracted to the sleeping figure's shining armour and thinks, not unreasonably, that it covers another man. Remember, at this point he has never seen a woman. He removes the helmet

Hugo L. Braune

Absorbed in their passion for one another,
Siegfried and Brünnhilde laugh at death and the end of the gods.

and long curling hair tumbles out. He still thinks it is a man, albeit a rather fair one. Then he tries to undo the breastplate and, finding this difficult, uses his sword to cut through the rings of mail on each side. When the breastplate is removed, Brünnhilde lies before him in soft woman's drapery. He stares in amazement, his heart pounds and he is filled with a new emotion – fear. His first reaction is instinctively to call out to his mother. 'Mother! Mother!' he says, 'Remember me!' It is an unbearably touching moment. He tries to awaken the sleeping figure but she does not respond. Only when he presses his lips to hers does she stir. To music which seems to be quivering with life and pulsating with long-restrained energy, she slowly rises to a sitting position and greets the sun and the light.

Significantly, her first words are addressed not to the man before her but to the sun. However, these are, in a sense, one and the same. In Norse mythology, the cycles of nature were often symbolised poetically as the trials of love. Sigurd (Siegfried) could be interpreted as a sun lord who, armed with a sunbeam (the sword *Notung*) dispels the darkness. Brynhild (Brünnhilde) was the dawn-maiden whose path he crossed each morning. In greeting the sun, Brünnhilde is greeting Siegfried himself at the start of this day of days, ushered in with a kiss. As events unfold in *Götterdämmerung*, the tragic separation and fiery reunion of the lovers mirrors the solar transit from dawn to dusk. Such was the symbolism of the old myths.

Brünnhilde's first words on her awakening, '*Heil dir, Sonne!*', which seem simple enough, have been variously translated as 'Hail to you, sun!' or 'Hail, Bright sunlight!' or 'Hail to thee, oh sun!' or 'Hail, my sunlight!' or 'I greet you, sun!', to quote just some versions. This points up the difficulties faced by any trans-lator, especially if the intention is also to match the German metre or even approximate the sound of German syllables. The best modern English translation of *The Ring*, to my mind, is that by Andrew Porter, whose version is clear, sensible and singable, and carefully avoids unintentional humour. Porter advises against colloquialisms such as 'Hi there, sunshine!', for obvious reasons.

Brünnhilde rejoices when she learns that it is Siegfried who has made his way through the flames to claim her. Siegfried praises the mother who bore him and Brünnhilde echoes his words. She tells him that she had always loved him and had cared for and protected him even before he was born. Siegfried responds softly and shyly: 'So my mother did not die then?' In his innocence he hopes beyond hope that perhaps this is his mother returned to him, not from death but from sleep. Brünnhilde gently dissuades him: 'O innocent child, never more will you look on your mother. But we are one if you can grant me your love'.

Then there unfolds a rapturous love duet. At one point, Siegfried's ardour gets the better of him and Brünnhilde tears herself away and flees to the other side of the stage. She is finding it difficult to come to terms with her newly discovered humanity. Siegfried suggests that she is still sleeping, and he wants to awaken her to be his bride. Her mind is in turmoil, and now it is her turn to be afraid. She imagines that night has fallen and all kinds of horrors loom up in the dark. Siegfried sees only the beginnings of a new life; Brünnhilde predicts its end. Eventually, he succeeds in turning her mind to other things, and she responds with a tender assurance of her constancy and love.

The music which Wagner introduces at this point has been the subject of much comment and conjecture. It is well known to concert audiences from the opening bars of the *Siegfried Idyll*, written to celebrate Cosima's birthday on Christmas Day 1870 and the birth of their son Siegfried in the June of the previous year. The music, which appears to have even earlier origins, had a very personal significance for both Richard and Cosima and it is as if, for a moment, they had identified themselves completely with the heroic pair whose love for each other had been awakened on that sun-lit mountain top. Something of a musical gear change occurs when this passage begins, and commentators have had very mixed feelings about it. The main objection seems to be that it is an extended, self-contained melody bearing little relationship musically to what has gone before. It is also said that the words seem to have been forced to accommodate a pre-determined melody, in contradiction of one of Wagner's main dramatic principles.

I would offer a few thoughts on this. It is true that Wagner considered it important to preserve the dramatic integrity of words and music; that is to say, both should be used in a complementary way to express the dramatic idea, and neither should be used simply as a peg on which to hang the other. However, we have also seen that he was quite willing to introduce extended lyrical passages when circumstances warranted this, especially to express feelings of love. He also breaks his own rule when other 'unusual' states of mind need to be expressed, and characters 'freeze the action', as it were, to enter a state of rhapsody or delirium or even just 'song'. In all of these cases, the extended melodic line is used to take characters out of themselves or at least out of the usual context of sung dialogue. Thus, we have Siegmund's Spring Song, Siegfried's Forging Song, Walter's Prize Song, the Quintet in *Meistersinger*, Wolfram's Song to the Evening Star in *Tannhauser*, Tristan's delirium, Isolde's *Liebestod* and so on. It seems to me that Brünnhilde's soliloquy falls precisely into this category.

From this point until the end of the act, the lovers lose themselves in an ecstatic outpouring of joy. The language is rhapsodic and the lines are highly compressed. Robert Donington has described the mood as one of manic over-elatedness. It is certainly the antithesis of the sombre, sinister beginning to Act One. We have moved from scheming and ill will to the most blatant baring of souls and declarations of love. We have gone from the ominous depths of Mime's cave to the giddy heights of Brünnhilde's rock. In the rare atmosphere and dazzling sunlight, we share the feeling that nothing could possibly detract from this moment of happiness. The music swells into a torrent of joy which sweeps everything before it. 'Farewell, Walhall's glittering world,' sings Brünnhilde, 'Farewell splendour of the gods ... Let the twilight of the gods – *Götterdämmerung* – now draw near ... I live by the light of Siegfried's star ... radiant love and laughing death'.

Just as the rhapsodic love music of Siegmund and Sieglinde crowned the first Act of *Die Walküre*, so the ecstatic music of their son and the reborn Brünnhilde is the high point of *Siegfried*. In both cases, the outpouring of love and optimism seems rather exaggerated, but it prepares the way for a tragedy which, by contrast, will be all the more devastating.

Far behind us now is the innocent boy who tormented Mime with a forest bear, reforged *Notung*, slew the dragon and communed with nature. We are about to enter a very different world, a world of men and women, a savage and complex world conjured up by some of the most astounding music ever written.

For the moment, the lovers have thoughts only for one another, and we leave them in the euphoria of their mutual awakening to new life and love as the curtain falls on *Siegfried*, the second day of the Festival Play *Der Ring des Nibelungen*.

Götterdämmerung

Götterdämmerung, like Shakespeare's *King Lear* and the *Agamemnon* of Aeschylus, offers an uncompromising picture of human frailty. Such works shock and dismay, but they can also inspire hope for a better world. By the time we reach the closing bars of this, the last and greatest part of *The Ring*, we are meant to feel that a better and more humane world is not only desirable, but possible as well. Certainly, we will have experienced some of the most beautiful and passionate music ever written.

Götterdämmerung can be puzzling on first acquaintance, as it contains a number of paradoxes. Although its scale is prodigious, it is concerned not with the cosmic ambitions of gods and goddesses, giants and dwarfs, but the day-to-day relationships of men and women. Its action takes place in real time and space but its characters often have recourse to supernatural aids and remedies. Its principal figures, Siegfried and Brünnhilde, spend much of their time behaving in ways that are totally out of character. Finally, of all the dramas of *The Ring*, it seems to be the least faithful to Wagner's early theories of *Gesamtkunstwerk* (total work of art), since the music, especially the orchestral music, has a dominant role in advancing the drama.

It has been suggested that Wagner might have lost the plot after so many years of working on his Nibelung story, that the work had become disjointed with its backwards expansion from one to four separate dramas, that his earliest *Ring* text and his most sophisticated musical score make uncomfortable bed-fellows,

1

The Norns contemplate the world and its future.

that he had abandoned his theories about new dramatic forms in favour of more traditional operatic practices, and that he just wanted to get the whole thing finished as quickly as possible and was careless about inconsistencies. I think we need to look a little deeper than this. After all, he had had more than twenty years to think about what he wanted to achieve.

Götterdämmerung is a work of mighty proportions, lasting four-and-a-half hours (not counting intervals), and the first act alone is longer than, say, the whole of *Tosca* or *La bohème* or *Elektra*. It displays Wagner's genius for creating and sustaining moods, manipulating climaxes, and exploring the deeper recesses of the human psyche. However, some of its greatest innovations are to be found in musical details.

By the time Wagner was ready to begin composing the music of *Götterdämmerung* in 1870, two significant developments had occurred. Firstly, most of the *leitmotivs* that form the basic genetic material of *The Ring* – its DNA if you like – had already been determined in the earlier dramas. Secondly, he had acquired unbounded facility as a composer in the writing of *Das Rheingold*, *Die Walküre*, *Siegfried*, *Tristan und Isolde* and *Die Meistersinger von Nürnberg*. Consequently, he was now able to handle his musical material without detectable effort or self-consciousness.

Twenty years after he had first mapped out a new path in his treatise *Oper und Drama*, Wagner was supremely confident of both his materials and his abilities and had nothing more to prove. He was now able to give himself completely to his drama, and to treat its themes and their relationships with the utmost freedom – one might almost say abandon. He could pick up motifs and drop them again, snatch bits from this and elements from that, mix and blend with unstudied ease, and create a complete musical language with which to convey every nuance of the story, without being tied rigorously to the text. And all the while, this musical language poured forth – as the critic from *The Times* wrote after the first

Ein Weib weiss ich,
das herrlichste der Welt:
Auf Felsen hoch ihr Sitz,
Ein Feuer umbrennt ihren
Saal.

Hugo L Braune

2

Hagen tells Gunther and Gutrune about a noble woman, high on a rock,
surrounded by fire.

performance – like a wind that is always blowing or a stream that is always flowing. In short, Wagner had created his own dramatic universe, with its own laws and its own logic, and there was nothing he could not accomplish within it.

We enter this universe like travellers from another time and place, to observe the three Norns, the daughters of Erda, who spin the rope of world knowledge which binds past, present and future. It is night on the Valkyrie's rock and firelight shines from round about. There is, according to the stage directions, gloomy silence and stillness. The prelude is of the briefest kind, but such was Wagner's ability to conjure up mood and atmosphere that eighteen bars is all that is required to set the scene with great effect. The woodwind chords which had heralded Brünnhilde's awakening at the end of *Siegfried* had been in the bright keys of E minor and C major. *Götterdämmerung* opens with similar chords, but this time in the ominous keys of E flat minor and C flat major. There could be no greater contrast with the euphoria of the closing scene of *Siegfried*, and yet it is achieved with the simplest of means. We know at once that all is not right with the world. The benign 'nature' motif, first heard in *Rheingold*, is hybridised with the 'ring' motif and produces, on muted strings, the strange, unworldly music of the Norns' rope of destiny.

One of the marvels of *Götterdämmerung* is the way in which, through harmonic design and instrumental colour, a sinister atmosphere pervades virtually all of the work. Many scenes are set in broad daylight but, somehow, the sun no longer shines as brightly as it did in the earlier works, and all nature seems burdened by things going wrong. Everywhere, the corrosive harmonies of the ring are eating their way into the score.

The Norns ponder with some anxiety the state of the world as they pass their golden rope from one to the other. Again, Wagner uses the rondo form in the musical structure. The Norns speak in poetic terms about the death of the world ash tree and the drying up of the spring of wisdom. They disclose that the remnants of the ash tree have been piled up around Valhalla to await the fire that will consume the gods. They tell of the greed that led to the theft of the Rhinegold and the making of the ring. The rope starts to fray. They speak of Alberich's curse. The rope breaks. Their wisdom ends. The Norns vanish. Day begins to dawn.

Softly, the horns give out the theme of Siegfried as hero, followed on the clarinet by that of Brünnhilde. The latter is carried higher and higher through the orchestra until it bursts gloriously onto the scene with the coming of day. Various themes are woven into the sound picture which follows, and the lovers emerge from their shelter. Brünnhilde is a Valkyrie no longer but, to use her words, she is strong in will and rich in love. Siegfried is about to set out on adventures and gives Brünnhilde the ring as a token of his love. He is, he says, not Siegfried but Brünnhilde's arm, endowed with her spirit. Her horse, Grane, will be his companion in the world of men which lies below. Amidst music of the greatest rapture, the pair farewell each other and Siegfried disappears from view. Then follows the extended orchestral interlude known as Siegfried's Journey to the Rhine.

This magnificent interlude is full of youthful vigour and energy, and motif after motif traces the young man's descent from the mountain and passage through the countryside until he reaches the broad expanse of the River Rhine. We are now well and truly in the world of human beings, rather than the timeless realm of mythology and fairy-tale.

Brünnhilde's horse, Grane, like his mistress, is no longer a supernatural being and walks on the ground instead of flying through the air. In most productions these days, Grane is conspicuous by his absence. Even the best-trained horses are not always reliable on stage. They can be distracting and are seldom satisfied with a supporting role. There is no place for them in modern, symbolic productions and even in old-fashioned, literal ones, they can look curiously out of place against painted scenery. But I see no reason why we shouldn't continue to talk about Grane even if we don't actually see him. After all, Brünnhilde and Siegfried talk about him, and even talk to him. Indeed, his greatest moment comes at the end of *Götterdämmerung* when Brünnhilde urges him to greet his master by carrying her into Siegfried's funeral pyre.

It is important to remember that *Der Ring des Nibelungen* is a 'Stage Festival Play for three days and a preliminary evening', to use Wagner's description. Note the words 'festival' and 'play'. It is a theatrical event to be presented according to the conventions of the musical theatre which are, inevitably, removed from every-day reality. They are concerned with representation rather than realism, with ideas rather than facts. The audience participates in the festival play through its own creative involvement; by using its understanding and imagination, even by being prepared to see horses where none are apparent!

Towards the end of Siegfried's Journey to the Rhine, the music, very gradually, begins to lose its vitality. The energy and con-fidence with which it began dissipate. When the curtain rises, we realise that a very different mood prevails in the palace before us: the hall of the Gibichungs on the banks of the Rhine. We are now at the true beginning of Act One of *Götterdämmerung*. All that has gone before has been by way of a prologue, reminding us of the mythological significance of what is about to unfold. Gunther and Gutrune, brother and sister, are the rulers of this place. With them lives their half-brother Hagen, son of Alberich.

Gunther is noble enough but he is somewhat weak of character. His sister is sweet and malleable. Hagen, on the other hand, is cold and sinister; a strong character but an evil one. The musical depiction of these characters is of the greatest importance in *Götterdämmerung*, and the motifs associated with them are strikingly apt. Gunther's music, for instance, suggests that he is

WILLKOMMEN GAST, IN GIEBICH'S HAUS!
SEINE TOCHTER REICHT DIR DEN TRANK·

3

Gutrune welcomes Siegfried.

outwardly bold but that his boldness is illusory. He will be a pawn in the hands of his half-brother. Gutrune's music is heart-rending. She is caught up in forces that are too much for her, and she too will fall victim to Hagen's evil ambition. There can be no doubt about Hagen's dark and sinister nature, which is laid out plainly in the music associated with him.

Gunther is very uncertain of himself and requires constant reassurance. He asks Hagen whether his fame along the Rhine is worthy of his father's name. Hagen replies that Gunther's fame is not what it should be because there are still things that he has not yet accomplished. Furthermore, he is still without a wife and Gutrune without a husband. Hagen suggests that Gunther's reputation would be enhanced if he won the hand of a particular woman whom he has in mind. She dwells on a rock surrounded by fire. But, adds Hagen, Gunther would not be able to penetrate the fire himself. That deed could only be accomplished by Siegfried the Volsung who, incidentally, would make a fine husband for Gutrune.

Hagen seems to be remarkably well informed, since he also knows that Siegfried has slain Fafner and won the hoard. Presumably he has learned all these things from his father, Alberich. Gunther reacts angrily, asking why Hagen should urge him to do the impossible. Hagen then sets out his plan. We hear the mysterious motif of the Tarnhelm in the orchestra as Hagen asks, 'What if Siegfried should bring home the bride to you, wouldn't Brünnhilde then be yours?' It is not clear at this point just what the 'Tarnhelm' motif signifies, but this is a good example of the use of a motif of anticipation. In due course we learn that the Tarnhelm will indeed have an important part to play. Hagen then outlines a plan to administer a potion to Siegfried, so that he might forget all memories of Brünnhilde, go to her through the flames and bring her to Gunther.

As is the way of myth, no sooner does the conversation turn to

Jetzt bist du mein! –
Brünnhilde, Gunther's Braut —

H. Braune

4

Siegfried, in the guise of Gunther, brutally abducts Brünnhilde.

Siegfried than the sound of his horn is heard in the distance. He has acquired a boat, and we imagine him rowing easily against the stream, with Grane the horse on board as well. Hagen hails him from the shore and he turns towards the bank. As he steps ashore, the trombones give out, with maximum force, the terrible motif of the curse. The tragedy of *Götterdämmerung* has begun.

Hagen offers to take care of Grane, and we hear in the orchestra the horse grumbling at being handed over to this dangerous stranger. Animals sense these things, it seems!

Siegfried greets Gunther who makes him welcome and puts all that he has at his disposal. Siegfried responds that he has nothing to offer in return, other than himself and his sword. Rather pointedly, Hagen asks about the Nibelung's hoard, for Siegfried attaches so little importance to it that it had completely slipped his mind. He replies that most of it had been left in the dragon's cave, but he had taken the object which now hangs on his belt. He has no idea what it is. Hagen, who is certainly more worldly wise than Siegfried, explains that this is the Tarnhelm, which will disguise its wearer at will, or take him in the twinkling of an eye wherever he may wish to be. 'Did you take anything else,' asks Hagen? 'Only a ring,' Siegfried replies, 'and that is now worn by a fair woman.' Hagen knows at once that he means Brünnhilde.

Gutrune enters and the music reveals her gentle and all too trusting nature. She offers Siegfried a drinking-horn, welcoming him as a guest in Gibich's house. He drinks, and his thoughts turn to Brünnhilde. The music wells up with memories of his love for her. Then, an extraordinary thing happens. The potion of forgetfulness with which Gutrune had laced his drink, begins to take effect. It is an eerie and terrible moment, and the music describes it with wonderful expressiveness. The twisted harmonies reflect what is happening to Siegfried's brain. He struggles to remember, but to no avail.

The potion does its obliterating work, and now Siegfried

cannot keep his eyes off Gutrune. He asks if Gunther has a wife. Gunther replies that he has his heart set on one who is beyond his reach; her home is on a towering rock, surrounded by fire. Only someone who can penetrate the fire would win Brünnhilde for wife. Siegfried repeats each of Gunther's sentences after him, as if dimly conscious that he should be remembering something important. However, in no time at all, the memories of those rapturous love duets on the Valkyrie's rock have gone completely. Even when Brünnhilde's name is mentioned, Siegfried betrays no glimmer of recognition.

As Hagen had anticipated, Siegfried offers to help Gunther by going through the fire to claim Brünnhilde for him. Using the Tarnhelm, he will change his form into that of Gunther. In return, Siegfried asks for the hand of Gutrune. Again and again, the motif of the curse surfaces in the orchestra, tainting the rest of the music and reminding us of its continuing destructive work. Gunther and Siegfried decide to pledge eternal loyalty to each other. Hagen fills a drinking-horn with fresh wine. He holds it out to the other two, each of whom cuts his arm with his sword and lets the blood fall into the wine. Then they swear blood-brotherhood before drinking from the horn in turn. The scene is chilling and barbaric.

Even more chilling is the atonement – if a brother breaks his bond, if a friend is false to a friend, then what has been drunk in drops today will flow in streams unceasing. Of course, neither believes that this will ever happen. Hagen cuts the horn in two so that it can never be used again, and explains that he had not joined in the oath because his blood runs pale and slow and cold. It would only poison their drink.

The two blood-brothers set off for the fiery rock. There, Gunther will hide while Siegfried assumes his appearance and abducts Brünnhilde. Hagen remains at the entrance to the Hall, to watch and wait. The sons of freedom, as he calls them, may despise him, but they will return with a bride for Gunther and the ring for Hagen. 'Then they shall serve the Nibelung's son.' Another orchestral interlude follows, during which Wagner demonstrates his remarkable ability to evoke character and mood with the most economical of means.

While Brünnhilde, on her mountain top, is lost in blissful memories of Siegfried, storm clouds gather, followed by the surprising arrival of one of her Valkyrie sisters, Waltraute, in a highly agitated state. Waltraute has come of her own accord to urge Brünnhilde to return the ring to the Rhinedaughters, so that the curse can be lifted from the gods and the world. In a long but moving monologue, Waltraute paints a sad picture of Wotan and the gods, sitting gloomily in Valhalla, awaiting their end. Brünnhilde is shocked at the suggestion that she should give up the ring. It means more to her than Valhalla or the gods, she says, for its golden gleam tells her 'Siegfried loves me! Siegfried loves me!' Her message for the gods is simple: she will never forsake love, and she will never part with the ring, even if Valhalla itself falls into ruins! So, Waltraute has her answer, and she rushes away in despair.

Evening has fallen and the glow from the fire that encircles the rock has become brighter. The flames leap and dance more wildly than usual and, suddenly, through the swirling but somehow more ominous music of the magic fire, the sound of a horn is heard with the motif of Siegfried, and then his horn call. Brünnhilde starts up in delight as she prepares to greet the returning hero.

Suddenly, Siegfried appears before her on a high rock, but he has the appearance of a stranger – Gunther. The horror of this moment cannot be described in words alone, and there are few more blood-curdling scenes in all opera. Brünnhilde cannot believe what she sees; a stranger has come through the flames. When Wotan had first conceived her punishment, he had intended to leave her to the mercy of the first stranger who encountered her. Now, it seemed, this terrible fate had befallen her.

Recovering some of her composure, she asks who it is who

5

Alberich visits his son, Hagen, by night.

dares to come to her. Siegfried, in a feigned and deeper voice, replies 'Brünnhild! A suitor has come. I have sought you through the flames. I claim you as my wife. Now you must follow me.' From the music that accompanies these words, we are left in no doubt that Hagen is the evil influence behind all that is happening.

In answer to her questions, Siegfried says that he is a Gibichung, and that his name is Gunther. Brünnhilde gives a despairing cry: 'Wotan! You vengeful and pitiless god! Now I know the true meaning of my sentence. I am condemned to shame and sorrow!' Siegfried (in the form of Gunther) tells her that there in the cave she must become his wife. Summoning her remaining strength, she holds out the ring towards him and invokes its power to protect her, but to no avail. It is Gunther's by a husband's right, says Siegfried, and promptly tears it from her finger. He then drives Brünnhilde before him into the cave. She is a shocked and broken woman. Siegfried draws his sword and, in his natural voice, cries, 'Now, *Notung*, witness here how I keep my vow. I keep my word to my brother. Separate me from Gunther's bride!' They disappear into the cave and the curtain falls.

In Act One of *Götterdämmerung*, we have seen some startling developments. As Erda had warned in *Rheingold*, Alberich has had a son, Hagen, by a mortal woman, just as Wotan had had a son, Siegmund, by a mortal woman. The marriage of gods or other mythical beings with men and women is common in both Greek and Norse mythology. The offspring of such marriages usually display distinctive personality traits, which can be very useful from a dramatic point of view. We do not know a lot about Hagen at this stage, other than his determination to manipulate everyone in order to get hold of the ring. He is resentful, humourless and single-minded.

We have also seen the use of the potion of forgetfulness, a mind-bending drug which selectively blots out Siegfried's memories of Brünnhilde and makes him lust after Gutrune. What do we

SPITZE, ACHTE DES SPRUCH'S! ———— DENN BRACH SEINE EIDE ER ALL,
SCHWUR MEINEID JETZT DIESER MANN!

6

A *furious* Brünnhilde *swears vengeance on the point of* Hagen's *spear.*

make of this? A modern audience might feel that recourse to such a device is an easy way out for the story-teller. After all, such potions are the stuff of fantasy. In the present context, we need to ask ourselves whether the story of Siegfried's memory loss and infatuation with Gutrune might not be just a case of a wandering eye in a virile young man a long way from home? Perhaps Siegfried's ardour cools as quickly as it overheats.

This view might be convincing were it not for his obvious feelings for Brünnhilde when his memory returns in the last scene, and his comment in the Rhinedaughters' scene in Act Three that he would happily have made the closer acquaintance of one of those watery nymphs had he not been betrothed to Gutrune! He is all alone when he says this and yet he thinks only of his betrothal to Gutrune, not his marriage to Brünnhilde. No, I am bound to conclude that Siegfried's underlying intentions are honourable and that the potion of forgetfulness, if not to be taken literally, might be regarded as a metaphor for Hagen's evil ability to cause naive, susceptible people to behave in completely uncharacteristic ways. There are many Hagens in the world who seem to be able to do just that. There is one other possible interpretation of Siegfried's fascination with Gutrune, but I shall come to that in a moment.

Finally, there is the assumption of Gunther's physical appearance by Siegfried in order to abduct Brünnhilde from the protective circle of fire. Shape-changing is another common feature of mythological stories and is certainly not just a Wagnerian device for livening up the drama. Wagner would have been familiar with many of the Greek poems and legends which refer to metamorphosis. The Greek gods changed their shape at the drop of a hat, assuming the form of animals, or masquerading as humans. For example, in the *Iliad*, Athene took the form of Hector's brother in order to lure the Trojan hero to his death at the hands of Achilles. Heroes and others could be transformed into plants or animals, and some shape-changers underwent a whole series of transformations of a magical kind.

But there is also a less mystical origin to the story of Siegfried's transformation into Gunther. In the thirteenth-century *Thidrekssaga*, we learn that Brynhild had agreed to wed Gunther but refused to consummate the marriage. So, Sigfrid dressed himself in Gunther's clothes and raped her. Obviously, such an account was not appropriate in the particular context of Wagner's story (or having regard to nineteenth-century sensibilities) but echoes of it remain in the atmosphere of horror and violence preserved in the music.

There is something Shakespearian about the opening scene of Act Two of *Götterdämmerung*. I think it is one of the most fascinating scenes in the entire *Ring*. It is especially interesting in terms of characterisation: Wagner lets us see Alberich and Hagen, father and son, not as they appear to us but as they appear to themselves. Alberich is completely justified, in his own eyes, in wanting the ring, especially after the wrong done to him by Wotan. Hagen will be his agent.

Hagen is discovered, as we left him, on watch outside the hall of the Gibichungs. When the curtain rises, it is night. Now and then, the moonlight breaks through the clouds and the music mirrors this when the dark, syncopated orchestral sound is suddenly broken by very high entries on flutes and oboes. We see the hall from a slightly different angle, and Hagen sits sleeping, leaning against one of the doorposts. He is waiting for the return of Siegfried and Gunther.

Oddly enough, in *Götterdämmerung* the gods have no direct part to play. In this drama, they are acknowledged only by altar stones on the hillside – stones dedicated to Fricka, to Wotan, to Donner and the rest. It is as if they are just memories of a distant past.

When the clouds separate for a moment, we notice that

Alberich is crouching motionless in front of Hagen. 'Are you sleeping Hagen, my son?' he asks. Hagen remains motionless as he answers, and the conversation which follows has a strange dreamlike quality. But whose dream? Alberich urges his son to take the ring from Siegfried, for if it is returned to the Rhinedaughters, the gold and the power which it confers will be lost to the Nibelungs for ever. 'Be true, Hagen, my son! Trusty hero! Be true! Be true!' Alberich vanishes as day begins to dawn.

The dawning takes place first of all in the orchestra, by the almost imperceptible transition to new harmonies and new motifs. The latter are introduced so subtly that it is difficult to be sure just when the transition begins; the process is almost organic. Wagner was especially proud of his skill in this respect and once characterised composition as the art of transition. The first soft rays of morning are accompanied by a beautiful canon for the horns and by the gradual emergence of the theme associated with Hagen's sardonic nature, later used by the vassals in their coarse celebrations. Clearly, it is Hagen's day that is now dawning.

Siegfried appears suddenly beside the river, in the act of removing the Tarnhelm from his head – he has used its magic to transport himself in advance of Gunther and Brünnhilde. Hagen calls Gutrune from the hall and there is an exchange between her and Siegfried, during which Siegfried reports on what had happened on the fiery rock. He has kept his part of the bargain; now he claims Gutrune as his own. The boat bringing Gunther and Brünnhilde is sighted and Hagen summons the Gibichung vassals to join the double wedding celebrations. He does this with a joke; a typically rough Hagen joke to be sure, but we are, for a moment, shown another side of his character which becomes all the more convincing because of it. He doesn't call the vassals to a wedding, but to war! 'Weapons! Weapons!' he calls, 'Bring your weapons! … Enemies are here!' He blows a steerhorn and other steerhorns answer from different directions off stage. The vassals rush on

*The mortally wounded Siegfried attempts to retaliate using his shield,
but his strength fails him.*

singly and then in growing numbers, assembling on the shore in front of the hall. They burst into raucous laughter when they discover the real reason for their summons.

Then follows the only chorus in *The Ring*; but what a chorus it is! After several hours of high drama, the effect of this lusty, barbaric, slightly old-fashioned music is to release emotional tension and to refresh the listener. At the same time it provides an unforgettable aural image of the brutal world of these Rhine dwellers, the subjects of Gunther and Gutrune and their half-brother, Hagen. It also prepares us for one of the greatest scenes in the whole work, the quarrel between Brünnhilde and Siegfried.

When the excitement has died down, both couples arrive in front of the hall. In the course of his welcoming remarks, Gunther speaks the name Siegfried. Brünnhilde, who has kept her eyes lowered all this time, is startled to hear the name and looks up to see Siegfried standing in front of her. She stares at him in amazement. Siegfried calmly presents Gutrune to her, clearly oblivious to their earlier relationship and pretending not to know of more recent events. Her bewilderment is compounded when she sees the ring, now on Siegfried's finger. If anyone should be wearing the ring, she says, it is Gunther, since he had torn it from her hand. Gunther has no idea what she is talking about.

Hagen is beginning to relish the complications which are now developing, especially when Brünnhilde finally realises that it must have been Siegfried who stole the ring from her. Siegfried replies that no woman gave him the ring; he won it from the dragon Fafner. Either he is protecting Gunther, or he has been caught out and is too ashamed to own up. Hagen decides to capitalise on the situation by asking Brünnhilde if she can identify the ring. If indeed it is Gunther's, then Siegfried must have been unfaithful to his friend and should pay for his treachery. Thus we reach a critical point in the drama.

Brünnhilde concludes bitterly that she has been betrayed and announces that not Gunther but Siegfried is her husband and that they had consummated their love. Not surprisingly, this causes much consternation in the Gibichung camp. Siegfried, who remembers only their second meeting, when he was disguised as Gunther, denies that anything happened between them. His sword *Notung* had lain between them, he says, and he had been faithful to his oath of blood-brotherhood. A furious Brünnhilde responds that when Siegfried had been with her, *Notung* had hung on the wall of their cave. Now Gunther feels betrayed and challenges Siegfried to deny the accusation. Siegfried replies that he will swear his innocence on the point of a spear, and asks who will offer him one for the purpose? Hagen is quick to oblige.

Siegfried lays two fingers of his right hand upon the spear point and addresses it as 'Shining steel! Holiest weapon!' He swears that if he betrayed Gunther, this spear should strike him down. We know that eventually it will but, for the moment, he firmly believes in the truth of what he says and fears no consequences. Then it is Brünnhilde's turn. She seizes the spear point and dedicates it to Siegfried's death. To her mind, he has betrayed every vow.

Baffled by these developments, Siegfried can only conclude that the Tarnhelm had not worked its magic well enough and that his disguise on Brünnhilde's rock had not been successful. He says so to Gunther and then leads Gutrune and the others into the hall to commence the celebrations. Only Brünnhilde, Gunther and Hagen remain behind.

It is difficult to imagine how Wagner could improve on what we have just heard, but he does just that with the trio which follows. This ensemble – one of the few in *The Ring* – is often cited, together with the vassals' chorus, as evidence of a regression in Wagner's style; a return to more traditional operatic forms. There may be some truth in this, resulting perhaps from a text which predates the music by some twenty-four years.

However, I am more inclined to the view that the trio and the chorus (and other instances of 'regression' which people have identified in *Götterdämmerung*) are simply musical forms deliberately chosen because they best serve Wagner's dramatic purposes. When he came to write the music in 1872, he could quite easily have recast these 1848 words if he had wanted to. That he did not do so, suggests that he had another purpose in mind. In any event, it is just as well that the trio survived because it is, dramatically, one of the greatest moments in *The Ring*.

Brünnhilde calls for vengeance, and Hagen decides how he will kill Siegfried. He will plunge his spear into Siegfried's back because, according to Brünnhilde, only his back remained unprotected by her charms. Siegfried would never turn away from an enemy. In non-magical terms, we can interpret this to mean that because Siegfried is exceptionally courageous, no enemy could hope to get the better of him in honourable combat. Only a cowardly attack from behind could succeed.

The third conspirator, Gunther, is misery personified and is taunted by Brünnhilde for being a pitiful creature who cannot even do his own dirty work. Hagen tells him that he should expect 'no help from brain, no help from hand'. His only hope is 'Siegfried's death!' Gunther recoils at this idea and the orchestra refers pointedly to the motif of 'blood-brotherhood'. Hagen persuades him that Siegfried has betrayed his oath and now can atone only with his blood. Brünnhilde replies that all the blood in the world could not wash away the guilt of those who have betrayed her but, she agrees, Siegfried must die. Hagen reminds Gunther that Siegfried's death will bring him the Nibelung's ring. Gunther is worried about the effect on his sister, the gentle Gutrune, but at last, he too agrees, Siegfried must die. Hagen decides that, in order to protect his half-sister's sensibilities, Siegfried's death will be staged to resemble a hunting accident involving a wild boar. And so this great and terrible trio reaches a climax with unanimity on Siegfried's untimely end.

Another composer might have brought down the curtain at this point, but Wagner has one more dramatic card to play. The touching music of Gutrune comes to our ears and a joyful bridal procession emerges from the hall. Siegfried and Gutrune are carried shoulder high; Siegfried on a shield. We know that he will soon return again to the hall on a shield, not for a wedding, but in death. The path is strewn with flowers, and sacrificial beasts are led to the altars of the gods. Gutrune smiles at Brünnhilde and signals her to join the festivities, but receives no response. The music of merry-making is intermingled with the sinister motifs of 'Hagen' and of 'vengeance'. Reluctantly, the conspirators join the procession, and the curtain falls on an act which must surely rank as Wagner's supreme achievement in the field of music drama.

Act Two has taken the drama in new and dangerous directions. Alberich has returned to offer his own ambition and resentment as added incentives for Hagen's actions. Hagen, we know, is jealous of his half-brother and sister, whose legitimacy he envies. He has his own reasons for getting hold of the ring. Indeed, there is some evidence that Hagen is not very susceptible to his father's entreaties, though their objectives coincide. Alberich keeps addressing him as 'Hagen, my son', but the most affectionate name that Hagen can give his father is 'crafty dwarf'. He also reminds Alberich vindictively that it was with gold that he had bought his mother. But before we become too sympathetic towards Alberich, we should heed his own admission that he had always encouraged in Hagen a deadly hatred of Siegfried. Vengeance is what he desires, and vengeance is what Hagen, in the end, will give him.

We saw the worst side of the new Siegfried at the end of Act One. Now we witness a similar development in the character of Brünnhilde. She has every reason to be angry and resentful. She has learnt the truth of Siegfried's masquerade as Gunther and is smarting at his treatment of her. Furthermore, Siegfried's answers about their time together were obviously at odds with her own recollections. But does any of this warrant his murder? She has become so outraged – one might even say deranged – that she is willing to be Hagen's accomplice, dedicating the spear to Siegfried's death, disclosing his area of vulnerability and inciting Hagen to avenge her. By these actions, Brünnhilde is just as guilty as Hagen of Siegfried's murder. It seems hard to credit that this is the same Brünnhilde who, in the presence of Sieglinde, had gloried in the thought of Siegfried's birth, had been a noble Valkyrie and daughter, and had then been a loving woman and wife.

And what of the unfortunate brother and sister, Gunther and Gutrune? They are victims of forces beyond their understanding, just like that other brother and sister, Siegmund and Sieglinde. There are some interesting parallels between the Volsung and the Gibichung siblings. Of course, Gutrune's lover is not her brother. But he is her brother's blood-brother, which makes him, if you like, her brother once removed. From Sieglinde, Siegmund received the water of life as he lay exhausted in the house of his enemy, and it was over a drinking-horn of mead that their love for one another was kindled. From Gutrune, Siegfried received the potion of forgetfulness in the hall of his enemy, and it was over that drinking-horn that their love for one another was kindled. Hagen stands in the same dramatic relationship to Gutrune as did Hunding to Sieglinde, and each killed their respective enemy with a spear – Siegmund receiving it in the chest and his son Siegfried in the back. In both cases, Brünnhilde was involved, but in contrary ways. She had tried, compassionately, to save Siegmund and in doing so had earned the wrath of Wotan and the gratitude of Sieglinde. She, misguidedly, encourages the murder of Siegfried and in doing so earns the gratitude of Wotan's dark counterpart, Alberich, and the curses of Gutrune.

It is the gentle, vulnerable, appealing Gutrune, not the wild and formidable Brünnhilde, who is most like the mother Siegfried

The vassals carry Siegfried's body back to the hall of the Gibichungs.

longed for. The characters of Sieglinde and Gutrune must have had similarities in Wagner's mind, for he considered using the same soprano, Mathilde Weckerlin, for both roles in the first production. In the end, she sang only Gutrune. Could it be that Siegfried was drawn, subconsciously, to Gutrune because, in her, he sensed similarities with his mother?

In mythology, magic (such as the potion of forgetfulness) symbolises any work of the unconscious which is not understood. Siegfried would hardly have understood the forces which compelled him, even after his encounter with Brünnhilde, to yearn still for his mother. Such feelings towards a mother are not usually confused with feelings towards a wife, although they may be, as in the so-called Oedipus complex, the infantile fixation on the mother. Siegfried's rather peculiar upbringing may have made him vulnerable to such a disorder. Of significance, too, for anyone familiar with the Oedipus story, is the fact that Siegfried had killed Mime, who had been *in loco parentis* for his father, and who had kept the identity of Siegfried's mother to himself for many years.

Could it be that Brünnhilde senses something deeper than ordinary attraction in Siegfried's feelings for Gutrune? After all, Brünnhilde is the only one present who had actually known his mother and she understands Siegfried's susceptibilities in this regard.

In Act Three of *Götterdämmerung*, an important change in mood and atmosphere takes place. Acts One and Two had involved strong characterisations, highly charged relationships and violent emotions. The characters of Siegfried and Brünnhilde underwent some very peculiar developments, each being distorted almost beyond recognition under the malign influence of Hagen. Now they recover their true natures and rise above the evil which had so corrupted their view of one another. In musical terms, Wagner accomplishes this by recapturing some of the lyrical atmosphere of the earlier dramas. Lyricism, as I have already suggested, was inseparable from love in Wagner's thinking. A complete reversion is not possible; too much has occurred that cannot be undone. However, enough of the earlier world of innocence is recreated to remind us of what has been lost, and to make the tragic events still to come seem almost unbearably poignant.

The earliest expression of lyricism in *The Ring* centres on the Rhinedaughters in *Das Rheingold*. Now, in Act Three of *Götterdämmerung*, we hear them again, those 'subservient creatures of the deep' as Wagner called them, lamenting the loss of their gold as they swim in the sparkling waters. This time however, the joy has gone from their song, and despite the great beauty and intricate filigree of the score, they are manifestly burdened with cares. A little later, when Siegfried begins to regain his memory and recounts how he listened to the Woodbird outside Fafner's cave, all of the beauties of nature come flooding back. Later still, when Brünnhilde realises that Siegfried 'the truest of all men, betrayed me, that I in grief may grow wise!' she acquires a nobility of character which transcends even that displayed in *Die Walküre*. Finally, the entire *Ring* is brought to a close with that most lyrical of outpourings, often called the motif of 'redemption by love', last associated with the frantic and exhausted Sieglinde responding to the news that she would bear the noblest of heroes. Wagner called it the theme 'in praise of Brünnhilde'. This ecstatic motif, with its sense of revelation, is Wagner's ultimate affirmation that hope resides in an inner wisdom born of love – love to the point of suffering and sacrifice.

Before the curtain rises on the final Act of *The Ring*, hunting horns alert us to what is happening on stage. Then we see the valley through which the great river flows. The Rhinedaughters are waiting for Siegfried, who is hunting with Gunther and Hagen and their men. Siegfried becomes separated from the others and appears on the cliff overlooking the river. The Rhinedaughters tease him and demand the ring which gleams on his finger. He refuses to give it to them and says that his wife would scold him if he gave away his goods so easily. Perhaps she beats him, one of the Rhinedaughters suggests and, laughing, they dive under the water. He weakens under the charms of such beguiling creatures and decides that if they returned to him he would give them the ring afterall. He takes the ring from his finger and holds it up.

When the nymphs surface again, it is to tell him solemnly to keep the ring and guard it well until he discovers what ill fortune it brings. Their warning could not be plainer. Anyone who possesses it is doomed to death. As Siegfried slew the dragon so he himself shall be slain this very day unless he returns the ring to the river. He replies that as he was not deceived by their wiles, so he will not be moved by their threats. They persist with their warnings but Siegfried tells them that he despises the worldly power which the ring is said to bring. He would barter it for the grace of love, but never under a threat. He counts life and limb of no more worth than the clod of earth which he then picks up and throws over his shoulder. The Rhinedaughters decide to leave this madman and foretell that, this day, a woman shall inherit the ring; one who will do what they ask. When they have gone, Siegfried muses that, were it not for his betrothal to Gutrune, he would have taken advantage of one of these playful creatures.

It is interesting to find in *Götterdämmerung* curious little details more appropriate to *Siegfrieds Tod*, that cling like barnacles to the revised poem. Surely, one such example is Siegfried's encounter with the Rhinedaughters in this scene. We suddenly come across a hero who is prepared to fling his life away, for he cares nothing for the ring's curse. This is not fearlessness – it is almost a death wish. Where does this strand in his character come from?

As we know, in Wagner's original conception, Siegfried confronts the gods and Brünnhilde purges their guilt by her act of self-immolation. In that version, Wotan continues to reign in glory

heiaho! Grane
GRÜSSE DEN FREUND!

Brünnhilde rides Grane into Siegfried's funeral pyre, to greet their heroic friend.

instead of perishing, and Brünnhilde and Siegfried rise above the flames like Senta and the Dutchman. This of course reflected Wagner's political ideas in 1848 (expressed in his June speech to the *Vaterlandsverein*), in which the aristocratic/plutocratic regime would be swept away but the Saxon king would remain as father of his people and head of a crowned republic. After all, in 1848 Wagner was still in the king's employ! So, in that early version, Siegfried must confront his fate, confront the gods, and risk all. The Greek notion of hubris comes to mind. If Brünnhilde will not give up the ring to save the gods, Siegfried will certainly not give it up to save himself.

In his prose sketch *The Nibelung Myth – A Sketch for a Drama*, which formed the basis of *Siegfrieds Tod*, Wagner describes the river bank encounter in these terms:

The Daughters hanker for the ring, and beg it of Siegfried, who refuses it. (Guiltless, he has taken the guilt of the gods upon him, and atones their wrong through his defiance, his self-dependence.) They prophesy evil, and tell him of the curse attaching to the ring: Let him cast it in the river or he must die today. Siegfried: 'You glib-tongued women shall not cheat me of my might: the curse and your threats are not worth a hair to me. What my courage demands governs my life; and what my mind determines I am destined to do. Call this a curse or a blessing, I'll follow this course and not act contrary to my nature.' The three Daughters: 'Would you out-do the gods?' Siegfried: 'Show me a chance to master the gods and I'll use all my might to vanquish them. I know three wiser women than you three; they know that the gods will one day struggle in fear. Well, so much for the gods – I'll do battle with them. So I laugh at your threats. The ring stays mine, and thus I cast my life behind me.' (He lifts a clod of earth and hurls it backwards over his head.) The Daughters scoff at Siegfried who thinks himself as strong and wise as he is blind and enslaved. 'Oaths he has broken and doesn't know it; a prize far higher than the ring he's lost and doesn't know it; runes and spells he was taught but he's forgotten them. Farewell Siegfried! We know a noble wife who this day will possess the ring when you are slaughtered. To her! She'll give us a better hearing.' Siegfried, laughing, gazes after them as they move away singing. He shouts: 'If I were not true to Gudrun, one of you three would have ensnared me!'

In this version there is no suggestion (as in *Götterdämmerung*) that he contemplates returning the ring to the Rhinedaughters for a bit of 'slap and tickle' in the bulrushes. In the finished drama we find that, once again, the Rhinedaughters are reluctant to play those kind of games, even though Siegfried is a better catch than Alberich. As with the Nibelung, they'll flutter their eyelashes and swish their tails but swim away just the same.

The other members of the hunting party arrive to rest and refresh themselves. During the exchanges that follow, Siegfried tells of his boyhood and of the remarkable things that had happened to him. The wonderful nature music of the previous drama floods into the orchestra, and Siegfried sings of the Woodbird that warned him about Mime and told him of the ring and the Tarnhelm. He repeats the bird's words and even the notes that it sang. Hagen drops the juice of a herb into Siegfried's drinking-horn and, gradually, his memory begins to return. The bird, he recalls, showed him where Brünnhilde lay, surrounded by fire. It is a moment of the greatest tenderness and, in a twinkling, we see the young Siegfried, the naive and innocent boy, restored to us again.

He had loosened her helm, he continues, his kiss had awakened her to life and, with a feeling like burning fire, she had held him in her arms. Gunther springs up in horror at this revelation. Two ravens fly up from a bush; they are Wotan's ravens, flying to tell their master that the end is near. Siegfried turns to look at them and Hagen asks him: 'Can you understand the language of those ravens? Vengeance, they cry to me!' And with that he plunges his spear into Siegfried's back.

Siegfried swings around in an effort to crush Hagen with his shield but his strength fails him and he crashes to the ground. Hagen slips away into the shadows but the others, including a remorseful Gunther, surround and comfort the dying man. Then, in a truly inspirational touch, Wagner draws from the orchestra the high, pure sounds to which Brünnhilde first opened her eyes and greeted the sunlight. Siegfried asks who has put her back to sleep. He had awakened her once; now he awakens her again to the truth. He shall live in Brünnhilde's love. With her name on his lips, he sinks back and dies.

Night has fallen. At a signal from Gunther, the vassals raise Siegfried's body and carry it in solemn procession over the rocky heights. All the while, the orchestra pours forth the Funeral Music, the effect of which is overwhelming. Laid before us, one by one in their grandest forms, are the various motifs associated with Siegfried's life, punctuated repeatedly with the shock of his death. Mists rise from the Rhine, obscuring the scene, and when they disperse, we find ourselves again before the hall of the Gibichungs.

Gutrune leaves her bedchamber and comes into the hall. Evil dreams have kept her awake. She fancies that she has heard the sound of Siegfried's horn and the neigh of his horse. She has heard Brünnhilde's laughter and has seen her steal silently towards the Rhine. Hagen's voice comes out of the darkness, calling for torches and rousing everyone from their sleep. With deliberate cruelty, he bids Gutrune greet Siegfried; the mighty hero has come home again! Never has music seemed more heartless and brutal.

Then Siegfried's body is set before her, to everyone's horror. Hagen explains unconvincingly that Siegfried has been killed by a boar. The shocked Gutrune accuses Gunther of murder and he in turn blames Hagen who finally admits to the deed and glories in it. When Hagen tries to claim the ring, Gunther insists that it

DENN DER GÖTTER ENDE DÄMMERT NUN AUF – ◊

10

*Valhalla burns as the twilight of the gods comes to pass,
and Alberich's curse is fulfilled.*

is Gutrune's dowry and tries to stop him. They struggle and Gunther is struck dead. Hagen goes to remove the ring from Siegfried's finger but, eerily, the hero's hand rises threateningly by itself.

Then Brünnhilde steps forward. From the Rhinedaughters she has learned how she and Siegfried have been the unwitting victims of Wotan's desperate bid to hold onto power. She instructs the vassals to erect a funeral pyre and to lift Siegfried's body on to it. Completely in command of events, Brünnhilde takes the ring and declares that it will be returned to the Rhinedaughters after being cleansed by fire. Then she takes a fiery brand and lifts it high. 'Fly home, you ravens!' she cries; 'tell Wotan what you have learned here by the Rhine! Wend your way to Brünnhilde's rock and bid Loge hasten to Valhalla, for the end of the gods comes at last! So I cast this brand on Valhalla's glittering towers!' Brünnhilde throws the brand on to the pyre which breaks into flame. Her horse, Grane, is brought to her and she speaks loving words to it about joining their hero in a fiery death. Then they leap into the flames.

According to Wagner's stage directions, the pyre blazes up, catching hold of the hall, the river swells mightily and pours its flood over the fire. The three Rhinedaughters swim forward to recover the ring. Hagen plunges into the river, still intent on claiming the ring, Alberich's ring. The Rhinedaughters draw him below the waves in an embrace denied his father before he had renounced love and set the whole drama in motion. The hall crashes in ruins and, in the fiery glow in the distance, Valhalla is seen, with the gods and heroes assembled, just as Waltraute had described. The men and women who have gathered near the river, look on fearfully. Fire seizes upon the hall of the gods, and when this is entirely hidden by flames, the curtain falls.

All this time, the orchestra has been weaving together numerous references to the events that have led to this tremendous conclusion. We hear again of the power of the gods and their downfall, Siegfried of glorious memory, and the Rhinedaughters joyously reunited with their gold. Then comes the sonorous motif associated with the majesty of Valhalla, before it is consumed in the flickering music of the magic fire. At last, only the high, sweet strains of the motif glorifying Brünnhilde remain to point the way to a new human understanding.

Epilogue

---◆---

The detailed stage directions that accompany the final pages of the *Ring* score are seldom taken literally these days and, frankly, there is no need for them to be. Wagner, for all his individuality, was a practical man of the theatre and he knew what the theatre did best. His priority was not outward display but inner meaning. The staging, just as much as music and words, had to serve this inner meaning. This was something he had felt strongly about since the days when, after his first successful opera, *Rienzi*, he had turned his back on the grand operatic style of Meyerbeer, with its emphasis on spectacle and theatricality and use of Italian and French conventions.

The textual ending of *Götterdämmerung* was the subject of at least nine revisions by Wagner, as he tried to make up his mind about the implications of the whole work. In early drafts, the ring was to be restored to the Rhine, Alberich and the Nibelungs were to be free again, the gods were to be forgiven for their wrong-doing, and Brünnhilde was to proclaim Wotan's power for all eternity. Wagner wrote several versions of this.

An important influence on his thinking at that time appears to have been the philosopher Ludwig Feuerbach, to whom he dedicated his 1849 monograph, *The Art-Work of the Future*. Feuerbach's humanist view prompted a final scene which elevated love above material possessions, authority, convention and even fate, to which the gods were subject as much as anyone else.

Then Wagner decided that the gods should be destroyed by fire. A marginal note about this in his own hand in 1851 reads 'self-annihilation of the gods'. He then discovered Schopenhauer and Buddhism, and his focus changed again. Wagner's 1856 version of the closing scene of *Götterdämmerung* was written contemporaneously with the sketch for *Die Sieger* and within months of the first sketch for *Parsifal*. In the text for this scene, Brünnhilde, the 'enlightened one', proclaimed her redemption from the endless cycle of suffering and rebirth, and her impending achievement of *Nirvana*, the 'blowing out' of the fires of greed, hatred and delusion; the extinction of 'self'. In this version, Brünnhilde's peroration over Siegfried's funeral pyre contained the following words: 'I flee for ever from the home of delusion; the open gates to eternal becoming I close behind me. To the holiest chosen land, free from desire and delusion the goal of world-wandering, redeemed from rebirth, the enlightened one now goes'. Two years after drafting this version, Wagner wrote to Mathilde Wesendonck: 'Only thoughtful acceptance of the idea of transmigration of souls has been able to show me the consoling point at which all in the end converge at an equal height of redemption after their differing paths through life, which in Time have run divided alongside one another, but which outside Time come together in full understanding.'[18]

Cosima commented that some of the composite words used in the 1856 text, notably '*Wunschheim*' and '*Wahnheim*', sounded rather artificial,[19] and so Wagner changed his mind about setting them. In the margin of the orchestral sketch we read: 'Enough! Anything to please Cosel!'[20] More to the point, he sensed that a prolonged vocal *scena* would be less effective than a symphonic orchestral passage in bringing the whole cycle to a close. In his 1872 definitive edition of the poem, he offered the following explanation for not setting all of the words, which were, nevertheless, still printed as a footnote: 'The musician had in the end' he said, 'in the act of composition, to sacrifice this passage, as its meaning is already conveyed with the greatest precision in the musical expression of the drama'.[21] It needs to be emphasised therefore that, far from denying the Buddhist imagery, he affirmed it; for, as he told Cosima, 'only music can convey the mysteries of reincarnation'.

It is interesting to trace the inspiration for Wagner's imagery as his ideas evolve for bringing the great work to a conclusion. In both the *Prose Edda* and the *Völsungasaga*, Brynhild ends up on Sigurd's funeral pyre, which is how Wagner depicted events in his original 1848 sketch for the drama. However, in the 1848 version, Brünnhilde, once more the Valkyrie, is seen rising above the flames and leading Siegfried heavenwards to his place in Valhalla – a suitably Nordic ending. There is no cataclysm, and the old order survives. Subsequently, in 1851, the idea of *Ragnarök* ('twilight of the gods') was introduced, in which the gods are to be destroyed, although, strictly speaking, this should occur after a great battle with the powers of evil rather than after a hero's funeral. The mythological account of battles with the frost giants, the fearsome wolf and the sea monster is rather different from Wagner's version, though there is some relevance in the flame giant, Surt, setting the heavenly rainbow bridge alight as the blazing world sinks beneath the ocean. However, in the accounts of the death and cremation of the Buddha, which attracted Wagner's attention in the mid 1850s, we learn that when the Sage entered *Nirvana* (which, remember, was also Brünnhilde's destination) the earth trembled and firebrands fell from the sky; the heavens were lit up by a preternatural fire and the rivers boiled over.[22] It is not difficult to recognise in a conflation of these images the amazing stage directions at the end of *Götterdämmerung*. Nor is it difficult to understand why Wagner, in a rare example of motif-labelling, referred to the exquisite closing theme (first used as Sieglinde's paean to Brünnhilde) as 'the glorification of Brünnhilde' or 'the theme in praise of Brünnhilde'. By embracing mortality and achieving wisdom through love, Brünnhilde had revealed the path to a better existence; one that was to be expressed definitively in the Christian/Buddhist syncretism of *Parsifal*. That is why it is Brünnhilde, not Siegfried, who is the real hero of *The Ring*, and why she is given the task of bringing the whole great adventure to a close.

Wagner once referred to *Götterdämmerung* as 'a tragedy of fate'. The gods, giants, dwarfs and humans are all trapped in a fateful web, from which they struggle, in their own ways, to be free. In the end, it is only by the destruction of the existing order in its entirety, and through the agency of love, that the human race can acquire wisdom enough to make a new beginning. Brünnhilde has the wisdom to see this at the end and, by her own sacrifice, sets in motion events which, ultimately, make possible a better world.

The German word *Dämmerung* means not only 'twilight' in the sense of 'dusk', but also 'dawn'. So, even the title of the drama carries the connotation of a beginning as well as an end, which is difficult to convey in a single English word. The death of Siegfried and the destruction of the gods are cataclysmic events but, in the language of myth, death symbolises transformation. Seen in its entirety then, the musical spirit of Act Three of *Götterdämmerung* is essentially lyrical, love-asserting and life-affirming.

I said at the outset that *The Ring* is a drama of ideas and that, ultimately, it is about us all. It is a parable of human folly and frailty, which uses mythology and music to tell its story. Its philosophical roots belonged to Europe of the industrial revolution, a time of unparalleled social and political change. But, like all great works of art, it really belongs to no particular time or circumstances and it is capable of, indeed demands, constant re-interpretation.

During the many years which passed between the first sketch for *The Ring* in 1848 and its completion in 1874, Wagner ventured on numerous occasions to comment on his intentions and to explain the meaning which lay behind aspects of the narrative. However, because he did not, himself, maintain a consistent view on every point over this long period of time, it is impossible to say that *The Ring* signifies this and only this, or that and only that. He came to realise that he was in danger of contradicting himself by being too specific in his interpretations, and said as much in a letter to his friend August Röckel as early as 1856:

> How can an artist expect that what he felt intuitively should be perfectly realised by others, seeing that he himself feels in the presence of the work, if it is true Art, that he is confronted by a riddle about which he too might have illusions just as another might.

However, one thing that did remain remarkably constant was the integrity of Wagner's musical language, from the opening E flat on the double basses in *Rheingold* to the closing D-flat chord in *Götterdämmerung*. We can only marvel at the infinitely flexible system of motifs which thread their way through the four dramas, his masterly handling of orchestral colour and texture, the expressiveness of his harmonies which convey, immediately and economically, the essence of a character or mood, and, above all, the skill with which he used all of these things as the raw material for a whole new mode of dramatic expression.

The critic Wilhelm Mohr, who attended the first performance, wrote afterwards that Wagner had 'won the battle' in the one area in which he was not trying to win it, namely in the field of music. The victory had gone to Wagner the musician, he said,

> because of his principles, irrespective of his principles, and contrary to his principles, he has created beauty, life in its fullness, and has brought into being musico-dramatic creations of a totally new kind. The old form has not been destroyed in this new beauty but has undergone a transformation like that of Siegfried's sword, *Notung*, which was filed down, melted, recast and forged ...'

It is a moot point whether Wagner's philosophical notions came first and were then given form by the music, or he looked for ideas which seemed promising vehicles for the music which welled up naturally within him. Many people would be inclined to think the former, but I think that the latter is closer to the mark. The best guide to his s in this regard is to be found in a letter of 1856 to Röckel, in which he said:

> While, as an artist, I *felt* with such convincing certainty that all my creations took their colouring from my feelings, as a philosopher I sought to discover a totally opposite interpretation of the world. This interpretation once discovered, I obstinately held to it, though, to my own surprise, I found that invariably it had to be abandoned when confronted by my spontaneous and purely objective artistic intuitions.

Whatever one might think of Wagner's idiosyncratic philosophical ideas, it is in the music that his true genius lay, and he came to trust his artistic judgement far more than the polemic that so distracted and even misled readers of his own and later times.

The music of Richard Wagner is no longer new, and *The Ring* has been performed on countless occasions over the past century-and-a-quarter. Nevertheless, it continues to be staged somewhere in the world each year, and performances are invariably sold out. Audio and video recordings of *The Ring* have never been more plentiful or accessible.

'Create something new!' was Wagner's advice, and he certainly followed this himself. These days, it is the staging of *The Ring* which is constantly being forged anew like Siegfried's sword, and many quite startling productions have offered new insights into this eternally fascinating and, in Tchaikovsky's words, 'epoch-making' work of art.

It seems to me that, if *The Ring* is to continue to make an impact on new generations of audiences, stagings require freshness, simplicity and a sense of immediacy. Audiences should be able to feel that they are involved in some way in the great drama which is going on in their presence. In 1850, Wagner wrote in a burst of idealism

> I would design and build a theatre made of wood, invite the most
> suitable singers, and organise everything necessary for a special event
> ... Then I would invite everyone interested in my works, make sure
> that the auditorium is filled properly, and give three performances in
> a week – *gratis* of course – after which the theatre would be pulled
> down and the whole thing would be over for good.[23]

We can be grateful that he did not go quite that far, but his comments do provide a clue as to how he regarded his works within a theatrical tradition going back to the amphitheatres of Athens, the street theatres of the Middle Ages, and Shakespeare's wooden 'O'. He wanted *The Ring* to be accessible to anyone who was interested in it, not just a wealthy or privileged section of society. He wanted a sense of festival, a celebration of life and ideas, to which ordinary men and women would come, before 'the whole thing would be over for good'.

As we look back over the war-torn twentieth century and forward to a new era in which all things seem possible, we still have good reason to be amazed by *Der Ring des Nibelungen*, the fruit of one man's intellect, and a most singular work of art.

Notes

An Introduction to *Der Ring des Nibelungen*

1 Selected Letters of Richard Wagner, trans. and ed. Stewart Spencer and Barry Millington (London, 1987), 319.
2 *'Zukunftmusik'* (1860).
3 Franz Liszt, *Richard Wagner's Lohengrin and Tannhäuser*, (Cologne, 1852)

Das Rheingold

4 Darcy, W., *Wagner's Das Rheingold*. (Oxford, 1993).
5 Wagner to August Röckel, 1854.
6 *ibid.*

Die Walküre

7 This was a theme to which Wagner returned on a number of occasions, emphasising the indivisible nature of love, be it sexual or otherwise.
8 Wagner to Karl Gaillard, 1844.
9 *About Conducting* (1869).

Siegfried

10 Wagner wrote this in a letter to the painter Ernst Benedikt Kietz.
11 J. and W. Grimm and others, *German Fairy Tales*, ed. Helmut Brackert and Volkmar Sander, (Continuum, New York 1985).
12 Berlioz, H., *Treatise on Instrumentation*, rev. by R. Strauss, (New York, 1948).
13 Cosima's Diary entry for 9 January 1873.
14 *Cosima Wagner's Diaries*, ed. M. Gregor-Dellin and D. Mack; trans. G.Skelton, New York 1978–80, Vol. 1, p. 215, 1 May 1870.
15 Ibid. Vol. 2 p. 117, 20 July 1878.
16 Quoted by Curt von Westernhagen, *The Forging of The Ring*, trans. Arnold and Mary Whittall, Cambridge University Press 1976, p. 169.
17 Melba, Nellie, *Melodies and Memories*, Hamish Hamilton, London, 1925. Annotated by John Cargher, 1980.
18 *Richard Wagner an Mathilde Wesendonk*, ed. W. Golther (Berlin 1904, p. 242). Trans. Lucy Beckett.
19 *Cosima Wagner's Diaries*, op. cit. Vol. 2, p. 448, 10 January 1872.

[20] Westernhagen, op.cit. p. 235.

[21] See Deryck Cooke *I Saw the World End*, London, Oxford University Press, 1979, p. 22.

[22] *Buddhist Scriptures*, selected and translated by Edward Conze, Penguin 1959, p. 63.

[23] Wagner to Ernst Benedikt Kietz, 1850.

The Ring Text in Prose

THE RHINEGOLD

Dramatis Personae

Gods

WOTAN	bass-baritone
DONNER	baritone
FROH	tenor
LOGE	tenor

Goddesses

FRICKA	mezzo-soprano
FREIA	soprano
ERDA	contralto

Nibelungs

ALBERICH	bass-baritone
MIME	tenor
NIBELUNGS	chorus

Giants

FASOLT	bass-baritone
FAFNER	bass

Rhinedaughters

WOGLINDE	soprano
WELLGUNDE	soprano
FLOSSHILDE	mezzo-soprano

Scene 1

Deep in the waters of the Rhine, three Rhinedaughters, Woglinde, Wellgunde and Flosshilde swim languidly amongst the rocks. They are guarding the Rhinegold, nature's gift to an innocent world. As the currents ebb and flow around the precious object, Woglinde sings a lullaby. Wellgunde joins her and they tease and chase each other until Flosshilde chides them for neglecting their charge.

From a dark chasm at the bottom of the river clambers Alberich, the Nibelung. He stops to watch the sisters and then calls to them, offering to join in their games. The Rhinedaughters are startled by this loathsome intruder and, recalling their father's warning, move to protect the gold. Alberich longs to enjoy their company and fantasises about holding one in his arms. The girls realise that it is not the gold he is after but one of them. They decide to teach this lecherous dwarf a lesson.

Woglinde flirts outrageously, inviting the Nibelung to climb a rocky outcrop to her. He slips and slithers on the slimy surface and then sneezes as the water tickles his nose. Compared with the graceful sisters, Alberich cuts an awkward and pathetic figure. Just as he reaches for Woglinde she swims to another rock. Then she invites him to join her in the depths, which seems a more convenient rendezvous. When he follows, she gives him the slip once again.

As Alberich stumbles about in pursuit of Woglinde, the voice of Wellgunde calls enticingly, hinting that she would be a much better catch. The Nibelung is quick to agree and encourages her to come closer. He wants her slender arms around him in order to caress her neck and hug her ample bosom. Wellgunde scrutinises this would-be lover and finds him to be a hairy, hunch-backed coxcomb; a black, calloused, sulphurous dwarf. 'Find a sweetheart who will have you', she declares. Alberich tries to take her by force but she evades his grasp and swims to a higher rock. The others laugh. He calls her a deceitful child and a cold and bony fish, adding that if she doesn't find him attractive, she can flirt with eels instead.

With feigned innocence, Flosshilde asks why he is grumbling. He has courted only two of the sisters; the third would be much more amenable. This is music to Alberich's ears. What luck that there are several Rhinedaughters! Surely one will find him attractive? But he is cautious this time. If Flosshilde means what she says then she must come to him. Flosshilde scolds her sisters for not recognising how attractive he is, and Alberich echoes her sentiments. Now that he has seen the third sister, the others appear silly and spiteful. Flosshilde flatters him and the Nibelung almost faints with excitement. 'Lovely man' she says, 'be kind to me'. In honeyed tones she extols his searing glance and stubbly beard, his bristly hair, toad-like form and croaking voice. Her sisters burst out laughing at this mockery.

In frustration, Alberich denounces all three sisters as a despicable, sly, lewd, evil gang. The Rhinedaughters tell him not to complain. They will be faithful to whoever catches them; why does he let them slip through his fingers? Then they swim in all directions, hither and thither, up and down, tempting him to chase them. Lust fuels his pursuit. He clambers awkwardly, jumping from place to place, falling down and staggering up. As the girls tease him relentlessly he shakes his fist.

Breathless with rage, Alberich is suddenly attracted by an extraordinary spectacle. An increasingly bright light penetrates down through the waters, gradually filling them with a blinding gleam of gold. The Rhinedaughters are entranced. The sun has awakened the Rhinegold, which seems to smile in the radiant light. The three sisters greet this beautiful vision with increasing abandon.

Alberich too is mesmerised by what he sees, and demands to know what it is. The sisters scorn his ignorance. Doesn't he know anything of the golden eyes that wake and sleep in turn? The Nibelung has little interest in an object whose only purpose is to illuminate underwater games. Woglinde remarks that he would not be so dismissive if he knew its wonders. Wellgunde adds that the world's wealth could be won by anyone who fashioned a ring from the gold – a ring that gave measureless power. Flosshilde tries to silence her chattering sisters, reminding them that their father had ordered them to protect the gleaming treasure from tricksters. But the others are not to be silenced. Woglinde reveals that only one who forswears the power of love and rejects its delights may forge a ring from the gold. Wellgunde concludes then they have nothing to fear, since no one will shun love. 'The lascivious gnome least of all', adds Woglinde. His greed for love is likely to be the death of him! 'Dearest gnome' they goad, 'won't you laugh too?'

Alberich no longer hears these taunts. His eyes are fixed on the gold as he broods: could he win mastery of the world through the gold? Could he forego love but, by cunning, satisfy his desires? In a new and frightening tone he shouts to the girls: 'Continue to mock! The Nibelung is near your plaything!' They respond in panic and the waters churn. Scrambling upwards, Alberich tells the sisters to woo in the dark. With fearful energy he tears the gold from the rock, proclaims that he will forge the vengeful ring, and curses love. Dense night suddenly falls everywhere as, with mocking laughter, he disappears below. Frantic at their loss, the girls dive quickly after him.

Scene 2

Gradually, the dark waters transform themselves into billowing clouds and then into fine mist, as the growing light of dawn fills the stage. In an open space on a mountain top, Wotan and Fricka are asleep on a flowery bank. In the distance are the gleaming battlements of a mighty fortress. Between the fortress and the foreground is a deep valley through which the Rhine flows.

Fricka rises and catches sight of the fortress. In alarm she attempts to waken Wotan but he is dreaming of eternal might and endless fame. She is impatient with such illusions and shakes him awake. He raises himself a little and hails the completion of the eternal work. On the mountain top stands the gods' fortress just as he had seen it in his dreams; just as he had intended it, strong, beautiful and majestic. Fricka is less enthusiastic. She fears for her sister Freia. Now that the building is completed, payment will be due. Has Wotan forgotten the price? He replies that he well remembers what the insolent builders had stipulated. He had bound them by a contract to build this glorious hall and, thanks to their strength, there it stands. The cost was immaterial.

Fricka has no time for this display of loveless optimism. Had she known of the contract she would have stopped it. The women had been kept deliberately at a distance so that the men could bargain with the giants. Shamefully and rashly, the lovely Freia had been promised in exchange, and the men felt satisfied with this arrangement. Do heartless men hold anything sacred when they hanker after power?

Was such hankering far from Fricka's mind, replies Wotan, when she begged him for such a building? She replies that it had been her husband's infidelity that had driven her to keep him by her side. She had visions of a splendid home, gorgeously furnished, in which they could relax, but he thought only of defences and ramparts, dominion and power. Only storm and strife had accompanied the building of the fortress. Amused, Wotan suggests that while his wife might want to keep him at home, she would still recognise that as a god, he had to win over the world. Ranging and changing are life's delights. These were pastimes he could not give up.

Fricka accuses him of being an unloving, disagreeable husband. For the worthless baubles of power and dominion, would he throw away love and a precious woman? Wotan replies that he forfeited one of his eyes when he wooed her for his wife; how stupid of her to scold him now. He admired women rather more than she wished. And as for Freia, it never really entered his head to give her up. To which Fricka replies that he had better help Freia now because she is coming running.

Freia rushes in, calling for help. She is being pursued by Fasolt, who wants to carry her off. Wotan is dismissive of Fasolt's threats and asks Freia if she had seen Loge. Fricka accuses her husband of always being too ready to trust that trickster. He has been bad news for the gods but continues to captivate Wotan. The god replies that when simple courage is called for he doesn't need anyone's help, but when jealousy has to be dealt with, only wily subtlety will serve. That is where Loge comes in. Loge had talked him into the agreement on the understanding that Freia would be released. Now Wotan is relying on him. Fricka notes that he seems to have been left in the lurch and the giants are approaching. Where is his wily assistant now? Freia calls plaintively to her brothers, Donner and Froh, but Fricka observes that they had all betrayed her in an evil pact and are now lying low.

The giants Fasolt and Fafner enter. Fasolt gives an account of the building of the fortress – built with tireless labour while the gods were resting. He tells them brusquely to take possession of their new abode and pay the fee. Disingenuously, Wotan invites the giants to name their fee, to which Fasolt inquires if his memory is really so feeble? It had been agreed that the giants should have 'Freia the fair, Holda the free' to take home with them.

They must be out of their minds, says Wotan. It is not for him to sell Freia. For a moment Fasolt is speechless. Is this betrayal? Are the runes on Wotan's spear just a joke? Does a sealed contract mean nothing to the chief of the gods? Fafner scornfully asks his brother if he now recognises fraud when he sees it.

Fasolt is wiser than he seems, for he tells Wotan that his

authority depends on observance of the law. His power might be
carefully calculated and he might be clever, but in order to keep
the peace he had bound by agreements those who were free. The
giant would curse Wotan's learning and reject his peace unless the
god honoured the contract. Thus a stupid giant gives advice to the
clever god.

Wotan replies that the giants had been perverse in taking seriously what had been contracted in jest. In any case, what use
would a lovely and charming goddess be to such louts? Fasolt
accuses Wotan of injustice. Rulers who attached so much importance to beauty had been willing to trade a beautiful woman for
turrets of stone. But when the giants, poor creatures, sweated and
toiled with calloused hands to win a beautiful and gentle woman,
this meant nothing.

Fafner has no patience for idle chatter. Clearly they will not
win this argument. Freia is worth little to the giants but her loss
would affect the gods greatly. Golden apples grow in her garden
and she alone knows how to tend them. By eating them, the gods
are able to remain perpetually young. If Freia were taken away,
they would become sick and pale, old and weak, and waste away.
Fafner is determined that the gods should lose Freia.

Wotan is irritated that Loge is so long in coming and he tells
the giants to ask for another form of payment. Only Freia will satisfy Fasolt, and Fafner orders her to follow them. She calls for help
and runs to her brothers. Froh takes her in his arms and Donner
threatens the giants with his hammer. The giants are mystified.
They don't want a fight, just their wages. Donner offers to pay
them with an appropriately measured blow and swings his hammer.
Wotan intervenes declaring: 'nothing by force!' The agreement is
protected by the shaft of his spear. Freia is appalled that Wotan
seems to be forsaking her, and Fricka labels him a cruel man.

At last Loge appears, and Wotan asks him sarcastically if he
were hurrying to keep his promise and to sort out the bargain.

Loge feigns surprise. What bargain? Did Wotan mean the contract with the giants that the god himself negotiated? Home and hearth are of no interest to Loge. Donner and Froh might worry about board and lodging, especially of they are looking for a marital home. Wotan wanted a stately hall, a mighty castle, and there it stands, strongly built. Hadn't Loge checked it himself to determine its quality? He had found Fasolt and Fafner to be entirely trustworthy; not a stone was out of place. He had been busy doing all these things, not lazing about like others he could name.

Wotan is not to be fobbed off with such talk. Loge needs to be careful. Amongst all the gods only Wotan is his friend, having backed him when the others were mistrustful. He should now advise skilfully. When the builders had negotiated Freia as payment, Wotan had only agreed on the basis of Loge's promise to secure her release. Loge is willing to admit that he did promise to give careful consideration to her release, but how could he promise to find what does not exist and can never be found? How could anyone promise such a thing? Fricka reproaches her husband for trusting such a treacherous rogue, Froh adds that 'Liar' not 'Loge' is his name and Donner threatens to quench his flame. Loge observes that these fools are abusing him in an attempt to hide their own shame. Wotan comes to his defence, claiming that Loge's advice is worth even more when it is cautiously given.

Fafner and Fasolt have run out of patience, and Wotan demands to know what Loge has been doing with his time. Loge declares that ingratitude has always been his lot. Concerned only for Wotan's interests, he had turned the world upside down in an effort to find a substitute for Freia. He had looked in vain and now realised that nothing was more precious to men than feminine charm. Wherever life was to be found, in the water, on land and in the air, Loge had inquired whether anything was deemed more important. This question had drawn only derision, for no one seemed prepared to forsake love. However, he had encountered one man who had renounced these favours in return for bright gold. The naïve children of the Rhine had told of their misfortune at the hands of Night-Alberich, the Nibelung. He had wooed them in vain and then, in revenge, had stolen the Rhinegold. He now valued it more highly than a woman's love. The Rhine-daughters had appealed to Wotan to bring the thief to justice and to return the gold to the waters, so that it could be theirs forever. Loge had promised to inform Wotan of this and so had kept his word.

Loge's account makes Wotan irritable. He has his own problems to worry about and is in no position to help others.

Fasolt begrudges Alberich the gold, for the Nibelung has been a source of trouble to the giants but always manages to avoid capture. Fafner fears even more trouble now and asks Loge how the Nibelung can benefit. The answer is that the gold is no mere plaything. A ring forged from it would give its owner the utmost power; it would win him the world. This news reminds Wotan that he too has heard of the Rhinegold, that riches lie hidden within its bright gleam, and that a ring could be the source of great power and wealth.

Fricka approaches Loge in confidence to ask whether glittering trinkets made from the gold could be used to adorn women. Loge assures her that a wife could command her husband's fidelity if adorned with gems wrought by dwarfs under the spell of the ring. Fricka suggests that perhaps her husband could win the gold himself.

Recognising the importance of the ring, Wotan asks Loge how it could be forged. Loge tells him that a magic charm turns the gold into a ring. Nobody knows the charm but it can be easily mastered by anyone renouncing love. Wotan turns away disconsolately and Loge observes that such a course is obviously not for him. In any case, he is too late. Alberich didn't hesitate. He won control of the spell and now possesses the ring.

Donner remarks that Alberich would have control over the gods unless the ring is taken away from him. Wotan resolves to have the ring. Froh suggests that the ring could now be obtained without having to curse love, and Loge adds that it would be ridiculously easy (child's play in fact) to get hold of it. 'Tell us how', asks Wotan. 'By theft!' comes the reply. What a thief stole, you steal from the thief. Nothing could be easier. But Alberich is wily. It would be necessary to act with cunning if the thief is to be brought to justice and the gold returned to the Rhinedaughters.

Wotan couldn't care less about the Rhinedaughters and Fricka disparages them as a watery brood. She recalls that many a husband (to her sorrow) has been lured away by their licentious bathing.

Fafner confers with his brother, suggesting that the gold would be of greater use to them than Freia. The gold's magic would confer eternal youth just as effectively. Fasolt has his heart set on Freia and is not convinced. Fafner then takes matters into his own hands and informs Wotan that the giants would forgo Freia and settle instead for the Nibelung's gold. 'Are you out of your minds?' replies Wotan, adding that what he does not have he cannot give. Fafner responds that it was hard to build the fortress but it would be easy by cunning and force to tie the Nibelung down. Wotan calls the giants shameless, over-greedy fools, and Fasolt promptly responds by seizing Freia as hostage until the ransom is paid. Both giants make it clear that if the golden ransom is not paid by evening, Freia will be forfeit forever. A distraught Freia calls for help to her sister and brothers who despite their bluster, stand pathetically, waiting for Wotan to make the first move.

Loge describes the giants' progress as they carry off the hapless Freia, over hill and dale, fording the Rhine, heading for Riesenheim, home of giants. Then he observes that a mist fills the scene and the gods are growing pale. Their cheeks have lost their bloom and their eyes their sparkle. Froh seems tired and Donner can no longer hold his hammer. Fricka is not herself either and

Wotan turns grey, as old age comes upon him. Loge soon realises what has happened. The gods have gone without their daily ration of Freia's apples, necessary to keep them vigorous and young. However, the keeper of the garden is now held for ransom. The fruit fades and withers on the branches and soon it will decay and fall. Loge is not affected because Freia was always stingy with her fruit for him and, after all, he is only a demigod. The giants understood how dependent the gods had become on the fruit. Without the apples, the race of gods would become old and grey, hoary and pitiful, withered and the butt of jokes, and will die.

Fricka castigates her husband for the abuse and shame that has befallen the gods. After a moment, Wotan pulls himself resolutely together and tells Loge that they will descend together to Nibelheim to get the gold. Loge raises the subject of the Rhine-daughters once more but is quickly silenced. Wotan's only thoughts are for Freia. He rejects the idea of approaching Nibelheim through the Rhine, and so Loge proposes that they descend through a crevice in the rocks, from which sulphurous fumes begin to issue. Loge goes ahead as Wotan promises the others that he will soon return to banish their ageing with redeeming gold. Donner and Froh offer good luck and Fricka urges her husband to return safely to an anxious wife.

The sulphur vapour darkens into an opaque black cloud extending from top to bottom. This becomes transformed into a dark rocky crevice, moving continually upwards so as to give the impression that the stage is sinking deeper into the earth. A dark red light glows in the distance on various sides. The growing sound of forging is audible everywhere. The din of anvils dies away. A subterranean cavern stretching far out of sight, becomes visible. It opens on every side into narrow shafts.

Scene 3

Deep in Nibelheim, Alberich pulls his howling brother Mime from a shaft. He threatens to pinch Mime painfully if the smith doesn't finish his work in time. Mime protests that the work is done and he pleads with his brother to stop tugging his ear. Alberich demands to know why he hesitated to produce the work, to which Mime replies that he feared something might be missing. When Alberich asks what is unfinished, Mime points with embarrassment 'here and there'. What 'here and there?' shouts Alberich, 'give me your work!'

In his anxiety, Mime drops a metal object that his brother picks up and examines. The object appears to be perfect in every respect and Mime is accused of wanting to keep for himself this splendid object that Alberich's cunning had taught him to forge. Alberich puts the object on his head as a *Tarnhelm* – a magic helmet. It fits, and he tries a spell: 'Night and mist resembling nothing'. He disappears, and in his place is a pillar of mist. He asks if Mime can see him and, when certain that he can't, says that he must feel him instead. Mime staggers under a rain of whiplashes, heard but not seen.

An invisible Alberich laughs cruelly, thanking his 'idiot' brother and commanding the Nibelungs to bow to Alberich. He will be everywhere, watching. They will never rest again. When they do not expect him he will be there, watching them. They will forever be his subjects. His voice is heard in the distance, and screams and cries answer from the lower caverns. While Mime cowers in pain, Wotan and Loge appear from a cleft in the rock face.

Loge notes the flash of sparks in the distance as Mime howls in fear and agony. Wotan discovers Mime, and Loge cheerfully enquires why he is whining; what cuts and torments him so?

Mime just wants to be left in peace. Loge offers to do that gladly, and also to help him. Mime doubts that anyone can help him, since he must obey his brother who put him in fetters. Loge asks how he came to be fettered. Mime tells how Alberich made the golden ring with which he enslaves his people. The Nibelungs were once carefree blacksmiths who made ornaments for their women, wondrous jewels and lovely trinkets. They gaily laughed at their work. Now the villain forces them to labour for him alone. With the help of the ring he discovers where new seams are to be found in the clefts and forces the Nibelungs to dig them out, melt, forge and cast without rest, and pile up their master's hoard.

Mime explains that it was not his idleness that drew Alberich's anger. Mime had been given the hardest task: to forge a helmet exactly as he instructed. But Mime took careful note of the extraordinary powers that belonged to the helmet and intended to keep it for himself and so escape Alberich's tyranny. Perhaps he could have outwitted his brother and snatched the ring and become his lord and master! Alas, Mime completed the work but could not use the binding spell, and now has discovered only too well the extent of the helmet's powers. Alberich vanishes from sight but doles out blows on the blind man. This is the way foolish Mime is being thanked for his efforts.

Loge suggests to Wotan that their task will not be an easy one, but Wotan puts his trust in Loge's cunning. Mime is struck by the gods' laughter and, studying them more closely, asks who they are. 'Your friends' says Loge. 'We shall free the Nibelung people from their troubles.' Alberich returns, driving before him a team of Nibelungs loaded with gold and silver that they heap up in a pile. The *Tarnhelm* is now hanging on Alberich's belt. Alberich is directing his slaves in piling up the treasure when he suddenly becomes aware of Wotan and Loge. He suspects that Mime has been prattling to the strangers and sends him off to his forging and moulding, threatening more whippings if anyone is idle. He draws the ring from his finger, kisses it and holds it aloft as he pro-nounces a command: 'Tremble and quake, wretched slaves! Quickly obey the ring's great lord!' With howls and screams the Nibelungs scatter in all directions to the shafts.

Alberich gazes mistrustfully at Wotan and Loge and asks them their business. Wotan says that they had heard of marvels being worked by Aberich in Nibelheim, and were anxious to see for themselves. Alberich can understand that others might be envious of him.

Loge tries a different tack, pointing out that without his fire, the caverns of Nibelheim would be cold and dark, and forging would be impossible. He has been a friend to the Nibelungs and finds Alberich's manner discourteous. Alberich says he knows that Loge is now consorting with the gods (light elves) and suggests that if he is as false a friend to them as he was once to Alberich, then there is nothing to fear. Loge asks if he is trusted, but Alberich replies that he trusts Loge's disloyalty, not his loyalty, and that he defies everyone.

When Loge expresses admiration for such confidence and strength, Alberich describes the wealth created by his minions and the scale of his wealth to come. Wotan asks what good such treasure will be since there is nothing to buy in Nibelheim. Alberich replies that Nibelheim serves to create treasures and hide treasures, but with this hoard he will win the world. Politely, Wotan asks how he intends to go about that.

Alberich says that amongst the gentle breezes up above, the gods laugh and make love. With golden hands he will capture the gods. As he had forsworn love, so all living things will forswear it. Dazzled by gold they shall hanker only for gold. Others lull themselves complacently on wondrous heights, feasting eternally and despising the dark spirit. They should beware! When their men are subjugated he will force himself on their women who shun his attentions and reject his love. Laughing wildly he continues: 'Did you hear? Beware the nocturnal army when the Nibelung hoard rises from silent depths to daylight!'

Wotan bursts out with invective but is urged to keep his head by Loge who continues to flatter the Nibelung. He acclaims him as the mightiest; even the moon, stars and shining sun must serve him! But – most of all – the race of Nibelungs obeys him. With a ring, he made his people cower. But if in sleep a thief crept up and snatched the ring, how would he defend himself? Alberich ridicules Loge for thinking himself clever and others stupid. The concealing helmet would allow him to assume any shape he desired. No one would see him but he would be everywhere and safe, even from such a kind considerate friend as Loge!

Loge says that he has seen much but has never witnessed such a miracle. He finds it hard to credit since, by this means, the Nibelung could retain power forever. Becoming excited at the prospect of demonstrating his own superiority, Alberich invites Loge to nominate a shape in which he would like him to appear. Loge replies that he should appear in any amazing shape he likes. Alberich puts on the Tarnhelm and recites: 'Giant dragon, wind and curl.' He disappears at once and, in his place, a giant serpent writhes on the ground. Loge pretends to be frightened while Wotan laughs and congratulates Alberich on his transformation. The serpent vanishes and in its place Alberich appears once more, pleased with his demonstration.

Loge seems suitably impressed but makes the point that Alberich grew bigger, but could he also become smaller, which might be the best way to escape danger? Perhaps that is too difficult? Alberich rises to the bait and Loge suggests that a toad would be able to hide in the smallest crevice. There is another invocation: 'Crooked and grey, crawl toad!' The Nibelung disappears and, when a toad appears, Loge urges Wotan to catch it. Together they grab the creature and wrench off the Tarnhelm. Alberich appears in his true shape, wriggling and cursing under Wotan's foot. Loge binds his hands and legs and the gods drag him, struggling, into a crevice and commence their ascent.

Scene 4

Wotan, Loge and the captive Alberich arrive on the open plateau on the mountaintop. Loge torments the prisoner, calling him 'cousin', showing to him the world he had intended to rule, and asking sarcastically what spot would be given to Loge for a stable. Alberich spits out abuse and Wotan savours the moment, explaining that a ransom would be required before the Nibelung could be set free.

Alberich laments his own foolishness and promises terrible revenge. Loge suggests that if he is considering revenge, he should think firstly about a ransom. 'Demand what you require', comes the reply. Loge stipulates 'the treasure and your bright gold'. Alberich is appalled but quickly realises that while he retains the ring he can soon win the treasure anew. This would be a salutary lesson to him and not too high a price to pay. Wotan demands that the treasure be handed over, and Alberich asks that one of his hands be untied so that he may comply. Loge unties one hand and Alberich touches the ring with his lips, whispering a secret order.

The Nibelungs emerge from the depths, dragging the treasure with them. Alberich asks that both of his hands now be untied but Wotan refuses until the ransom is paid. As the Nibelungs pile up the hoard, Alberich is appalled that his minions should see him reduced to captivity. However, this doesn't deter him from shouting abuse at his people, commanding them not to look at him and threatening punishment if they are idle. Once again he kisses the ring and holds it aloft. As if struck by a blow, the Nibelungs hurry in fear to the crevice and disappear from sight.

Alberich argues that, since he has now paid up, he should be released. He asks for the return of the finely wrought helmet, the Tarnhelm, that Loge is holding, but Loge throws it on the heap, declaring it to be part of the ransom too. Alberich curses under his breath but consoles himself with the thought that he who made the old Tarnhelm can make him another.

Wotan points to the golden ring on Alberich's finger and says that it too is part of the treasure. Horrified at this demand, the Nibelung cries out: 'My life but not the ring', to which Wotan responds: 'It is your ring I require. With your life you may do as you please'. Alberich is beside himself and says that if he loses his life then he must lose the ring, but heart and head, eyes and ears are truly not more essential to him than is the bright ring. He is shameless, says Wotan, in claiming ownership of the ring. From whom did he take the gold with which the ring was made? The Rhinedaughters would be able to confirm whether they had given the gold to Alberich for his own use.

Alberich condemns this shameful deceit and monstrous trickery. Wotan would happily have stolen the gold from the Rhine if he had known how to harness its power. How convenient for him that Alberich, in distress and anger, had won this magical thing. Would a royal plaything be so attractive if the price of winning it had been the renunciation of love? The god should take care. If the Nibelung sinned, it was only against himself, but the immortal one would sin against everything that was, is and will be, if he seizes the ring.

Wotan is not to be put off by such chatter and violently tears off the ring. Alberich utters a terrible cry. He is ruined, crushed – the most tragic of slaves.

Wotan has eyes only for the ring which, he says, will make him the mightiest of mighty lords.

Loge, with Wotan's concurrence, releases Alberich and tells him to slip off home. Alberich then asks hysterically if he is free, really free? If so, he will give freedom's first greeting. As he acquired the ring by a curse, so let the ring itself be cursed. As its gold gave him power without limit, now let its magic bring death to the one who wears it. No happy man will want to have it. No fortunate man will benefit from it. Whoever possesses it will be afflicted with trouble and whoever lacks it will be consumed by envy. Everyone will hanker for its possession but no one will enjoy it to advantage. Its owner won't benefit from it, for it draws him to his assassin. Assured of death, the coward will be in the grip of fear. As long as he lives, he'll thirst for death. The ring's master will be the ring's slave until Alberich holds again what was stolen from him. This is the blessing with which the Nibelung, in dire distress, invests his ring. He laughs bitterly as he tells Wotan to guard the ring well for he will not escape this curse. Then Alberich disappears quickly into a crevice.

Loge asks Wotan if he had been paying attention to this affectionate message. The god is not perturbed by the Nibelung venting his spleen.

Froh, Donner and Fricka return and inquire anxiously about the journey to Nibelheim. Loge, with self-satisfaction, points to the piled treasure that will ransom Freia. Froh remarks on the sweetness of the air and his quickening senses as Freia draws near with the giants Fasolt and Fafner. The gods' appearances have regained their youthfulness. Fricka hurries to embrace her sister but Fasolt refuses to let Freia go until the ransom is paid, adding that he had brought her back reluctantly.

When Wotan indicates that the ransom is ready, Fasolt confesses that being deprived of the woman will make him sad. If she is to vanish from his mind, the treasure must be so heaped up that it hides her completely from his sight. Wotan tells the other gods to pile up the treasure so that it conceals Freia's form. The giants thrust their staffs into the ground on either side of her and Loge and Froh begin to stack up the hoard. Fafner is concerned that it should be stacked tightly so that he cannot see any gaps. Wotan cannot bear to watch, and Fricka observes that Freia looks ashamed and humiliated, pleading silently with her eyes. How wicked is her husband who asks this of a loved one.

Fafner demands that more be added to the pile. Donner can

hardly contain his rage and threatens again to use violence. Once again, Wotan restrains him, adding that Freia now seems to be hidden by the gold. The treasure has been used up. Fafner looks carefully for gaps and, catching a glimpse of Freia's hair, orders that the Tarnhelm be thrown on the pile. Loge hesitates but Wotan tells him to let it go.

Fasolt takes one last look, lamenting the loss of beautiful Freia, then catches sight of an eye. As long as he can still see those lovely eyes, he cannot give up the woman. Fafner won't accept Loge's protestations that there is no more gold left, and points to the gleaming gold ring on Wotan's finger. Wotan is taken aback at the suggestion that he should give up the ring, and Loge reminds everyone that this gold belongs to the Rhinedaughters, to whom Wotan will return it. Wotan responds tartly that he fully intends to keep the ring and does not consider himself bound by Loge's commitment. Fafner insists that the ring be surrendered, to which Wotan replies that while he would part with anything else, he would not, for the world, give up the ring.

Fasolt angrily pulls Freia from behind the pile and announces that the deal is off. Freia will remain with the giants forever. Freia cries out in alarm and Fricka instructs her husband to give the giants what they want. Froh and Donner also urge Wotan to hand over the ring. He refuses absolutely to do so.

As Wotan turns angrily away, darkness falls. Erda appears, rising from the ground. She tells Wotan to yield the ring and thereby escape the curse that would bring about his destruction. When Wotan asks who she is, Erda replies that she knows how all things were, are and will be. She is the everlasting world's primeval woman. She had borne three daughters, the Norns, who tell Wotan each night what Erda has seen. But now the greatest danger brings her personally to him. He should heed this: all that exists will end. A dark day dawns for the gods. Wotan must shun the ring.

Wotan asks her to stay, so that he might learn more, but she disappears saying that he knows enough and should ponder with fear and trembling what she has told him. Fricka and Froh prevent Wotan from following her. Donner assures the giants that they will receive the gold. Wotan broods deeply over all that he has heard and then decides resolutely to secure Freia's release and hand over the ring. He throws the ring onto the pile as Freia rejoins the gods who embrace her joyously.

Fafner spreads out a huge sack and, as he begins to stow the treasure, Fasolt stops him, demanding a fair share. Fafner, irritated, says that the girl meant more to his brother than the gold, and that he is a lovesick ass. Fasolt had only been persuaded with difficulty to exchange Freia for the gold, and he certainly wouldn't have shared her. Fafner insists on taking the greater part of the treasure. Fasolt calls on the gods to divide the treasure equally but Wotan turns away contemptuously. Loge advises Fasolt to worry only about the ring. Fasolt at once hurls himself at his brother and, in the ensuing struggle, takes the ring which, he says, Freia's eyes had won for him. With a blow from his staff, Fafner fells his brother and quickly seizes the ring from the dying man.

The gods are appalled at what they have witnessed. Fafner continues to load his sack and makes off. A shocked Wotan comments on the terrible power of the curse. Loge congratulates him, observing that while he had gained much by acquiring the ring, he had benefited even more when it was taken from him. Now his enemies are killing each other for the gold he had given away.

Wotan is gripped by fear but resolves to learn from Erda how this fear may be calmed. He is comforted by Fricka who asks why he hesitates; the noble fortress awaits its owner. Wotan replies that an evil wage had paid for the building.

Donner observes that a sultry mist hangs in the air, and he decides to gather it into a thunderstorm that will sweep the sky clean. He climbs onto a high rock and swings his hammer.

Summoning the mists, he disappears behind dark clouds. His hammer blow is heard striking the rock. There is a flash of lightning and a violent clap of thunder. Donner calls to his brother to show the way over a bridge.

From where Froh and Donner are standing, a rainbow bridge is seen, stretching across the Rhine gorge to the fortress bathed in evening light. The gods are overwhelmed at the marvellous sight. Wotan rhapsodises about the splendid fortress and, struck by a grand idea, picks up a sword left on the ground when Fafner collected the treasure. The god salutes the fortress and invites his wife to follow and live with him in Valhalla. Fricka asks about the name, which is unfamiliar to her, and Wotan replies that, when all he has dreamt of has come to pass, when victory is his, then its meaning will come clear.

Loge has been listening to these exchanges but does not share Wotan's optimism. He sees the gods hurrying to their doom even though they imagine the opposite. He is embarrassed at collaborating with them. He toys with the idea of transforming himself into flickering flame in order to burn them up rather than accompany them to oblivion. He'll think about it. Who knows what he'll do?

As Loge strolls nonchalantly to join the others, the plaintive voices of the Rhinedaughters float upwards: 'Rhinegold, Rhinegold, pure gold! How bright and pure you once shone upon us. For you and your brightness we are now lamenting. Give us the gold! Oh give us back the pure gold.' Wotan pauses with one foot on the bridge and asks what the mournful sound is that reaches his ears. Loge says it is the children of the Rhine lamenting the theft of their gold. Irritably, Wotan tells him to silence them. Loge calls to the Rhinedaughters and asks what they are weeping about. The gold may no longer shine on them but they can bask in the gods' new radiance instead. The gods laugh and begin to cross the bridge.

Once again the voices of the Rhinedaughters float upwards: 'Rhinegold, Rhinegold, pure gold! If only your brightness could shine in the depths. Goodness and truth dwell but in the deep: false and base are those who dwell up above!'

The curtain falls as the gods cross the bridge to the fortress.

THE VALKYRIE

Dramatis Personae

SIEGMUND	tenor
SIEGLINDE	soprano
HUNDING	bass
WOTAN	bass-baritone
BRÜNNHILDE	soprano
FRICKA	mezzo-soprano
Valkyries	sopranos and contraltos
GERHILDE	
ORTLINDE	
WALTRAUTE	
SCHWERTLEITE	
HELMWIGE	
SIEGRUNE	
GRIMGERDE	
ROSSWEISSE	

Act I

The interior of a hut. In the middle of the room stands the trunk of a mighty ash tree, whose prominent roots stretch far along the ground. The tree is separated from its top by a roof. The walls are made of roughly chopped logs, covered here and there with rugs. In the foreground is the fireplace. Behind the fireplace is a storeroom. In the background is the main door, fitted with a simple wooden latch. On the left is a door to an inner bedroom.

During a stormy night, an exhausted man enters the hut and collapses at the hearth. The room is empty and the man –

obviously a fugitive – decides that regardless of who owns the hut, he must rest there. As he lies motionless, Sieglinde enters. She had heard a noise and had assumed that her husband had returned. She is surprised to see a stranger lying by the fireplace. Who is this man, she wonders; has he fainted? Is he ill? She notes that he is still breathing and has only closed his eyes. He appears to be strong even though he has fallen exhausted.

The man suddenly raises his head and asks for a drink. Sieglinde fetches a drinking horn and leaves the room to fill it. Returning, she hands it to the man. As he nods in thanks, he studies her face with growing interest. He speaks of the cool and reviving water that has eased his tiredness and refreshed his spirits. He says he is glad to find her and asks who she is. She replies that both she and the house belong to Hunding. She urges the man to rest here as Hunding's guest until he returns home. The man comments that her husband has nothing to fear from an unarmed and wounded guest. Sieglinde asks anxiously to see his wounds but is told that they are slight and not worth talking about. His body remains in tact and his limbs are strong. He adds that if his spear and shield had proved half as strong, he would not have needed to flee his enemies. They had smashed his spear and shield and had pursued him in a pack. The thunderstorm had sapped his strength. However, he had now thrown off his tiredness faster than he had fled from his foes. Night had fallen on his eyelids but the sun now shone on him once again.

Sieglinde goes to the storeroom and fills a horn with mead, which she hands to the man with a concerned gesture. He invites her to taste it first – which she does – and then she hands it back to him. He takes a long drink, all the while looking at her with growing fascination. He sighs deeply and gazes sadly at the ground. He says that he is an unfortunate man and hopes that she will be spared such misfortune. Now that he has rested, he must go on his way. Sieglinde asks who could be pursuing him that makes him want to leave so soon. He replies that bad luck pursues him wherever he goes. It catches up with him wherever he stops. He prays that it will stay away from her, which is why he must go elsewhere. As he walks to the door and lifts the latch she calls to him to stay, saying that he can't bring bad luck into a house where it already dwells. The man, deeply moved, gazes into her face. She lowers her eyes in embarrassment and sadness. He tells her that he calls himself 'Woeful' and that he will wait for Hunding.

Sieglinde hears a noise outside and goes to the door. She opens it and Hunding enters, armed with a spear and shield. Catching sight of the stranger, he stops in the doorway and turns to his wife with a look of stern inquiry. Sieglinde explains that she had found the man exhausted, lying by the fireplace. Distress had driven him to the house. Hunding asks if she had been looking after him and Sieglinde replies that she had refreshed him and treated him as a guest. The stranger adds that he has her to thank for shelter and drink and he hopes that this would not cause trouble for her. Hunding replies that his hearth is sacred and his house should be considered sacred too. He tells Sieglinde to prepare a meal for the men.

As she makes preparations, Hunding observes how like his wife the stranger is. The same mark of the dragon glints in his eye. He says to the man that he must have travelled a long way. He was not on horseback, so he wonders what rough paths had caused his exhaustion. The man replies that he was driven through forest and field, heath and thicket by storm and desperation. He didn't know which way he had come or where he was now, and would be glad to be told. Hunding invites the man to sit at the table and adds that the roof that covers him, the house that shelters him, are owned by Hunding. To the west lie the wealthy estates of his kinsmen, who defend his honour. The guest would also honour him by disclosing his name. Perhaps the stranger is wary of confiding in him? If this were the case, he should tell his story to his wife, who is obviously curious to know. Sieglinde confirms that she would indeed like to know who the guest is.

The stranger replies that he could never call himself 'Peaceful', and although he wishes he were 'Cheerful', his name has had to be 'Woeful'. 'Wolf' was his father. He had come into the world with a twin sister but, prematurely, his mother and twin sister had been taken from him. He hardly knew either of them. Wolf was warlike and strong and made plenty of enemies. As a boy, he had gone out hunting with the old man. One day they returned from skirmishing, to find the wolf's lair empty. The fine room was burnt to ashes and the oak tree reduced to its stump. His mother lay slaughtered and his sister was nowhere to be found. This harsh fate had been inflicted on them by a cruel band of Neidings. Father and son had fled into exile. For many years the boy lived with Wolf in the forest. They were hunted by enemies but the wolf pair stoutly defended themselves. He adds that a wolf-cub is telling this story and it is as 'Wolf-cub' that he is known to many.

Hunding comments that these are remarkable and strange tales on the part of Woeful the Wolf-cub. He has indeed heard dark rumours of this warlike pair but had never come across Wolf or Wolf-cub. Sieglinde asks where the man's father now lives, and he replies that when the Neidings had set upon father and son, many of the hunters had fallen to the wolves. However, he had become separated from his father and had lost all trace of him. He had searched everywhere. He found an empty wolf's skin in the forest but he did not find his father. Something urged him to leave the forest. He was drawn to other people, but whenever he had tried to find a friend or a wife he was outlawed. Ill fortune followed him. Whatever he thought right, others considered wrong. What seemed bad to him, others approved of. He got into disputes wherever he went. He encountered anger, and when he sought joy he aroused only sorrow. He was obliged to call himself 'Woeful', for sorrow was all that he possessed.

Hunding says that the Norn who had allotted him so wretched a fate clearly did not love him. No man would welcome such a stranger seeking hospitality. Sieglinde responds that only cowards would fear an unarmed man travelling alone. She urges the stranger to tell them more about how his weapons were lost in battle. He explains that a girl in distress had called on him for help. Her family had wanted to marry her to a man she didn't love. He had gone to her defence and, in battle, the enemy was overcome. But her brothers lay dead and the girl embraced their bodies. Grief replaced anger and, in floods of tears, the unhappy bride wept on the battlefield for the death of her brothers. The kinsmen of the slain enemy attacked in overwhelming numbers, crying for vengeance. They came from all sides against him but the girl did not leave the field. He had protected her with shield and spear until these were hewn to pieces. Wounded and weapon-less, he stood and watched the girl die. The furious attackers pursued him while she lay dead on the bodies. That is why he cannot be called 'Peaceful'.

Hunding rises gloomily and says that he knows the savage race who do not respect things others hold sacred. It is hated by others and by him. He was summoned to seek atonement for his kinsmen's blood. He had arrived too late, and now he had returned home to find the fleeing criminal in his own house. In this house that harboured him, there would be shelter for the night, but next day the stranger must defend himself with stout weapons. Hunding would choose the day of battle and the stranger would atone for the dead.

Hunding tells Sieglinde to leave the room, to prepare his nightly drink and to wait for him in the bedroom. She sets about preparing the drink and, after filling the drinking horn, sprinkles some spices into it. Before leaving the room, she looks again towards the stranger, who has never taken his eyes off her. She looks pleadingly, directing his attention to a place on the great ash tree that occupies the centre of the dwelling. Hunding drives her away with a threatening gesture and, with one last look at the man, she goes into the bedroom and closes the door. With a final remark about the impending battle, Hunding also enters the bedroom and leaves the stranger alone by the dim light of the fire.

After brooding for some time, the man anxiously recalls that his father had promised him a sword in his greatest need. Unarmed, he had now stumbled into his enemy's house. He had found a woman, lovely and dignified. Strange feelings gnaw at his heart. He feels for her and has fallen for her sweet enchantment, but she is in the power of a man who treats an unarmed stranger with hostility. Agitated, he cries out: 'Wälse! Wälse! Where is your sword?' If only this strong sword, needed in adversity, could burst from his breast where it lies hidden in his heart.

The flickering fire in the hearth illuminates a sword hilt buried in the tree trunk. The man wonders what it is, gleaming in the firelight. Is it a glance that the lovely woman has left behind? Night and darkness closed his eyes but then her eyes fell on him, bringing warmth and daylight. Now the splendour fades, the light dies out but, deep in his breast, a flameless fire still smoulders.

The fire in the hearth has burnt out and in the ensuing darkness the door to the bedchamber opens. Sieglinde enters and moves quickly towards the hearth. She asks if the guest is asleep. He asks who is there, and she replies that Hunding is sleeping soundly since she drugged his drink. Under cover of night, the stranger should save his life. He replies that her presence gives him life. Sieglinde says that she will show him a weapon. If only he could win it she would call him the noblest of heroes, for it belongs to the strongest.

She tells him that kinsmen once sat in this hall at Hunding's wedding. He was marrying a woman who, without being asked, had been forced to be his wife. She had sat there miserably during the drinking. A stranger came in – an old man in a grey cloak –

with his hat pulled down to cover one eye. However, the glint of his other eye made them all afraid. To her alone his eye revealed a sweet, longing sadness; tears and consolation combined. He had looked at her and glowered at the men, while a sword flashed in his hand. This he had thrust into the tree trunk, up to the hilt. The blade would belong to anyone who pulled it out of the tree. All the men bravely tried but failed to win the weapon.

Guests came and guests went. The strongest pulled at the blade but it didn't budge an inch. There the sword silently remains. She realised who the stranger was – the stranger who had consoled her in her grief – and she knew too for whom he intended the sword. How she wishes that she might find that friend, come from far away to a most wretched woman. Whatever grief she suffered, whatever pain she felt in her shame and dishonour, sweetest revenge would make up for it all. Thus she would have regained all she had lost, all she had wept for. She would have won, if only she could find the blessed friend and her arms could embrace the hero.

The stranger embraces Sieglinde fervently and tells her she is in the arms of the friend for whom weapon and wife were decreed. An oath that makes her his noble wife burns fiercely in his heart. All that he longed for he sees in her. Although she suffered disgrace and he knew sorrow, although he was outlawed and she was dishonoured, joyful revenge would bring them both happiness. He laughs aloud as he holds her and feels her beating heart.

Suddenly, the main door to the room flies open. The storms have abated and it is a marvellous spring night. The full moon shines in and throws its light onto the couple who are suddenly able to see one another clearly. Sieglinde starts with surprise and asks who went out? Who has come in? The man replies that nobody went but someone had come. The spring now smiles into the room.

He says that winter storms have vanished before the month of

May. In a gentle light, springtime shines, softly and wonderfully. The spring works his wonders. Through woods and meadows his breath blows, his eyes are bright with laughter. The lovely songs of birds sweetly proclaim him as he exhales blissful scents. From his warm blood bursts gorgeous flowers. Buds and shoots grow from his strength. Armed with fragile weapons he conquers the world. Winter and storm forsake their defences. To his bold blows, stout doors yield, for they too lock out the spring. To his sister he has flown – love enticing the spring. Spring was deeply hidden in their hearts but now smiles joyfully in the light. The sister-bride is freed by her brother. Everything that kept them apart is in ruins. Joyfully, the young couple greet one another. Love and spring are one.

An ecstatic Sieglinde replies that he is the spring for which she longed in the frosty wintertime. Her heart responded to him with holy terror when his glance had first stirred her. She had only ever seen strangers, and her surroundings were friendless. But she knew as soon as her eyes beheld him, that he was hers. What she had hidden in her heart – her very being – had come to light as clearly as day. It was like the pealing of a bell reaching her ear when, in this cold, strange, bleak place, she first beheld her friend.

For the stranger, the words of this blessed woman are sweetest bliss. Sieglinde presses closer to him so that she may see clearly the radiant light that shines from his eyes, and his face that sweetly overwhelms her senses. He tells her that, in the spring moonlight, her face shines brightly, framed by her lovely waving hair. He now recognises clearly what had bewitched him. Rapturously he feasts his eyes. Caressing his brow, Sieglinde notes how open it is and how the veins wind in his temples. She trembles with delight and her memory is strangely stirred. Although she had beheld him for the first time today, her eyes had seen him before. He confesses that a dream of love reminds him too that, in fervent longing, he had seen her before. Sieglinde says that, in a stream, she had seen her own image, and now she sees it again. He replies that she is the image he preserved within him. She says that, listening to his voice, she thinks she remembers it as a child. No, she had heard it recently when her own voice echoed in the woods. For him, these are sweet sounds indeed.

Sieglinde gazes rapturously into his eyes and tells him that their gleam had shone on her before. She recognised them in the old man who looked kindly at her, consoling her in her grief. By that glance his child recognised him and almost spoke his name. She asks the stranger if he really is called 'Woeful', and he tells her not to call him that, now that she loves him and he enjoys the greatest happiness. She suggests that he should now call himself 'Peaceful' and he replies that he would accept whatever name she gave him. Sieglinde recalls that his father's name was 'Wolf' and he replies that he was certainly a wolf to cowardly foxes. But he whose eyes shone as splendidly as hers was really called 'Wälse'.

Sieglinde is now ecstatic. If Wälse was his father and he is a Volsung, it was for him that the old man had left the sword! So she would call him by the name she loved: 'Siegmund'! Thus he is named.

Siegmund springs to his feet and seizes the hilt of the sword. 'Siegmund by name and Siegmund by nature!' he cries. Wälse had promised him the sword in his moment of greatest need. The highest need of holiest love, yearning love's consuming desire burns brightly in his breast, urging him on to deeds and death. 'Notung' (Needful) – he names the sword. This precious blade should now reveal its sharp, cutting edge and slip from its scabbard. With a mighty heave, he pulls the sword from the tree and displays it to Sieglinde, who is overcome with astonishment and delight.

He is Siegmund the Volsung he says, and, as a wedding gift, he brings this sword. Thus he weds the fairest of women and will take her far away from his enemy's house into the joyous house of spring. For protection she would have *Notung* the sword, even if Siegmund were to die of love.

She tears herself from his grasp and, intoxicated with love, faces him. Can this truly be Siegmund who stands before her? She is Sieglinde who longed for him – his own sister. He has won both her and the sword. She flings herself into his arms, and Siegmund declares her to be his bride and sister, through whom the race of Volsungs will flourish.

Act II

In a wild, rocky pass, Wotan is seen armed for battle, carrying his spear. Brünnhilde is also fully armed as a Valkyrie. The god tells Brünnhilde to bridle her horse because soon, bitter strife will flare up. She must enter the fray and bring victory to the Volsung. Hunding will have no place in Valhalla.

Brünnhilde gives her wild battle cry as she surveys the scene and then tells her father to prepare himself for a storm. Fricka is approaching in her chariot drawn by rams. The beasts are bleating with fear and the wheels are clattering madly. She is coming to pick a quarrel. Brünnhilde doesn't enjoy such strife, although she is at home amidst the conflict of brave warriors. She leaves her father to face his consort alone.

Wotan doesn't relish the thought of the same old storm, the same old strife, but he decides to make a firm stand.

Fricka says that she has sought him out here in the mountains where he has been hiding, because she wants his assistance. She has been listening to Hunding's complaints. He has called on her as the guardian of wedlock for vengeance. She has promised to punish severely the shameless and impious pair who so wronged this husband. Wotan asks what the couple, whom spring had united in love, have done that is so terrible. The magic of love had enchanted them and who can atone for the power of love?

Fricka accuses him of pretending to be stupid and deaf. As if he

didn't know that her complaint is about the flouting of marriage –
a holy vow. Wotan replies that he considers unholy the vow that
unites without love. He doesn't intend to intervene in something
that is not Fricka's concern. If issues do arise, then he advocates
settling them in battle.

Fricka tells him that if he grants respectability to adultery, then
he will also have to sanctify the incestuous fruit of this liaison
between twins. The very idea stops her heart and causes her brain
to reel. Marital intercourse between brother and sister – when was
such a thing ever witnessed? Wotan replies calmly that today she
had seen it happen. She should learn from it that things may happen even though they have not occurred before. It is patently
obvious that the two are in love, so Fricka should listen to sensible
advice. She would be better off smiling on love and blessing the
union of Siegmund and Sieglinde.

With extreme indignation, Fricka asks if this then is the end of
the everlasting gods. Her husband thinks nothing of the sacred
kinship of the gods and rejects everything that he once used to
value. He tears apart the bonds that he himself had tied.
Laughing, he relaxes his rule in heaven so that pleasure and whim
may be gratified by these wanton twins, the licentious fruit of his
unfaithfulness. She wonders why she bothers to protest about
marriage and its vows since her husband was the first to break
them. He has constantly deceived his faithful wife. In the depths
and heights he has looked with a lecherous eye to see how his
fickle fancy might be gratified and thereby mock and wound his
wife to the quick. It grieved her, but she was forced to bear it when
he went into battle with the uncouth girls he had fathered. He
had retained enough respect to make the Valkyrie gang, and even
Brünnhilde – the bride of his wishes – respect Fricka as their sov-
ereign. But now he had taken to assuming new names, and as
Wälse had roamed the forest like a wolf. He had reduced himself
to begetting a pair of common mortals. Now he would debase his

wife before the she-wolf's litter. So, he might as well finish his work, fill the cup full and trample on the wife he cheated.

Trying to maintain his composure, Wotan replies that his wife has never learnt – even though he tried to teach her – to recognise events before they happened. She only understands the conventional whereas he is concerned with things that have never happened before. Just for once, she should listen to him. Their crisis calls for a hero who, free from divine protection, is not bound by divine law. He alone will be able to perform the deed that is so vital to the gods but which a god is prevented from doing.

Fricka dismisses such talk as an attempt to baffle her with profundities. What lofty deed could heroes perform that could not be performed by the gods? Wotan asks if a hero's bravery means nothing to her? Fricka responds by asking who had inspired men with such heroic thoughts? Who lit up their foolish eyes? Under Wotan's protection they appear strong, and spurred on by him they follow their ambitions. He alone was responsible for those whom he now praises to a goddess. With new tricks he is trying to dupe her, but he will not keep this Volsung for himself. In him she sees only Wotan, since it is only through him that Siegmund can act boldly.

Wotan replies that Siegmund grew up alone in bitterness and sorrow. His father's protection never sheltered him. 'Then do not shelter him today', says Fricka. 'Take away the sword that you gave him.' Wotan insists that Siegmund won the sword himself in the midst of his desperation. From this point onwards, Wotan's expression and demeanour grow more and more profoundly dejected. Fricka senses that her husband is defensive. She says that he created Siegmund's distress, just as he had created the flashing sword. It was the god who had thrust the sword into the tree trunk and who had promised Siegmund the splendid weapon. Can he deny that it was his cunning alone that had brought

Siegmund to where he would find it? No one of high birth would fight as an equal with a bondsman. A free man is merely punishing an outlaw. Siegmund the serf is forfeit to Fricka.

Wotan is all too conscious of his own powerlessness in the face of such arguments. Fricka asks if Wotan's eternal consort is to be subject to a bondsman and slave? Surely her husband would not profane the goddess in this way. Wotan asks what it is she desires, and she replies: 'Abandon the Volsung!' In a subdued voice, he offers to remove his protection from Siegmund and leave the Valkyrie free to act as she chooses. Fricka replies that the Valkyrie fulfils only Wotan's wishes, therefore he must forbid Siegmund's victory. Wotan says that he cannot slay Siegmund for he found the sword, to which Fricka responds that the sword's magic should be withdrawn and that it should break and leave him defenceless. As Brünnhilde's voice is heard in the distance, Fricka again insists that the Volsung should fall for the sake of her honour. She insists that Wotan give her his oath that this will be so. In a state of profound dejection, Wotan swears agreement. As Fricka strides away she encounters the approaching Brünnhilde. The two women regard each other for a moment in silence. Fricka tells the Valkyrie that the Father of Legions awaits her and will inform her how the lot is to fall.

Brünnhilde anxiously approaches the brooding Wotan and asks why he is so downcast. He explains that he is caught in fetters of his own making. He is the least free of all the living. Brünnhilde is shocked and asks what gnaws at his heart. Wotan is overwhelmed with a sense of humiliation, grief, disgrace and despair. Brünnhilde implores him to confide in her. He sinks into deep thought and then says that if he speaks about his concern, won't he then lose control of himself? Softly she assures him that he is speaking to himself when he speaks to her. Who is she if not his other self? He acknowledges that what he doesn't say remains unspoken forever, and that he is only talking to himself when he speaks to her. His voice becomes even more muted and fearful as he continues.

When the pleasures of young love had waned in him, he says, his spirit longed for power. Impetuous desires had roused him to madness and he won the world for himself. With no thought of integrity he had acted disloyally. By treaties he made alliances with powers concealing evil. Loge's cunning tempted him and Loge is now not to be found. Yet he couldn't let go of love. With all his power, he longed for love. The child of darkness, Alberich, had cursed love and through his curse had won the glittering Rhinegold and, with it, immeasurable power. The ring that he had made was taken from him by trickery but it was not returned to the Rhine. With it he paid the price for Valhalla, the fortress built by the giants and from which he then ruled the world. Erda, who knew everything that ever was, the wisest of women, told him to give up the ring and warned him of an end to everything. About that end he wanted to know more, but she vanished. Then he lost his joy in life. As a god he longed for knowledge. He travelled into the depths of the earth and, with the magic of love, he over-powered the wise woman, overcame her pride, and she talked to him. He learned her secrets but she exacted a fee.

The world's wisest woman bore him Brünnhilde, whom he brought up with eight sisters. By means of the Valkyries he sought to avert what the woman had told him to fear – a shameful end to the immortals. To protect the gods from their enemies, Valkyries were sent to fetch heroes, men who were held by laws in bondage, mortals whose pride had been curbed and who, through deceitful treaties, were bound in obedience. The Valkyries' task was to spur them into storm and strife, to tempt their strength in bitter war-fare, so that armies of bold warriors would be fit for Valhalla.

Brünnhilde assures her father that the Valkyries had never hesitated in finding many heroes to fill Wotan's hall. Why then should he be troubled?

Wotan replies that Erda had warned him that Alberich's power would bring about the end of the gods. The Nibelung nurses his resentment but Wotan doesn't fear the forces of darkness. His heroes would give him victory. But if the ring ever found its way back to Alberich, Valhalla would be lost. He who cursed love could use the ring's magic to turn Wotan's heroes against him. With their strength he would wage war.

Wotan has thought carefully about how the ring could be kept from his enemy. One of the giants, Fafner, to whom he had given the accursed ring as payment, now guards the treasure for which he slew his brother. From him, Wotan would have to seize the ring. But since the god is bound by his agreement with Fafner, he could not attack him. Such are the chains that bind Wotan. He became a ruler through treaties, and by those treaties he is now enslaved. Only one person could do what he is unable to do – a hero who acts without the god's assistance. Only a free man, unwitting and unprompted, driven by his own motives and using his own weapons, could do the deed which Wotan must avoid and could not even propose, though it is his greatest wish.

How can he find this man who is opposed to the gods but will fight for Wotan – this friendly foe? How can he create a free agent whom he has never protected and who, by defying him, will be dearest to him? How can he make that other one, who is no longer part of him, do of his own accord what Wotan alone desires? What a predicament a god finds himself in! With loathing, he finds only himself in everything he has created. That other man for whom he longs, that other one, he can never find. A free man has to create himself. Wotan can only create slaves.

Brünnhilde is astonished. Doesn't the Volsung Siegmund act on his own? Wotan explains that he had wandered through the woods with him. Against the counsel of the gods he had encouraged him to act boldly. Against the vengeance of the gods, his only protection now is the sword which Wotan's favour had bestowed on him. Why did Wotan try a trick to defraud himself? It was easy for Fricka to spot this deception. To his deep disgrace, she saw through him. Now he must yield to her will.

Brünnhilde is shocked and asks whether Wotan will deprive Siegmund of victory? Her father responds that he had touched Alberich's ring. Greedily he had held his gold. The curse from which he had fled has still not left him. He must forsake what he loves, murder the one he cherishes, deceive and betray someone who trusts him.

Wotan is now overwhelmed by the most terrible despair. Away then with lordly splendour, divine pomp and shameful boasting. Let everything that he has built fall to pieces. He will give up his work. Now he desires only one thing: the end, the end! And for that end, Alberich is working. Now Wotan understands the hidden meaning in Erda's wild words: 'when love's dark enemy begets a son in anger, the end of the blessed ones will not be long delayed'. He has heard a rumour that Alberich had seduced a woman for money, and the woman is now carrying the fruits of the Nibelung's hatred. This miracle had benefited the loveless creature but Wotan, who ruled by love, could not beget a free man.

Then Wotan offers a blessing to the Nibelung's son: what deeply revolts the god is bequeathed to him, to feed his hate on the empty glory of divinity.

Brünnhilde is stunned by what she has heard and asks her father what he requires of her. He tells her bitterly to fight for Fricka and guard marriage and its vows for her. What Fricka had decided must be his decision too. What use is his own will? He cannot will a free man into life, and so Brünnhilde must fight for Fricka's subjects.

The Valkyrie urges him to take back these words. He loves Siegmund and she knows that she must protect the Volsung. Wotan replies that she must kill Siegmund and procure victory for Hunding. She must be on her guard and summon all her bravery, for Siegmund wields a conquering sword and he will not die a coward. Brünnhilde says that her father has always taught her to love Siegmund and that he is dear to his heart. She will never be turned against him by her father's self-deceiving orders!

Wotan becomes angry with this presumptuous, rebellious girl. What is she but the blind means of carrying out his intentions? When he confided in her, did he so demean himself that abuse from his own offspring should be the result? She knew the extent of his anger. Her courage would fail if just a spark of his rage fell upon her. In his heart he concealed a fury that could reduce the world – once so pleasing to him – to dust and ashes. Woe to any-one whom this fury strikes; their pride would be transformed into misery. Therefore he advises his daughter not to provoke him. She should remember his command: Siegmund shall die. That is the Valkyrie's task. Wotan turns away and quickly vanishes amongst the mountains.

For a long time, Brünnhilde stands shocked. She has never seen the Father of Victories like this, even when he has been upset by some quarrel. Her armour now seems to weigh heavily on her. When she fought as she wished, how light it was. Into this evil fight today she creeps as though she were afraid. Oh, the poor Volsung. In his deepest sorrow his friend must disloyally forsake him. She looks down into the valley and sees Siegmund and Sieglinde approaching. She watches them for a moment, then walks into the cave where her horse is, and disappears from view.

Siegmund and Sieglinde appear. She is hurrying on ahead and he is trying to restrain her. He urges her to rest but Sieglinde wants to press on, further, further. At last he clasps his sweet wife to him and persuades her to wait. From their night of love she had rushed away in such haste that he can barely keep up. Speechless, through woods and meadows, past cliffs and rocks, she ran on ahead. His calls were unable to stop her. Now he wants her to rest and speak to him. Her silence frightens him. The brother is holding his bride. Siegmund is with her.

She gazes into his eyes with growing delight and embraces his neck passionately. Then suddenly, she jumps up in terror, urging him to be off and to keep clear of the curse that is upon her. The arm that clasps him is unholy. Her body is dishonoured, disgraced and has died. He should run from this corpse; let go of it. Let the wind blow away what she had vilely given to a hero. He has held her lovingly and she had found the greatest joy. He had given her his love and had woken all her love. Through the sweet bliss that filled her mind and pierced her soul came fear and terror, a ghastly shame that gripped her in horror and disgrace, even though she had belonged to a man who had obtained her without love. She is accursed and wants to flee from Siegmund. She is condemned and worthless. He is the most pure of men. She must hurry away from him. She can never belong to this wonderful man. She brings shame on her brother, disgrace on the friend who has won her.

Siegmund replies that whatever disgrace she had suffered would be paid for by the villain's blood. She should run no further but wait for their enemy who would die at Siegmund's hand. When Notung strikes at his heart, then she would be revenged. Sieglinde starts in terror and listens. She hears horns in the distance and asks her brother if he hears them too. All around echoes the fearsome noise, sounding in forest and fields. Hunding has woken from his sleep. He has assembled his dogs and his kinsmen. Roused to frenzy, the pack is howling. They cry to heaven for the marriage vows that have been broken.

Sieglinde stares wildly into the distance. Calling for her beloved Siegmund, she wants the stars in his eyes to shine on her once again, and pleads with him not to spurn the kiss of his outcast wife. She throws herself sobbing on his breast and then jumps up terrified. Again she hears Hunding's horn. His men are approaching, fully armed. No sword will be sufficient when their dogs attack. She urges Siegmund to throw the sword away, and then she begins to hallucinate. She imagines a terrible sight. The dogs are baring their teeth at his flesh. They do not respect his noble features. Their teeth fasten on his feet and he falls. The sword shatters in pieces, the ash tree topples, the trunk breaks. She cries out for her brother Siegmund, and faints in his arms. Siegmund listens closely to her breathing. He sits with her head resting on his lap, leans over her and implants a long kiss on her forehead.

Brünnhilde appears in the background and moves slowly towards Siegmund. She gazes at him with a grave expression and says to him: 'Siegmund, look at me! I am the one whom you will soon follow.' Siegmund looks up at her and asks who she is. Brünnhilde replies that only those doomed to die meet her gaze. Whoever looks on her must leave the light of life. Only on the battlefield does she appear to heroes. Whoever is aware of her has been chosen in the battle.

Siegmund asks where will she lead him if he follows her? Brünnhilde replies that she will take him to the Lord of Battles, who chose him. He must follow her to Valhalla.

Siegmund asks if, in Valhalla, he would find only the Lord of Battles? She replies that dead heroes will embrace and welcome him. Siegmund asks whether, in Valhalla, he would find Wälse, his own father. Brünnhilde replies that he will indeed find his father there. Siegmund asks whether, in Valhalla, he would be welcomed affectionately by a woman? Brünnhilde replies that wishmaidens abound there and Wotan's daughter will gladly serve him his drink.

Siegmund says that he recognises the holy daughter of Wotan but he asks one thing: can this brother take with him his sister and bride? May Siegmund embrace Sieglinde there? Brünnhilde replies that Sieglinde must still breathe the air of the world. He would not see Sieglinde there.

Siegmund leans tenderly over Sieglinde and gently kisses her, before turning to Brünnhilde. He tells the Valkyrie to greet Valhalla for him, to greet Wotan and Wälse too, and all the heroes, to greet as well the lovely wishmaidens, but he will most certainly not follow her to them. Brünnhilde replies that he has seen the Valkyrie's glance and must go with her. Siegmund says that wherever Sieglinde lives, in happiness or in sorrow, there he will also remain. The Valkyrie's gaze will never force him to leave. Brünnhilde says that as long as he lives, nothing can compel him, but death will force him and she has come to announce it to him.

Siegmund asks where the hero is to whom he must fall victim? Brünnhilde replies that Hunding will kill him in battle. Siegmund says that she must threaten with stronger blows than Hunding's. If she hankers for a battle then she should settle on Hunding as her prize, for Siegmund intends to kill him. Brünnhilde shakes her head and informs him that he has been chosen by fate. He asks if she knows the sword, and who had made it for him and promised victory? With it he defies her threats. She replies that he who made it for Siegmund has decreed his death and he will remove the power from the sword.

Siegmund tells Brünnhilde to be silent and not terrify the sleeping woman. With much sadness, he leans tenderly over Sieglinde. He addresses his sweetest wife, saddest of all faithful women. Against her rages the whole world, and he is the one whom she trusts and for whom she defied the world. Can he not shield her? Must he betray a heroine in battle? Shame on him who made the sword if he decreed shame and not victory for Siegmund. Siegmund decides that, if he has to die, he would never go to Valhalla but remain in Hell.

Brünnhilde is shocked by this response and asks him if he values everlasting bliss so little. Does this tired and sorrowful woman mean everything to him? Is nothing else important? Siegmund looks up bitterly at the Valkyrie and says to her that although she looks young and fair and dazzling, her heart must be cold and hard. If she can only scoff, then she should leave him. She is cruel and unfeeling. If she had come to gloat over his misery then she should enjoy his suffering but not speak of Valhalla's frigid delights.

Brünnhilde is greatly moved. She sees the distress that gnaws at his heart and feels sympathy for this hero's sorrow. She assures Siegmund that she, the Valkyrie, will take care of his wife. Siegmund replies that he and no other will touch her while she lives. If he is doomed to die, then he will kill her first in her sleep. Brünnhilde calls him a madman and urges him to leave his wife and go with the Valkyrie for the sake of the child that their love has conceived. Siegmund draws his sword, this trusted weapon, given so treacherously to him, a sword which, so cowardly, must betray him to his enemy. If it cannot prevail against his foe then let it succeed against his friend. He points the sword at Sieglinde and says that two lives are open to the Valkyrie here and that *Notung* shall take them with one blow.

In a violent outburst of sympathy, Brünnhilde stops him and tells him to listen. Sieglinde will live and Siegmund will live with her. She has decided to change the outcome of the battle and to ensure victory for Siegmund. Horn-calls are heard in the distance and Brünnhilde urges Siegmund to prepare. He should rely on his sword and wield it boldly. The weapon will be true to him just as the Valkyrie will truly protect him. She farewells Siegmund and assures him she will see him again on the battlefield. She rushes away and disappears from sight.

In the gathering darkness, warlike horn-calls are heard again coming from all directions. Siegmund bends over Sieglinde and listens to her breathing. He takes comfort from the fact that she is now sleeping peacefully and so will avoid witnessing the terrible battle. He tells her to go on sleeping until the battle has been fought and peace brings her joy. He lays her gently down and kisses her good bye. Then he hears Hunding's horn call and prepares for the fight.

As Siegmund draws *Notung* and disappears into the surrounding gloom, Sieglinde begins to move uneasily in her dreams. She imagines that she is waiting for her father to come home from the woods with the boy. She tells her mother she is afraid – the strangers do not look friendly. There is black smoke and flames. The house is burning. She calls to her brother for help – 'Siegmund! Siegmund!' A violent clap of thunder awakens her. She jumps up, staring about with growing terror. Hundling's horn call is heard, not far off, and then comes his voice: 'Wehwalt! Wehwalt! Stand and fight or my dogs will stop you!' Siegmund's voice is heard, telling Hunding to stand so that he may face him. Sieglinde listens in terrible anxiety as Hunding calls to Siegmund to come to him so that Fricka can smite him down. Siegmund scoffs at being threatened with a woman and says that he fearlessly drew the sword from the tree trunk and Hunding will now taste its blade.

There is a lightning flash, and Hunding and Siegmund are seen locked in battle. Sieglinde calls to them with all her strength to stop and murder her first.

Brünnhilde is seen hovering over Siegmund, protecting him with her shield, telling him to rely on his sword. Siegmund aims a fatal blow. Then Wotan appears, standing over Hunding and holding out his spear. 'Get back from my spear!' he calls. 'To pieces shatters the sword!' Brünnhilde recoils in terror and the sword is broken on the outstretched spear. Hunding thrusts his spear into the breast of the defenceless man and Siegmund falls dead on the ground. Sieglinde, hearing his death cry falls down with a scream. In the ensuing darkness, Brünnhilde is seen running hastily to Seglinde, urging her to run to the horse and she will save her. She lifts Sieglinde onto the horse and disappears with her.

The clouds separate and Hunding is clearly seen pulling his spear out of Siegmund's chest. Wotan stands behind him, leaning on his spear and looking sadly at Siegmund's corpse.

Finally, Wotan turns his attention to Hunding who, he says, must kneel before Fricka as a slave and tell her that Wotan's spear had avenged her shame. Then, with a contemptuous wave of his hand, the god strikes Hunding dead.

Wotan bursts into a terrible rage, vowing that Brünnhilde will regret her crime; her rashness will be punished. He disappears amidst thunder and lightning.

Act III

On the summit of a rocky mountain, Brünnhilde's eight Valkyrie sisters – Gerhilde, Ortlinde, Waltraute, Schwertleite, Helmwige, Siegrune, Grimgerde and Rossweisse – gather en route to Valhalla with the bodies of heroes plucked from the battlefield. They call to each other as they arrive:

'Put your stallion next to my mare. Your bay will enjoy grazing with my grey.'
'Who's that hanging from your saddle?'
'Sintolt the Hegeling.'
'Then take your bay away from my grey. The mare carries Wittig the Irming.'
'They were always fighting, Sintolt and Wittig.'
'My mare is being kicked by the stallion.'
'The warriors' quarrel makes even the horses fight.'
'Be still Bruno! Don't disturb the peace!'
'Here, Siegrune. What kept you so long?'
'There was work to do. Have the others arrived?'
'Grimgerde and Rossweisse!'
'They're riding together.'

'Take your horses into the woods to graze and rest.'

'Keep the mares far apart until our heroes' hatred has subsided.'

'Were you girls riding together?'

'We rode separately and have just met up now.'

'If we're all here then let's not wait any longer. We'll make our way to Valhalla, to bring Wotan his warriors.'

'There are only eight of us. One is missing.'

'Brünnhilde will still be with that tanned Volsung.'

'We must wait for her. Father would be angry if we arrived without her.'

'Brünnhilde's riding furiously; she's coming this way.'

'She's riding towards the fir trees.'

'How Grane is panting after galloping so quickly.'

'I've never seen such furious galloping by any Valkyrie.'

'What's that on her saddle?

'That's no hero!'

'She's carrying a woman.'

'How did she find the woman?'

'She can't be bothered with her sisters.'

'*Heiaha*, Brünnhilde, can't you hear us?'

'Let's help our sister dismount.'

'Mighty Grane falls to the ground.'

'She lifts the woman from the saddle.'

'Sister, sister, what's happened?'

A breathless Brünnhilde pleads with her sisters for protection. They ask why she has ridden at such a speed, since only fugitives flee like that. She replies that, for the first time, she is running away. The Father of Battles is pursuing her. The others are astonished. Why should Battle Father be chasing her? She pleads with them to go to the high ground and look to the north, to see if War Father is coming.

Ortlinde reports that there is a thunderstorm coming from the north. Others remark on the gathering clouds and that Battle Father is riding his sacred horse.

Brünnhilde tells them he is hunting her in anger. She seeks the protection of her sisters and asks them to save the woman. They ask what is the trouble, and Brünnhilde explains that this is Sieglinde, Siegmund's sister and wife. Wotan is fuming with rage against the Volsungs. Brünnhilde should have withheld victory from the brother but she had disobediently protected Siegmund with her shield, and the god had killed him himself with his spear. Siegmund fell but she had fled far away with his wife. She had hurried, fearfully, to her sisters to save the woman.

The Valkyries are in great consternation. Brünnhilde asks which of her sisters will lend her a horse to carry the woman away, but her sisters feel compelled to obey their father. Brünnhilde pleads with them, but Sieglinde, who has been observing these events, tells her not to worry, death is what she wants. She would rather have been struck down by the same weapon that killed Siegmund. She would have met her fate united with him. She longs for death and urges Brünnhilde to plunge her sword into her heart.

Brünnhilde replies that she must live for the sake of a child – the Volsung who is already stirring in her womb. Hearing this news, Sieglinde is at first terrified, but then her face lights up with sublime happiness. She asks Brünnhilde and the other Valkyries to save her and to save her child. But the Valkyries are frightened of their father and dare not protect her. Only Brünnhilde is pre- pared to stay and face Wotan's vengeance. She urges Sieglinde to escape quickly while she delays her father and takes the full force of his rage. Sieglinde asks in what direction she should head. The others tell her that to the east lies a forest into which Fafner has taken the Nibelung treasure. He has changed his form into that of a dragon and, in a cave, keeps watch over Alberich's ring. Although it isn't a pleasant place for a defenceless woman, it is safe from Wotan's anger since he dislikes going there and keeps away from it.

Brünnhilde urges Sieglinde to flee to the east, to be brave and defiant, and to put up with all dangers – hunger and thirst, thorns and rocks – to laugh, whatever her distress and suffering. One thing will sustain her. In her womb she is carrying the noblest hero in the world. She should keep for him the fragments of the sword, collected from the place of his father's death. He will forge them anew and, one day, will wield the sword. Brünnhilde gives the unborn child his name: 'Siegfried' – 'Peace through Victory'. With great emotion, Sieglinde hails this sublime miracle and praises Brünnhilde as the most glorious of women. She thanks her, and promises that she will save the dear child for him whom they loved. With a parting blessing, the unfortunate Sieglinde hurries away.

In the midst of a terrible storm at the top of the mountain, Wotan's voice is heard calling for Brünnhilde. She pleads with her sisters to help her, and they hide her in their midst. Wotan enters in a towering rage and strides vehemently up to the group looking for Brünnhilde. They try to deflect him but he will have none of it. They tell him she has fled to them with fear and trembling and awaits his anger. For their poor sister's sake they beg their father to control his rage.

He describes them as a soft-hearted gaggle of women. Did they inherit this feeble spirit from him? Had he brought them up to ride boldly into battle, did he make their hearts hard and keen so they would weep and wail the moment he punishes disloyalty? He tells them to stop whimpering and hear what their sister did. No one but she knew his innermost thoughts but she had broken the sacred alliance, and disloyally defied his will. She took up arms against him. Does she now hide in terror and run away from punishment?

Brünnhilde leaves the protection of the Valkyries and walks

towards her father, offering herself for punishment. He says that he does not punish her, for she made her own punishment. She existed only through his will and had wilfully opposed him. She was the agent of his wishes but she had turned against him. She was the bearer of his shield but against him she had raised that shield. He had made her the disposer of fates but she had disposed fate against him. He had made her the inspiration of heroes but against him she had inspired heroes. Wotan had told her what she once was. Now she should tell herself what she is. She is no longer the agent of his will. She had been a Valkyrie but, from now on, she would be something less.

Brünnhilde is deeply shocked and asks if her father would cast her out. Wotan replies that he would no longer send her on missions from Valhalla to fetch heroes from the battlefield. Never again would she bring heroes into his hall. At the solemn banquets of the gods she would never again offer him the drinking horn. Never again would he kiss her as his child. From the company of gods she would be exiled and she would be banished from his sight.

The Valkyries react in great agitation and Brünnhilde asks her father if he would take from her all that he had given her. Wotan replies that he who overpowers her would take it. Here on the mountain she would be confined in defenceless sleep. Any man who finds her by the wayside and wakes her could have her.

The Valkyries react with horror that their sister should become the victim of any passing man, and offer to share her fate. Wotan tells them that their sister is banished from their company. They will never ride together again. The flower of her youth will wither away. A husband will win her, and from that day forth she will belong to him. She will sit by the fire and spin and be the butt of jokes.

Brünnhilde falls to the ground with a cry and the Valkyries shrink in horror from her side. Wotan tells them to keep their distance from her. If any of them dares to disobey him and cling to her in her misery, that foolish one will share her fate. He orders them to disperse and, with wild cries of anguish, they rush into the woods. A flash of lightning reveals them flying away into the clouds. As they vanish, the storm dies down and the weather becomes calm.

Brünnhilde lies motionless at Wotan's feet, and there is a long silence. Slowly, she begins to raise her head a little and timidly asks whether her action was so shameful that it should be punished so shamefully? Did she do something so base to her father that he should humiliate her so profoundly? Was her action so dishonourable that it should now rob her of honour? Gradually she raises herself into a kneeling position and asks her father to look into her eyes, to control his rage and explain the hidden guilt which has forced him to exile his favourite child. Wotan replies that she should think about what she did, since that will explain her guilt.

Brünnhilde says that her father had given an order and she had carried it out. He asks if he had ordered her to fight for the Volsung. She replies that he did so command as Ruler of Battles. But, says Wotan, he withdrew his decree. Brünnhilde observes that Fricka had persuaded him to change his mind and he adopted her point of view. He was his own enemy. Wotan replies that he believed Brünnhilde had understood him but she had obviously thought him cowardly and foolish. Was he not obliged to react to her disloyalty? Did she think she meant nothing to him? Brünnhilde says that she might not be clever but she did know one thing – that Wotan loved the Volsung. She knew the dilemma that compelled her father to forget this. It had caused him great pain to realise that Siegmund should be denied his support. Wotan expresses surprise that, knowing this, Brünnhilde had still dared to protect Siegmund. She replies that because her eyes were her father's, she held faithfully to the one thing that her father's painful dilemma was forcing him to deny. When Wotan was at war she guarded his back, and this time she saw what he could not see. She had to see Siegmund. She went to him to warn him of death. She saw his eyes, heard his words and realised the depths of his distress. She heard the sounds of a brave man's lament, boundless love, heartfelt sorrow and terrible defiance. Her eyes saw what her heart sensed. She stood astonished and ashamed. Victory and death were the options to share with Siegmund and she knew that victory was the lot she must choose. One man's love breathed this into her heart. It was one will that allied her with the Volsung and kept her faithful to her father's innermost wish, even though she disobeyed his command.

Wotan acknowledges that she did what he wanted so much to do, even though hypocritical necessity compelled him to do otherwise. Did she believe that love's happiness could be attained when a burning pain had stabbed her father to the heart, when desperation had roused his anger, and when love of the world had allowed the source of that love to be rejected? He had turned himself against himself. He had risen in rage above agonising sorrows. An angry longing with its burning desires had brought him to a dreadful decision. In the ruins of his own world he would end his eternal sadness. Was Brünnhilde savouring a sense of fulfilment, smiling as she drank the draught of love, while his divine distress was mingling with uncontrollable bitterness?

Wotan continues that Brünnhilde has her carefree heart to guide her but she has renounced her father, and he must keep away from her. Never again will they be able to do things together. They are separated, and while life and breath remain, the god must never meet her again.

Brünnhilde replies that the simple girl is no longer of use to him – the girl who, while obedient to his orders, did not understand him. Her own intelligence had told her one thing – to love what he loved. If she must leave him and meekly avoid him, if he must tear apart what once linked them, if half of himself must keep its distance from him, then he should not forget what once was completely his. An everlasting part of him cannot want to be dishonoured – cannot want to disgrace him. He would demean himself by seeing people mock and laugh at her.

Wotan says that she was happy to follow the power of love. Now she should follow one whom she is obliged to love.

Brünnhilde replies that if she is no longer to be sent on missions from Valhalla to work and govern with her father, if an overbearing man must henceforth be her master, then let no coward take her as his prize. Whoever wins her must not be worthless. Wotan responds that she had renounced War Father, and he is unable to choose for her.

Softly Brünnhilde observes that he had fathered a noble family and no faint-heart can ever spring from it. The greatest hero, she knows, will be born to the Volsung race. Wotan snaps back that she should hold her tongue about the Volsungs. When he had given her up, he had given them up too. His hatred had obliged him to dispose of them. Brünnhilde says that by tearing herself from him she had saved them. Sieglinde was carrying the holiest child in sorrow and pain and would give birth to him. Wotan replies that she should never ask him to protect the woman and, still less, the fruit of her loins. Brünnhilde replies quietly that Sieglinde is looking after the sword that Wotan had made for Siegmund. 'And which I broke in pieces', responds the god angrily. Brünnhilde should not try to alter his decision but await her lot. He cannot choose for her and must now travel far away. As she had once turned away, so he must turn away from her. He is not interested in what she wishes for herself but only in her punishment.

She asks what it is she has in mind for her. He replies that he will enclose her in a deep sleep, and whoever wakens the defenceless maid will have her for his wife.

Brünnhilde falls on her knees. If the chains of sleep are to bind her fast, a prey even to the feeblest man, she begs one thing in her divine anguish. Let her sleep be protected by fearful terrors so that only a free and fearless hero will climb the rock and find her. Wotan says that she asks too much, too great a favour. Brünnhilde implores him. He may destroy his child who clasps his knees, trample on his favourite, crush the girl, let all trace of her body be destroyed by his spear but he should not be so cruel as to condemn her to vile disgrace. He could command fire to blaze up around the rock, burning with glaring flames and fiery tongues, its teeth devouring any coward who dares to approach the rock.

Persuaded and deeply moved, Wotan raises Brünnhilde to her feet and gazes emotionally into her eyes. 'Farewell, you bold, wonderful child!' he says, 'you, holiest pride of my heart. Farewell, farewell, farewell!'

He decrees that if he must reject her and not greet her again in love, if she may no longer ride beside him or bring him mead at the table, if he must lose the one whom he loved – the apple of his eye – then a bridal fire will burn for her as never blazed for any bride. A fire shall burn around the rock with a devouring terror to scare away the faint hearted. Let cowards run away from Brünnhilde's rock, for only one person shall win the bride – one who is freer than Wotan, the god.

Brünnhilde falls on her father's breast and he holds her in a long embrace. He gazes into her eyes – that bright pair of eyes that he had often caressed with smiles, when the excitement of battle had won her a kiss and child-like praise of heroes had flowed from her lips. That gleaming pair of eyes that had often flashed at him in storms, when his heart had yearned and desired worldly joy amidst so many fears. This day, for the last time, let them delight him with a final kiss of farewell. May their star shine for a happier man, but for the luckless immortal they must close in parting.

Wotan takes her head in both hands and kisses the godhead from her. Brünnhilde sinks back into unconsciousness in his arms.

He lays her gently down and gazes at her once more, covering her body with her shield.

Slowly, Wotan walks away before turning around again with a look of sadness. Then, solemnly, he walks to the centre of the stage, points with the tip of his spear to a rock and summons Loge; Loge, whom he had first found as a fiery blaze and who had then vanished again as an unpredictable fire. As they were once allies, so Wotan summons him to arise and surround the rock with fire. He strikes the rock three times with the spear and calls Loge to him. Flames spring from the rock and gradually grow brighter and spread. Wotan, with his spear, describes the circumference of the rock, indicating the direction the fire must take. Eventually, it spreads to the background and blazes continuously around the edge of the mountain. Wotan decrees that whoever fears the point of his spear shall never pass through the fire.

He looks back sadly at Brünnhilde and turns slowly to go. Again he gazes back, before vanishing through the flames.

SIEGFRIED

Dramatis Personae

SIEGFRIED	tenor
MIME	tenor
THE WANDERER	bass-baritone
ALBERICH	bass-baritone
FAFNER	bass
ERDA	contralto
BRÜNNHILDE	soprano
VOICE OF A WOODBIRD	soprano

Act I

A forest. We see Mime's forge, bellows and anvil in a cave in the rocks. Mime is sitting at the anvil, hammering at a sword blade with growing anxiety. At last he stops disconsolately. He complains about the pointless effort of welding a sword which, though strong enough for giants, is broken by the boisterous youth for whom it was made. The boy hurls it in pieces as if it were just a toy. But there is one sword that he wouldn't smash. The remnants of *Notung* couldn't be abused in this way. If only Mime could weld those pieces together, if only he could forge it for the boy, this would be compensation for his shame. Fafner the savage dragon lives in the dark wood. He guards the Nibelung treasure with his great body. Siegfried's boyish strength might well slay Fafner and he would then get the Nibelung's ring for Mime. Only one sword would enable him to do this. Only *Notung* could serve Mime's ambition, but Mime can't weld it. His effort is pointless. The best sword he has ever welded will never do for the one deed for which it is needed. He taps and hammers away because the boy makes him – the boy who snaps the sword and throws it away, and then is angry if Mime doesn't do what he wants.

Siegfried enters from the forest, driving before him a large bear tethered with a bit of rope. He is in cheerful high spirits and sets the bear on Mime, telling the creature to get the ugly old blacksmith and eat him. Mime drops the sword in terror and runs behind the hearth. Siegfried makes the bear chase him all over the place. Mime orders him to take the animal away; what good is a bear to him? Siegfried says that the two of them came to encourage Mime, and he tells the bear to ask for the sword. Mime implores him to let the beast go, and then displays the sword he has finished forging.

Siegfried chases the bear out. Mime says that he doesn't mind Siegfried slaughtering the bears but why bring them home alive? Siegfried replies that he was looking for a better mate than the one who sits at home. In the deep forest he had blown his horn to see if he could find some cheerful, friendly company. A bear came out of the bushes and growled at him as he listened to the music. Siegfried prefers the bear to Mime, though he might find someone better. With the rope he quickly tied the bear up and brought him to Mime to ask for the sword.

Mime gives Siegfried the sword and says he hopes he will enjoy using its blade. Siegfried replies that the blade is no use to him if the steel is not hard. He asks if Mime calls this flimsy toy a sword, and promptly smashes it on the anvil so that the pieces fly about. Mime shrinks in terror. Siegfried says that he should have smashed the pieces on Mime's head. The smith prattles on about giants and bold deeds and valiant weapons, and he wants to forge armour for Siegfried and make swords that will win him praise. Yet as soon as Siegfried lays hands on what he had made, he is able to smash the rubbish. If he didn't think Mime far too scrawny, he would melt the absurd old gnome down along with his work, and then his aggravation would be ended!

Mime cautiously replies that he finds this ingratitude vile. The boy forgets all that he's done for him. Won't he ever remember what he taught him about gratitude? He should be glad to obey the man who did so much for him. The boy might not want to hear about that again but he probably would like some food? Mime offers to fetch him some meat from the spit, or would he like some broth? He had cooked it well for him. He offers the food to Siegfried who, without looking, knocks the pot and the meat out of Mime's hand. Siegfried says that he can roast meat himself and Mime can drink his slops alone.

Mime whines and screeches about this being love's bitter reward! This is the disgraceful way in which effort is repaid. When Siegfried had been a suckling child, says Mime, he had brought him up, made clothes to keep him warm, had brought him food and drink and had cared for him as if he were his own. As the boy grew, Mime waited on him and made him a bed so that he could sleep comfortably. He made toys and a ringing horn. Mime was happy to work to make the boy happy. He helped him with good advice and learning. He sharpened his wits. While he sits at home, toiling and sweating, the boy gads about. Mime worries about him and wastes away, the poor old dwarf that he is. And for all those troubles his reward is that this bad-tempered boy scolds and hates him.

In response to this performance, Siegfried stares into Mime's eyes. Mime slyly looks away.

Siegfried says that Mime has taught him much, and he has learned a lot from him. But what Mime had most wanted to teach him he had never managed to learn: how to put up with him! Although the dwarf brings him food and drink, it is loathing that nourishes Siegfried. When Mime makes him a soft bed, he finds it hard to get to sleep. Though Mime had tried to teach him to be bright, he'd rather not listen and remain stupid. Whenever he looked into Mime's eyes, he saw evil in everything he did. When he watched him standing, shambling as he walked, shuffling and nodding and blinking his eyes, the boy longed to take him by the scruff of his nodding neck and make an end to his ghastly blinking. That's how he's learned to put up with Mime!

Siegfried tells the dwarf that if he were clever, he would help him understand something that he's pondered in vain. He runs into the forest to get away from Mime; so why does he come back? The animals mean more to Siegfried than Mime. Trees and birds, fish in the stream – he puts up with them more easily than he puts up with him. How then does it happen that he returns? If Mime is so clever he can tell him.

Mime says that this just goes to show how dear to Siegfried's heart he is. Siegfried laughs and says that in fact he can't stand him. Mime says that Siegfried is a bad boy. His wildness is to blame and he must learn to control it. Young creatures pine for the nests of the older ones. That longing is love. And so too does Siegfried love his Mime. Just as a bird feeds a baby bird in its nest before the fledgling can fly, so too does Mime teach and tend Siegfried. It must be so.

Siegfried replies that if Mime is so bright then he could tell him something else. The birds sang sweetly in springtime and one courted the other. Mime himself had said that they were husband and wife. They snuggled lovingly together and never left one another's side. They built a nest and hatched their eggs in it. Out fluttered young birds and the two tended their brood. Resting amongst the bushes, deer mated too, as did wild foxes and wolves. Food was brought by the husband to the nest and the wife suckled the young ones. Thus he had learned what love is. He never took one of the young ones away from its mother. Siegfried asks where Mime keeps his loving wife, so that he may call her 'mother'.

Mime is cross with such talk and says that Siegfried is foolish. Is he a bird or a fox? The boy goadingly reminds Mime that, as a whimpering child he had brought him up and made clothes to keep him warm. Where did the child come from? Did Mime really make him without a mother? Greatly embarrassed, Mime replies that he must believe it when he tells him that he is both his father and mother. Siegfried replies that the odious wretch is lying to him. The young look like their elders. He had noticed that when he had come to a stream and had seen the trees and animals reflected in it – sun and clouds appearing just as they are, appearing in the glittering waters. He saw too his own shape, which was completely different from Mime's. He no more resembled him than a glistening fish resembled a toad, and a fish was never born to a toad.

Mime becomes angry at such talk and tells the boy he is talking nonsense. Siegfried responds that he has now worked out what has long puzzled him: when he ran into the woods to get away from Mime, he still returned. It was because he needed to learn who his father and mother were. Mime shrinks away from him shouting: 'What father; what mother – foolish question!' Siegfried seizes Mime by the scruff of his neck and says that he has to rough him up in order to discover anything. He has learned nothing by being gentle. He had to force everything out of him. Now at last he should say who were Siegfried's father and mother.

Mime gasps and says that the boy is almost killing him. What he greedily wants to know, he will tell him, exactly as Mime understands it. He is a thankless, cruel child.

Mime admits that he is not the boy's father, nor any relation, and yet the boy should be grateful to him. He is a total stranger but his only friend. Out of pity he had sheltered him here, and what reward does he receive? He was a fool to hope for thanks. Once a woman lay whimpering out in the wild forest. He helped her into the cave and tended her by the warm fireside. She carried a child in her womb. Sadly she gave birth to it here. She writhed back and forth. He had helped her as well as he could. She was in great distress. She died but Siegfried lived.

Siegfried asks quietly if his mother died because of him. Mime explains that she had given the boy into his protection, which he had gladly provided. He had gone to no end of trouble out of kindness to relieve suffering. Mime starts his old refrain: *'I brought you up as a whimpering child'*.

The boy then asks why he is called Siegfried. Mime says that his mother had told him to give the boy that name – that as Siegfried, he would grow up strong and handsome. *'I made warm clothes for the little mite'*.

Siegfried asks what his mother was called. Mime claims not to know. *'Food and drink I brought for you'*.

The boy insists that he must tell him her name. At first, Mime says it has slipped his memory, but then – perhaps she was named 'Sieglinde'. She had given the boy to him in sorrow. *'I cared for you as my own flesh and blood'*.

Siegfried then asks what his father was called, to which Mime impatiently replies that he had never seen him. Siegfried asks if his mother had mentioned his father's name. Mime replies that she had said that he had been killed; that's all he remembers. Since the child was fatherless, he had been given to Mime. *'As you grew up I waited on you; I made you a bed for comfortable sleep'*.

Siegfried is fed up with this old 'starling song' and tells Mime to stop going on about it. The boy says that if he is to believe this story then he must see some proof. Mime asks how can he prove it, and Siegfried replies that he won't believe his ears, only his eyes. After thinking for a moment, Mime fetches two pieces of a broken sword and says that the mother had given them to him. She had left them as poor payment for all his trouble in feeding and caring. She had said that his father had used the sword when he had perished in his last fight.

Siegfried becomes very excited and insists that the pieces be forged together, so that he can then wield a real sword. He orders Mime to stir himself and demonstrate his skill. He must not deceive Siegfried with shoddy trash; he will put his trust only in these pieces. If he finds that Mime has been lazy and rivets badly or repairs the steel poorly, he will have his cowardly scalp. He would teach Mime what a scolding was because, he swears, he wants that sword and shall have it today.

A terrified Mime asks what he plans to do with the sword. Siegfried says that he'll run away into the forest, out into the world, and he'll never come back. How happy he is to be free. Nothing holds or compels him. Mime isn't his father and he'll feel at home far away from here. This hearth is not his, his lodging isn't under this roof. As happily as the fish swims in the stream, as free as the finch flies, he will flee – float away like the wind over the forest. He will blow away and never see Mime again! And with that, Siegfried rushes off into the forest.

Mime, with the utmost anxiety, tries to stop him, shouting at the top of his voice. The boy keeps going and, eventually, Mime returns to the forge and sits down behind his anvil. He laments that here he sits already burdened with old troubles, and now he has a new one that really confounds him. How can he help himself now? How can he keep the boy? How shall he lead this hoodlum to Fafner's lair? How shall he repair the pieces of this impossible steel? No furnace fire could forge such an object; no dwarf hammer could shape such hard pieces. Neither Nibelung envy nor trouble and sweat would rivet *Notung* or weld the sword together. Mime slumps down in despair behind the anvil. While he sits dejectedly, the Wanderer (Wotan in disguise) appears out of the forest and enters the cave.

The Wanderer greets Mime as 'worthy smith' and says that a visitor, weary from travelling, requests the favour of his house and hearth. Mime jumps up in alarm and asks who is searching for him; who is pursuing him in the desolate forest. The stranger says that the world calls him 'Wanderer'. He has travelled a long way over the face of the earth and is always on the move.

Mime says that if the world calls him Wanderer, he should keep on wandering and not stop here!

The stranger replies that he has enjoyed the hospitality of good men, many of whom have been generous to him. Only those with something to hide have anything to fear.

Mime says that ill fortune lives with him all the time. Does the stranger want to bring more on a poor man? The Wanderer replies that he has explored a lot and has learned a lot. There are important things he has told many people, and he has been able to protect them from worries gnawing at their hearts.

Mime says that the stranger might be a clever thinker and have spied out much, but he doesn't need thinkers or spies here. He wants solitude and his own company. He lets loiterers go their way.

The Wanderer moves a little closer and says that some think they are wise but they don't know what causes them trouble. In order to assist them he asks them questions and they benefit from his words. Mime becomes more anxious when he sees the stranger moving closer to him.

Many people hang on to useless knowledge, says Mime. He knows enough for his needs. His wits are sufficient; he doesn't want any more. He offers to show this wise man on his way.

The Wanderer sits down by the fire and says that he would be willing to stake his life in a contest of knowledge. His head would be forfeit if Mime doesn't learn something useful from him. Mime shudders to himself and wonders how he can get rid if this pest. He would have to question him very cleverly.

Mime then tells the stranger that he would accept his head in return for hospitality, and that he should now try to redeem it by skill. Mime will ask him three questions. The Wanderer agrees that he must answer them correctly.

Mime notes that the stranger has ranged a great deal over the face of the earth and has travelled far and wide. Therefore, he should tell him what race dwells in the depths of the earth. The Wanderer replies that in the depths of the earth dwell the

Nibelungs, and their land is Nibelheim. They are the spirits of darkness. Dark Alberich was once their lord. With a magic ring, with its power to compel, he tamed his hard-working people. Rich treasures they heaped up for him in a gleaming pile. These should have won him the world. What is the dwarf's second question?

Mime thinks deeply. He says that the wanderer has told him much about the earth's navel, so now he should tell him what race dwells on the earth's face. The Wanderer responds that the giants live on the face of the earth. Riesenheim is their land. Fasolt and Fafner, chief amongst these thugs, envied the Nibelung's power. They won for themselves a huge treasure and acquired the ring as well, over which a quarrel flared up between the brothers. Fasolt was killed and Fafner, now in the guise of a savage dragon, guards the treasure. What is the third question, on which his head depends?

Mime seems lost in thought and says that the Wanderer has told him much about the earth's rugged face. Now he should tell him what race lives on the cloudy heights. The Wanderer replies that the gods dwell on the cloudy heights. Their home is called Valhalla. They are spirits of light and their lord, Wotan, rules over them. From the primeval ash tree's sacred branch he had cut himself a spear shaft. The trunk may whither but the spear will never rot away. With its point, Wotan controls the world. On the shaft he carved sacred treaties with binding runes. Authority over the world belongs to the hand that controls that spear, and Wotan's fist clasps it. Before him bowed the Nibelung army. The race of giants was tamed by his might. They all obey forever the powerful lord of the spear.

As if by accident, the Wanderer lets the tip of his spear touch the ground, and distant thunder is heard. Mime shrinks in terror. The Wanderer then asks if he had answered the questions and was free to keep his head. Mime, who has been watching the Wanderer and his spear attentively, becomes very anxious, looks around for his tools and turns shiftily away. He says that the Wanderer has won the quiz, and his head, and should now be on his way.

The Wanderer replies that Mime should have asked what he needed to know. The Wanderer had staked his head on telling him, and since the dwarf still did not realise what he needed to know, the Wanderer would now claim Mime's head as security. The dwarf had greeted him inhospitably, and the Wanderer had yielded his head into his hands in order to receive hospitality. By the rules of the wager, he would now claim Mime's head if he did not answer three questions with ease. So, he should marshal his wits.

Mime replies with miserable resignation that he had left the land of his birth long ago, and had been born long before that. Wotan's eyes had settled on him and had looked into his cave. Mime's native wit is a poor thing against the stranger but now he needs to be clever. The Wanderer should ask away. If he is lucky, perhaps he will manage to save his dwarf head.

The Wanderer flatters Mime by calling him 'honest dwarf'. He asks him what is the tribe that Wotan has treated harshly though it is dearest to him. Mime cheers up and says that he has studied a little heroic genealogy. The question is one he can answer. The Volsungs are the love children that Wotan fathered and dearly loved though he also showed them displeasure. Siegmund and Sieglinde were fathered by Wälse. They were a wild and desperate pair of twins. They produced Siegfried, the strongest Volsung child. So, he asks, does he keep his head this time?

The Wanderer replies in a friendly fashion that Mime has named the family accurately. He is obviously a cunning fellow. He solved the first question, and now for the second one. A wise Nibelung is caring for Siegfried, who must kill Fafner for his guardian so that he may win the ring and be lord of the treasure. What sword must Siegfried wield if it is to bring about Fafner's death? Mime is warming to this game and rubs his hands with glee. 'Notung' is the name of the glorious sword! Wotan had thrust it into the trunk of an ash tree, so that it would belong to whoever pulled it out. None of the strong heroes could manage this – Siegmund alone was able to. Bravely he carried it in battle until it snapped on Wotan's spear. The pieces are now guarded by a wise blacksmith, who knows that only with Wotan's sword will the brave and stupid child, Siegfried, slaughter the dragon. So, asks Mime delightedly, does he keep his head the second time too?

The Wanderer laughs. Mime is the wittiest of wise men. Who can equal him in cleverness? But if he is so clever as to get the young hero to do his bidding, then he must answer the third question. The wise armourer should say who will take the strong pieces of the sword Notung and weld them anew?

At this, Mime jumps up in terror, crying out and nearly fainting. How should he begin? What can he think of? The wretched weapon – why did he steal it? It has caused him nothing but pain and distress. Its hardness resists him, he cannot hammer it, and rivets and solder have both failed him. He hurls his tools about and bursts out in utter despair that the wisest of smiths doesn't know what to do. Who can weld the sword if he can't? How can he fathom this mystery?

The Wanderer calmly rises. He says that Mime had asked three questions, which had been answered correctly. These had been about pointless, remote topics, but it didn't occur to him to ask about what was close to him – what he needed to know. Now when he tells him he'll go crazy. The Wanderer has won his clever head. Now Fafner's bold destroyer – the wretched dwarf – should take heed: only one for whom fear has never existed shall forge Notung anew.

Mime stares wide-eyed as the Wanderer turns to go. The visitor warns him that he should take care of his clever head from now on, for it would be left in forfeit to him who has never learned fear. With that, the Wanderer smiles and turns away, and quickly disappears into the forest.

A stunned Mime collapses behind his anvil. He stares out into the sun-lit forest and starts to tremble. Cursing the light, he imagines that the air is on fire, that there is a flickering and flaring, a glimmering and buzzing, with things floating and spinning and quivering. Something is gleaming and glistening in the sunshine. There is a rustling, humming and roaring – a rumbling, howling and crackling coming nearer. It bursts through the forest, heading towards him. He imagines a dreadful mouth, gaping at him. The dragon is after him – Fafner! Fafner! Uttering a loud cry, he collapses again behind the anvil.

Siegfried appears from out of the forest and calls to Mime, asking if the lazy fellow has finished his work. How is the sword? At first, he can't find Mime, and he wonders if Mime the coward has crept off. Is he hiding? Mime, in a small voice from behind the anvil, asks if the boy is alone. Siegfried laughs and asks what Mime is doing there. Was he sharpening the sword? Mime emerges highly disturbed and asks how he could possibly repair the sword since only one for whom fear has never existed shall forge *Notung* afresh. Obviously, he is too clever for such a job.

In an irritated tone, Siegfried asks if he must give him a hand. Mime says he has too much on his mind. Where can he find good advice? He'd gambled away his clever head. He'd forfeited it to one who has never learned fear. Siegfried asks if this nonsense is for his benefit. Is Mime trying to get out of it? Gradually, Mime takes control of himself and says he would gladly escape from anyone who knows fear, but he had omitted to teach it to the boy. Stupidly he had forgotten the one important thing. The boy was supposed to love Mime but even that went wrong. Now, how should he instil fear into him?

Siegfried grabs hold of Mime and asks if he needs to help him. What has the dwarf made today? Mime says that, in worrying about him, he had become distracted thinking about how to show him something important. Siegfried laughs. Mime seems to have been distracted under his seat – what was the vital thing that he'd found there?

Mime replies that he had learned fear in order to teach it to the stupid boy. Siegfried asks what is this fear that he's talking about? Mime is surprised that although Siegfried has never known it, he intends to leave the forest and go off into the world. What good is the strongest sword if fear is alien to him? Siegfried says that this is all useless advice. Mime tells him that it is his mother's advice that he's repeating and he must keep his promise to her. He cannot let Siegfried go into the dangerous world until he had learnt fear. Siegfried says that if this is a skill he needs to know, why hasn't he been taught it already? What is this fear?

Mime asks if, in the dark forest at twilight, at some dark spot, he has ever felt a rustling far off, a humming and a buzzing, a wild roaring that booms closer towards him, a dizzy flickering that flares around him, a swirling that grows louder and flies towards him. Didn't he then feel a furious shudder seizing his limbs? Didn't burning fear make him shake, trembling in his breast with anxiety? Didn't his heart burst with pounding? If he has never felt like that, then he doesn't know fear.

Siegfried is puzzled, since his heart is strong and firm. This fury and shuddering, burning and quaking, fever and dizziness, pounding and trembling – he'd like to feel such anxiety and longs to sample the pleasure of it. But how would Mime teach it to him? How could a coward like Mime be his master? Mime tells the boy just to follow him. He would be his guide. He knows an evil dragon that has killed and eaten many people. Fafner would teach Siegfried fear if he followed it into its lair. Siegfried asks where this lair is to be found. Mime replies that its name is the Cave of Envy. It is to the east, at the end of the forest. Siegfried says that it can't be far from the outside world. Mime assures him that the outside world is quite close to the Cave of Envy. Then, says Siegfried, he must be taken there. He'll learn fear and head off into the world. So Mime should hurry up and make the sword, for he wants to use it in the outside world.

Mime despairs. The sword – what a disaster! Siegfried tells him to run to the smithy and show him what he's done. Mime curses the weapon. He can't tell the boy how to mend it. It is so strongly influenced by magic that no dwarf could control it by force. Someone who doesn't know fear might more easily discover the technique. Siegfried tells this idle creature that he is speaking in riddles. He should admit that he's a bungler, and that he lies and cheats his way out of doing things. He tells Mime to fetch the pieces and, striding to the fireplace, proclaims that it would be easier for him to mend his father's blade. He'll forge the sword himself.

Siegfried boisterously sets to work, throwing Mime's tools about. Mime says that if the boy had concentrated on learning technique, he might manage the job. But he had been so flippant during his lessons – how could he possibly succeed? The boy replies that when the master can't do it, how could a pupil possibly learn – even if he were paying attention? He tells Mime to be off and not mess about or he'll fall into the fire too. He heaps up a large quantity of charcoal on the hearth and keeps the fire going while he fastens the pieces of the sword in a vice and files them to shreds.

Mime sits to one side and watches Siegfried at work. He asks what the boy is doing and advises him to take the solder, which he's been warming for a long time. Siegfried tells him to take the stuff away. He doesn't need it since he doesn't bake swords with glue!

Mime notes that the boy has worn away the file and rubbed the rasp to pieces. How is he going to work the steel when it's in fragments? Siegfried replies that he must reduce it to splinters. When something's broken, that's how he fixes it. He goes on filing vigorously while Mime talks to himself, grumbling that an expert is no help here, he can see that. The help for this fool comes only from his folly. He is working busily and energetically. He's filed the steel to nothing but he isn't sweating at all. Mime is as old as the caves and the woods but he's never in all his life seen anything like this. He just knows that the fearless boy is going to restore the sword. The Wanderer understood this well. Now where should he hide his poor head? It will fall to the boy if Fafner doesn't teach him fear. But then, how can Siegfried slay the dragon if he learns fear? How can he get the ring? This is a terrible dilemma for Mime, and he'll be caught in it unless he finds some cunning way to get the fearless boy under his thumb.

Siegfried has now worn the pieces down to filings and has put them in a crucible that he sets on the heat. He calls to Mime, asking what is the name of the sword he's now reduced to fragments. Mime replies that the coveted sword is called 'Notung'. That is what the boy's mother had told him.

Siegfried now fans the fire with the bellows, singing as he works: 'Notung, Notung, coveted sword. Why did you have to break? Your sharp splendour has been reduced to filings that are melting in the crucible. Blow bellows, blow the fire!

A tree growing wild in the forest was felled. The brown ash tree was burned to the charcoal now lying heaped on the fire. Blow bellows, blow the fire!

The charcoal from the tree burns bravely. How bright and splendid it glows. Jumping sparks are sent aloft as it smelts the steel. Blow bellows, blow the fire!'

Mime admits to himself that the boy will forge the sword and will kill Fafner, he can see that. He'll win the treasure and the ring in the fight, but how is Mime to be victorious? He must use cleverness and subtlety to get it all and still keep his head. When Siegfried is tired from fighting the dragon, a drink will refresh him.

From the spices that he's picked, he'll brew a drink for him. Only a few drops will be necessary and he'll fall unconscious. With the sword that the boy has won for himself, Mime will easily dispatch him and acquire the ring and treasure. He rubs his hands with delight at these thoughts. The Wanderer might have considered him foolish but what would he think of his cleverness now? At last Mime has a plan.

Siegfried sings that he has smelted the fragments of *Notung*, which now swims in its own sweat. He pours the glowing contents of the crucible into a mould and holds it aloft. Soon he will wield it as his sword. He thrusts the full mould into the water trough and steam and loud hissing arise from it as it cools. Siegfried sings that a fiery stream flows into the water. With fierce rage it hisses. It flowed like a wound but now in the water it flows no longer. It has become strong, hard and masterful. Hot blood will soon run upon it. He thrusts the steel into the forge fire and energetically pulls at the bellows. Now the steel must sweat once more so that he can forge it – *Notung*, the coveted sword.

Mime jumps up with glee. He fetches various jars, shakes herbs and spices from them into the cooking pot and attempts to put this on the fire. Siegfried watches as Mime places the pot on the embers at the other end of the fireplace. He wonders what the idiot is doing with the pot. While he melts steel, is Mime cooking slops?

Mime says that a smith is put to shame when the pupil teaches the master. The old man is finished now at his trade and is working as a cook for the boy. While Siegfried reduces the steel to a pulp, old Mime is brewing a broth from eggs.

Siegfried observes that Mime the craftsman is now learning to cook; forging doesn't suit him any more. All his swords have been smashed and what he is cooking isn't worth tasting. Mime wants to carry him off to teach him about fear but someone else had better do that. Mime's efforts have no effect whatever. He is a bungler with everything.

Siegfried sings that his hammer forges a tough sword: blood once made its blue surface blush. Coldly it laughed as it licked the warm blood cool. Now the fire has heated it red. It's hardness yields to the hammer. He had tamed its pride and angrily, it showers him with sparks.

Mime observes that the boy is making a sharp sword to slay Fafner, the dwarf's enemy. He has brewed a drugged drink to trap Siegfried when Fafner is laid low. His cunning will succeed and he'll enjoy its reward.

While Mime busies himself, pouring the contents of the pot into a flask, Siegfried continues to sing and work on the sword. The bright sparks make him glad. The sword's valour is strengthened by a hot temper. Cheerfully, the blade laughs, though it appears to be fierce and angry. The fire and the hammer have brought him luck. The sword has been straightened with hard blows and now will be rid of its shameful blushes. It must become as cold and hard as it can. He brandishes the blade, plunges it into the water trough and laughs loudly at the hissing.

Mime recalls that his brother had made the gleaming ring and had given it a spell of irresistible power. The bright gold that makes one the lord – Mime has won it. Mime possesses it!

As Siegfried works, tapping with the small hammer and sharpening and filing, Mime skips about in a lively fashion, growing increasingly ecstatic. He concludes that even Alberich who once enslaved him is now doomed. As lord of the Nibelungs, Mime will go back there and command obedience from them all. The dwarf they despised – how respected he'll be! To the treasure they'll flock, those gods and heroes. When he nods his head the world will bow down. When he is angry they'll tremble. Then Mime will not have to work any more and others will make him endless treasures. Mime the brave, Mime is king, lord of the elves, ruler of the universe! Hei, Mime, how lucky you are. Who would have thought it?

Siegfried, with a few final blows, hammers home the rivets on the hilt and then holds up the finished sword.

'Notung, Notung, coveted sword, now re-set in your hilt. Although you were broken, now your're restored. No blow shall ever smash you again. When my father died, the blade snapped. His son lived to make a new one. Now its brightness gleams, its sharpness will cut keenly.

Notung, Notung, coveted sword, you have been brought back to life. You lay dead in ruins, now you shine defiantly and gloriously. Villains shall see your brightness, the deceiver will be struck down and the scoundrel laid low. Mime the smith should watch how Siegfried's sword can strike.'

Siegfried then brings the sword down on the anvil, which splits in two and falls apart with a tremendous crash. Mime, who had jumped onto the stool in his state of ecstasy, falls to the ground in fright. Jubilantly, Siegfried holds his sword aloft.

Act II

In the forest at night, Alberich watches over the Cave of Envy. He is listening hard and watching carefully. Is the fearful day beginning? Is dawn emerging from the gloom? What is that light shining? It is coming closer, speeding like a glowing horse, breaking through the forest. Is this the dragon's killer? Is this the one who will destroy Fafner? The light fades, the brightness is hidden, and night returns once again. The Wanderer enters from the forest and stops near Alberich, who wonders who is emerging from the shadows.

The Wanderer speaks, saying that he has come to the Cave of Envy at night. Who is it there in the darkness? Moonlight breaks through a sudden gap in the clouds and illuminates the Wanderer's face. Alberich recognises him and shrinks back fearfully. Then he bursts out in a violent rage, asking why he dares to be seen here – the shameless thief should get out of his way.

The Wanderer is surprised to see Black Alberich loitering here.

Is he guarding Fafner's house? Alberich says that if the Wanderer is intent on new crimes, he needn't remain. There had been enough villainy plunging others into distress. Now he should leave them alone. The Wanderer replies that he has come to observe, not to participate. Who would bar his way?

Alberich laughs maliciously and says that Wotan's is the voice of desperation. If Alberich was as foolish as he had been when captured so easily, how simple it would be to take the ring from him again. But he is now familiar with Wotan's methods and he has not forgotten the god's vulnerability. Wotan had paid his debts with Alberich's treasure. His ring had rewarded the giants for their work in building the fortress. Even now, the treaty agreed with that pair remains inscribed on the shaft of Wotan's spear. Having paid the gold as wages, the god dare not snatch it back from the giants. By doing such a thing, he would himself be splitting the shaft of his spear. This instrument of his power would disintegrate in his hands.

The Wanderer replies that no treaty binds him to Alberich. His spear had subdued the Nibelung by its power, and it is now kept ready for war. Alberich observes that while the god proudly boasts about his strength, he is, at heart, fearful. The guardian of the treasure is doomed by Alberich's curse. Who will inherit it? Will the precious treasure belong to the Nibelung again? That is the source of Wotan's unending concern, for if Alberich grasps it again – just once in his fist – he shall use the power of the ring. Then the protector of the heroes will tremble and Valhalla's heights will be stormed by the hosts of Hell. Then Alberich shall rule the world!

The Wanderer replies quietly that he is well aware of Alberich's intentions but they do not worry him. The ring shall be controlled by whoever wins it. Alberich says that Wotan is speaking mysteriously about things that the Nibelung understands perfectly well. The god depends on hero sons sired by amorous blood. Isn't he raising a boy who will pluck the fruit that the god himself isn't allowed to touch?

The Wanderer replies that Alberich's quarrel shouldn't be with him but rather with Mime, for his brother is bringing danger. He is leading a boy who must kill Fafner for him. The boy knows nothing of Wotan. The Nibelung is using him entirely for himself. So, Alberich should do what is in his own interest. He should note carefully that the boy knows nothing of the ring, but Mime has learned about it.

Alberich asks if the god will keep his hands off the treasure. The Wanderer replies that the one he loves will be able to look after himself. He will stand or fall as his own master. Only heroes are useful to the chief of the gods.

Alberich asks if his fight for the ring will be with Mime alone. The Wanderer replies that, apart from Alberich, only Mime lusts after the gold.

Alberich asks if he might not still win the gold, to which the Wanderer replies calmly that a hero is approaching to free the treasure. Two Nibelungs covet the gold. Fafner will die and the one who snatches the ring wins it. Does Alberich need to know more? The dragon is lying in his cave. If Alberich warns him of death, perhaps he'd be glad to give up his trinkets.

Wotan offers to wake the dragon himself. He stands in front of the cave and calls into it to Fafner to wake up. Alberich is alarmed by this behaviour and wonders what the madman is doing. Will he really let him have the ring?

From the dark depths of the cave, Fafner's voice is heard, asking who is disturbing his sleep. The Wanderer replies that someone has come to warn him of trouble. He will reward the dragon with life if he pays him with the treasure he's guarding. Fafner asks what he wants. Alberich moves to the Wanderer's side and calls into the cave to the dragon to wake up. A strong hero is coming who wants to overcome Fafner. The dragon replies that he is hungry for him. The Wanderer says that the boy is bold and strong and his sword cuts keenly. Alberich adds that the golden ring is all that he longs for. If Fafner could give Alberich the ring he would prevent the fight. The dragon could continue to guard the treasure and live long in peace. Fafner replies that he lies here in possession. He yawns and asks to be left to sleep.

The Wanderer laughs loudly and then turns to Alberich, noting that they had not got anywhere with that attempt. But, he says, the Nibelung should stop accusing him of being the villain. Everything is as it was meant to be. He can alter nothing. He would leave this spot to Alberich to make a firm stand and try his luck with Mime, his brother. He might do better with him. As for what is to come, that too he will learn in due course.

The Wanderer disappears rapidly into the forest and Alberich gazes after him. Now he is left alone to anxiety and humiliation. The pleasure-seeking gang of gods could go on laughing but Alberich would see them all pass away in time. For as long as the gold gleams, he who knows about it will keep guard, and his tenacity will get the better of the gods. He slips into a cleft in the rock face at one side as day begins to dawn.

Mime and Siegfried enter, and Mime decides they should stop here. Siegfried sits down under a large Linden tree and asks if he will learn fear here. They had been walking all night long through the forest, and if he doesn't learn what he needs to know here, he will continue on alone. Then, at last, he'll be rid of Mime.

Mime replies in ingratiating tones that if Siegfried does not learn fear at this spot, then he will hardly find it anywhere else. In that dark cavern lives a savage dragon. It is huge, with a terrible pair of jaws, and it can gobble anyone up with one gulp. Siegfried suggests that it would be a good thing to close its mouth, and then the dragon couldn't bite him. Mime says that the beast drips poisonous venom, capable of eating away skin and bone. Siegfried says that the poisonous venom wouldn't hurt him, since he would keep to one side of the dragon. Mime adds that a snaky tail will thrash about behind it, and if it coils around Siegfried and grasps him tight, his limbs would break like glass. Siegfried replies that when the tail swings around, he would defend himself and keep a close eye on the beast. He asks if the dragon has a heart. Mime replies that it has a cruel, hard heart. The boy asks if its heart beats in the usual place. Mime assures him that it does and he asks if Siegfried is starting to feel fear. Siegfried replies that he would plunge *Notung* into this proud heart – is that what's called fear? If this is all that the old fool can teach him, then he should be on his way. He won't learn fear here.

Mime admits that what he is saying might sound like empty babbling. Siegfried needs to see and hear the beast itself, and then he would lose his senses. When his sight blurs and the ground sinks under him, and the fear in his chest makes his heart quake, then he will thank Mime for bringing him, and he will know how much Mime loves him.

Siegfried replies that Mime mustn't love him – hasn't he told him so? He should get out of his sight and leave him alone. He will put up with it no longer if he carries on about love. The loathsome nodding and the twitching of his eyes – when shall he see them for the last time? When shall he be rid of this fool?

Mime says that he will leave him now. He'll just be down by the stream. Siegfried should stay here and when the sun is high he should watch out for the dragon which will come out of its cave and come past here on its way to drink at the stream. Siegfried laughs and says that if Mime waits by the stream he'll certainly let the dragon go there. He'll plunge *Notung* into its vitals, but only after it's swallowed Mime with its drink. So he should take Siegfried's advice and not rest by the stream but go away as far as he can and not come back.

Mime says that surely the boy wouldn't turn him away if, after the fight, he brings him some refreshment? He should call out for him too if he needs advice – or if fear overtakes him. Siegfried stands up and drives Mime away with angry gestures. As Mime leaves, he mutters to himself: 'Fafner and Siegfried, Siegfried and Fafner. Oh, if only they'd kill one another!'

Mime disappears into the forest and Siegfried lies down comfortably under the Linden tree and ponders his predicament. Mime is not his father – how glad that makes him feel. At last he can enjoy the forest's coolness and feel the smile of daylight upon him. Now that the ugly gnome has gone, he won't see him again. Siegfried wonders how his father looked, and concludes that it must have been like him. If Mime had had a son, wouldn't he be the perfect likeness of Mime? Just as ugly and grizzly and grey, small and crooked, hunch-backed and hobbling, with droopy ears and bleary eyes. Away with the goblin! He never wants to see him again.

And then Siegfried wonders what his mother looked like. He can't imagine that at all. Surely her bright gleaming eyes shone like the doe's, but much more beautifully. When she had borne him in sorrow, why did she have to die? Do all mothers die giving birth to their sons? If that were so, how sad it would be. Ah, if only this son could see his mother – his mother, a human wife! He sighs gently and leans further back. Above him, the sounds of the forest increase and eventually, his attention is drawn to the song of the forest birds.

He listens with growing attention to a bird in the trees over his head. Then he addresses it, saying that he has never heard it before. Is its home in the forest here? If only he could understand its sweet call, it would surely tell him something – perhaps about his dear mother.

The dwarf had told him that a bird's talk could be understood – that one could learn it. How would this be possible? He sees a clump of reeds growing not far from the Linden tree and decides he would try to recreate the bird's song. He would copy its notes on a pipe. If he got the words wrong but copied the tune, he would still be singing its language and, perhaps, could learn what the bird says.

He cuts a reed with his sword and quickly whittles it into a pipe. He notes that the bird stops and listens, and so, he'll chatter away. He blows on the pipe and sits down and works on it. He plays it again and shakes his head and makes further improvements. He tries again, gets cross and pinches the reed with his hand and tries again. Then smiling, he gives up, saying that it didn't sound at all right. He couldn't get the lovely tune to work on the pipe. He thinks he'll have to stay stupid. Learning from the bird isn't easy.

He listens again to the bird and looks up at it, feeling ashamed that the rascal is listening to him. It watches but still hasn't heard anything – so it should hear his horn! He'd had no success on the silly reed. The bird would now hear a forest tune, one that he could really play – a cheerful one. He had used it to try to attract a companion but nothing better than wolves and bears had answered. Now he would see what it would bring him. Perhaps a friend he could love.

Siegfried takes the horn from his hip and blows a loud, sustained note on it. He looks up expectantly at the bird but instead, he disturbs Fafner in the shape of a monstrous, serpentine dragon. It lurches from its cave and breaks through the bushes, giving a loud yawn. Siegfried looks round in astonishment. His tune has brought him something lovely! A fine friend indeed!

Fafner sees Siegfried and asks what he is. Siegfried thinks that if this is an animal that has learned to talk, perhaps he could learn something from him – like fear. Fafner asks if he is being presumptuous, and Siegfried retorts that brave or presumptuous, he doesn't know. But he would make mincemeat of him if he doesn't teach him fear.

Fafner emits a laughing noise and says that he was after a drink but now he's found food as well. He shows his teeth and Siegfried comments that this is a pretty mouth he is showing off: laughing teeth in a dainty mouth! It would be a good thing to stop up the gap for him, for his jaws are gaping too wide. Fafner replies that they are no good for empty chatter but they are just right for gobbling him up.

Siegfried tells the gruesome, angry fellow that being digested by him is a bad idea but it would be a good idea if he dropped dead without delay! Fafner roars and urges the boastful child to come and get him. Siegfried tells him to watch out, for the braggart is coming. He then draws his sword and jumps towards Fafner. In the fight that ensues, Fafner bears his breast. Siegfried quickly sees the location of his heart and plunges his sword in it up to the hilt. Fafner rears himself up high with the pain and collapses onto the wound as Siegfried releases the sword and jumps to one side.

Siegfried shouts that the hateful creature should lie there with *Notung* in his heart. Fafner, in a weaker voice, asks who the boy is who has pierced his heart. Who had incited his childish courage to commit murder? Did his own brain plan what he had done? Siegfried replies that there is still much that he does not know – even who he is. He adds that Fafner himself had roused him to fight to the death.

Fafner replies that he will tell the bright-eyed boy – who knows so little about himself – who it is he has murdered. Amongst the race of giants, Fasolt and Fafner were brothers, and both are now dead because of the accursed gold that they had got from the gods. Fafner had put Fasolt to death and now, as a dragon guarding the treasure, Fafner the last of the giants, has fallen to a pink-cheeked hero. But the bright-eyed boy should watch his step. Whoever prompted him to do this deed is now plotting his death. With his last gasp he warns him to note how things will turn out.

Siegfried wants to know his origins, and thinks that the beast in his death throes seems to be wise. He might recognise his name.

He says that he is called Siegfried. Fafner repeats the name and then expires.

The boy concludes that dead men tell no tales, so his living sword must lead him. He pulls his sword out of Fafner's breast and, in the process, his hand is smeared with blood. He draws his hand back with a jerk and notes that the blood burns like fire. Involuntarily, he puts his finger to his mouth to suck away the blood. His attention is drawn increasingly to the song of the forest birds. It seems almost as if the birds are talking to him, and he wonders if this is the result of tasting the blood. A curious bird is singing to him and he wonders what it is saying. Then he hears the voice of the bird on a branch of the Linden tree, high above his head. The bird says: *'Hei, Siegfried now owns the Nibelung treasure. He'll find it in the cave. If he wants to take the Tarnhelm it will help him work wonders. And if he can get the ring, that will make him master of the world'*.

Siegfried, greatly impressed, thanks the bird and decides he will take its advice. He climbs down to the cave where he disappears from sight.

Mime creeps in, peering timidly about to convince himself that Fafner is dead. At the same time, Alberich comes in from the other side out of the rocks. He closely watches Mime who, since he no longer sees Siegfried, is moving towards the cave. Alberich rushes over to him and blocks his path. Where is he creeping, so slyly and quickly? Mime curses his brother and tells him he's not needed here. Alberich asks if he is greedy for his gold? Does he fancy Alberich's property? Mime says that the place belongs to him. Why is his brother rummaging about here?

Alberich suggests that he might be disturbing Mime in his quiet little enterprise, if he's come here to steal. Mime replies that what he's achieved by hard work he isn't going to give up. Alberich asks if Mime had gone to the Rhine and stolen the gold for the ring. Was it he who cast the powerful spell on it? Mime responds by asking who made the Tarnhelm that changes people's shapes? His brother needed it but he didn't create it. Alberich calls Mime a bungler who knew nothing about spells. It was the magic ring that was the source of Mime's skill. Mime taunts: where does Alberich keep the ring now? The giants took it from him, the coward. What he had lost, Mime's cunning would recover.

Alberich asks if this pitiful creature wants to profit from what the boy had done. The shining boy himself is the ring's master. Mime replies that he raised the boy, who'll now repay him for this upbringing. This has been a long time coming in return for Mime's toil and sweat.

Alberich says that, for rearing the lad, this pathetic serf has the nerve to make himself king. The most miserable dog has more right to the ring than Mime. This lout will never get his hands on the ring of power.

Mime tells Alberich he can keep the ring and look after it well. He can be the master but he should treat Mime as his brother, who would be satisfied with the pretty charms of the Tarnhelm. That way, both would win by sharing the booty. Alberich laughs mockingly. If he shared the Tarnhelm with the devious Mime, he would never sleep soundly again.

Mime is beside himself: not even an exchange? Not even a share? Must he go empty-handed without any reward? Can't he have anything?

Alberich replies that he can't have a thing – not even a nail!

Mime, in passionate fury, says that Alberich shall have neither the ring nor the Tarnhelm. He will call Siegfried and his valiant sword to come to his aid. The hero will enforce his rights.

Alberich sees Siegfried approaching and informs his brother. Mime says that the boy is sure to have chosen childish playthings.

Alberich notes that the boy has the Tarnhelm, and Mime sees that he has the ring as well. Alberich curses under his breath and

Mime, laughing maliciously, says that his brother should make Siegfried give him the ring, for Mime will soon get it for himself.

Mime then slips back into the forest and Alberich, swearing that the ring's master would eventually have it, disappears into a rocky crevice.

Siegfried considers the objects he has brought out with him. He doesn't know what to make of them. He had taken them from a pile of golden treasure because he had been advised to do so. Their beauty would serve as a souvenir of his exploits. These pretty objects would prove that he fought and killed Fafner, though he had still not learned fear. He hangs the Tarnhelm on his belt and slips the ring on his finger.

Once again he hears the voice of the bird, telling him: 'Siegfried now has the helm and the ring. He mustn't trust Mime, who is treacherous. Siegfried must listen carefully to Mime's flattering words. He'll be able to tell what he really means in his heart. Tasting the dragon's blood has taught him that'.

The boy then sees Mime approaching. The dwarf stops and studies Siegfried, wondering if he is weighing up the value of his spoils. Perhaps the Wanderer had hung about and chatted to the boy? Therefore, Mime must be doubly clever. He will now set his cleverest trap and, with friendly and deceptive speeches, he'll fool the insolent child.

He approaches Siegfried and welcomes him in honeyed tones. He asks the brave boy if he has learned fear. Siegfried replies that he still hasn't found a teacher. Mime asks if he killed the dragon – wasn't that a difficult bout? The boy replies that fierce and spiteful as the dragon was, its death saddened him. Scoundrels who are even more evil are still living. He hates the one who made him kill Fafner more than he hated the dragon itself.

Mime, in ingratiating fashion (but unable to disguise his true thoughts from Siegfied) tells the boy that he should calm down because he won't be seeing him for much longer. He'll soon be shutting his eyes in everlasting sleep. Mime's purpose has been accomplished. Now he just wants to get the spoils, which shouldn't be hard since Siegfried is such a booby.

So, Mime is planning to hurt him then, asks Siegfried. Mime is shocked and asks why Siegfried should think such a thing. He attempts to clarify what he means. In beguiling tones he says that he loathes his little son Siegfried and all his kind. It had not been out of feelings of love that he had raised such a pest. The treasure in Fafner's care – the gold – was what he had worked for. Believing that he is saying something pleasant, Mime asks the boy to give him the treasure or else (says Mime, with particular jocularity) he must pay with his life!

Siegfried observes that he is glad to hear that Mime hates him, but is it necessary to give him his life too? Crossly, Mime replies that he didn't say any such thing. Siegfried has misunderstood him. He takes out a flask and again, with great pains to conceal his true feelings, says that the boy looks tired after his strenuous efforts; his body must be on fire. Mime has gone to a lot of trouble to refresh him with a drink. While the boy had smelted his sword, Mime had prepared this broth. Now he should drink it – then Mime will have the sword and the Tarnhelm and the treasure with it.

Siegfried notes that the dwarf wants the sword. Would he steal the ring and the loot as well? Mime insists that his intentions are being entirely misunderstood. Is he stammering or slobbering at the mouth? He says that he has gone to the greatest trouble to hide his true intentions by flattery, and the silly boy has got it all wrong. He should open his ears and listen carefully to what Mime means.

Again, with amiability and effort, he invites Siegfried to take and drink the cordial. The boy has often liked Mime's drinks, even when he acted in a surly way and pretended to be cross. Even when he was in a bad temper, he always drank them. Siegfried replies that he's always glad of a nice drink, and asks how this one was made. Mime explains gaily (as if describing a state of merry intoxication) that the boy should just drink it and trust to his skill. His senses will soon fail in night and mist. Unwaking and unconscious, he'll soon stretch out his limbs. Mime says that he could easily take the spoils and hide them while the boy lies there, but when he woke up Mime would never be safe, even if he had the ring. So, with the sword that Siegfried had made so sharp, he'll first of all hack off the boy's head. Then he'll have peace and the ring as well. Mime chuckles to himself.

Siegfried seeks to clarify that, when he is asleep, Mime intends to murder him? Mime is furious and asks if that is what he said? In his most charming voice, he explains that he only wants to chop off his head! Then he adds, with meticulous clarity, that even if he hated Siegfried less, and even if the boy's insults and Mime's shame and trouble didn't give him so much to avenge, he still wouldn't hesitate to get him out of the way. Otherwise, how would he get the loot, since Alberich has his eye on it too?

Mime then pours the drink into a horn and presses it on Siegfried, at the same time inviting the Volsung – Wolf's son – to drink and choke himself to death! Siegfried raises his sword an, overwhelmed with revulsion, Siegfried aims a quick blow at Mime, who falls to the ground, dead. Alberich's mocking laughter is heard from a cleft in the rocks.

Siegfried looks at the corpse on the ground. Mime the loathsome prattler had tasted the sword. *Notung* had paid the wages of hatred, for which purpose it was forged. He grabs Mime's body and drags it to the mouth of the cave. Here it will lie on the treasure that Mime had so deviously sought. Now he is the lord of its splendour. Siegfried will give him a good watchdog too, to protect him from robbers. With a great effort he rolls the dragon's body in front of the cave to block it completely. The dark dragon can guard the glittering treasure, together with the dragon's greedy enemy. Thus they can both find rest.

Siegfried turns slowly away from the cave and wipes his hand across his forehead. It is noon and he is hot after his hard work. A storm is racing through his fiery blood and his head is even making his hand feel hot. The sun is high, and from the blue sky it shines straight down on his temples. He moves to the cool shade of the Linden tree, lies down and once again gazes up through the branches. He hopes that, after that annoying interruption, the dear bird will sing once again. He sees it happily perched on a branch, twittering and fluttering, with its brothers and sisters lovingly surrounding it. Siegfried is lonely and has no brothers and sisters. His mother had died, his father had fallen in battle; their son never saw them. His only companion had been a horrible dwarf. No sense of kindness had ever blossomed into love. The evil dwarf had set cunning traps for him, and so Siegfried had had to kill him. He looks sadly up into the branches and asks if the friendly bird could find him a good companion. He needs its advice. He had often wanted a companion but had never found one. This little friend might do better. Its advice has been good so far. It should sing and Siegfried would listen to the song.

The bird sings: 'Siegfried has killed the evil dwarf and can now be told of the most marvellous woman. She is asleep high on a rock and a fire burns around her home. If he can walk through the fire and wake the bride, then Brünnhilde would be his'.

Siegfried jumps up with excitement. What a lovely song he is hearing: a breath of sweetness. Now its meaning burns into his longing breast. How violently it tugs and inflames his heart. He asks the bird what is it that is running so quickly through his heart and senses? The bird responds that: 'cheerful in grief, it sings of love; blissful in woe it weaves its song. Only lovers know its meaning'.

Siegfried says that it is driving him onwards, shouting for joy, out of the forest and up to the rocks. He asks again of this sweet singer if he can break through the fire? Can he awake the bride? The bird replies that: 'winning the bride and waking Brünnhilde is not *for a coward but only for one who knows no fear'.*

Siegfried laughs with delight at what the little bird has said, for he realises that the stupid boy who doesn't know fear is himself! Only today he tried in vain to learn fear from Fafner. Now he's burning with desire to learn it from Brünnhilde. How does he find the way to the mountain?

The bird flutters up, circles around Siegfried and flies about hesitantly. Siegfried shouts for joy that the way will be shown to him. Wherever the bird flutters, he will follow it. He runs after the bird, which teases him for a while by leading him hither and thither. Finally it decides on a course and flies off, with Siegfried in pursuit.

Act III

A wild landscape at the foot of a rocky mountain. It is a stormy, rainy night with lightning and violent thunder that gradually abates. The Wanderer enters and walks deliberately to the cavernous mouth of a cave in the rocks. He calls on Erda, the Wala, to awake from her long sleep. He commands her to rise from her misty chasm – from the depths of night where the immortal woman sleeps. He says that he sings a waking song to her, to rouse her from her thoughtful slumbers. He rouses her in song, the all-knowing, eternally wise, immortal woman. The Wala must awake!

The mouth of the cave grows brighter with a bluish light. In this light, Erda rises very gradually from below. She says that the song calls powerfully to her; the magic draws her strongly. She has woken from the sleep of knowledge. Who has banished sleep from her?

The Wanderer replies that he is the one who has wakened her and has used charms that would rouse her from far away, where sleep held her fast in its grip. He has travelled the world to gain information, to learn primeval wisdom. As a fount of knowledge, no one surpasses her. She knows what is hidden in the depths, what links the mountains and valleys, the air and water. Wherever life exists, her breath blows. Wherever brains are active, her mind is attuned to them. It is said that all things are known to her and so, to seek information, he has wakened her from her sleep.

Erda says that her sleep is dreaming, her dreams are thoughts and her thoughts control wisdom. But while she is asleep, the Norns are awake. They weave the rope and innocently spin what she knows. Why doesn't he ask the Norns?

The Wanderer replies that the world determines the Norns' spinning. They cannot alter or reverse events. From Erda's wisdom he would like to know how to stop a revolving wheel. Erda says that human actions cloud her mind. With all her knowledge, she was once mastered by a ruler. She bore to Wotan a wish-maiden who selected heroes in battle for him. She is brave and clever as well. Why does he waken Erda rather than seek knowledge from the child of Erda and Wotan?

The Wanderer asks if she means the Valkyrie maid Brünnhilde? She defied the Master of Tempests at the very moment when he had mastered himself. What the Lord of Battles wished to do, but refrained from doing, the stubborn girl Brünnhilde dared to accomplish in the heat of battle against his will. The War Father punished the girl. He pressed sleep on her eyes. She is fast asleep on the rock and will only waken when a man woos her for his wife. Would there be any point in questioning her?

After a long silence, Erda speaks. She is dazed. How wild and awry the world's course is. Is the Valkyrie child of the Wala sentenced to fetters of sleep while her mother's wisdom slept? Does he who preached rebellion now punish rebellion? Does he who conceived the deed become angry when it is done? The defender of justice and guardian of oaths, does he shun justice now and govern by breaking oaths? She wants to descend again, to let sleep seal her wisdom.

The Wanderer says he will use his magic to prevent this earth mother from leaving. By her timeless knowledge, she once plunged the dagger of worry into Wotan's reckless heart. Her knowledge filled him with fear of a shameful, catastrophic downfall, and his spirit was bound with fear. He asks that if she is the world's wisest woman, then she must tell him how a god can conquer his dread.

She replies that he is not what he calls himself. Why did he come so wild and storm-like to disturb the Wala's sleep? He replies that she is not what she thinks herself to be. The primeval mother's wisdom will come to an end; her knowledge will vanish before his will. Does she know what Wotan intends?

After a long silence, he says that because she is unwise, he will open her ears and then she can sleep without care forever. The downfall of the gods does not fill him with fear because it is now what he desires. Once he found himself on the horns of a dilemma and, maddened with sorrow, he resolved in despair on a plan that now he puts into effect, joyfully and freely. In rage and loathing he gave the world to the spiteful Nibelung, but now to a glorious Volsung he bequeathed his inheritance.

Though the boy was chosen by Wotan, he still does not know him. This brave lad, unaided by advice from the god, acquired the Nibelung's ring. Happy in love, innocent of envy, his noble nature will neutralise Alberich's curse, for fear is still foreign to him. She whom Erda had borne, Brünnhilde, will be wakened by the hero. When she awakes, she will behave as a child of her mother's wisdom and redeem the world. So Erda can sleep now and close her eyes. In her dreams she can watch Wotan's downfall. Whatever the enemy may do to the eternally young hero, the god is happy to yield. Erda may descend then – mother of primeval fear and source of worry – away, away to everlasting sleep!

Erda has closed her eyes and is gradually sinking lower and lower. She disappears completely. Moonlight illuminates the scene.

The Wanderer sees Siegfried approaching. The boy notes that his bird has left him. It had happily shown him the way but now has vanished. He tells himself that it will be best if he finds his own way to the mountain. He'll continue to follow the path that his guide had shown him.

The Wanderer asks the boy where his road takes him. Siegfried is surprised to hear someone speak – perhaps he'll show him the way. He says he is looking for a rock surrounded by fire. A woman is asleep there and he wants to wake her. The Wanderer asks him who told him to look for a rock? Who spoke of the woman and made him desire her? Siegfried replies that he was told by a singing forest bird that gave him good advice. The Wanderer replies that a bird may chatter about all sorts of things but no human can understand it. How could he make sense of what it sang?

Siegfried says it was achieved through the blood of a savage dragon that he had killed at the Cave of Envy. The fiery stuff had hardy touched his tongue when he understood the language of the birds. The Wanderer asks who suggested that he, giant slayer, take on the mighty dragon? Siegfried replies that he was led by Mime, the deceitful dwarf who wanted to teach him fear. But the sword stroke that killed the dragon was prompted by the beast itself when it snapped its jaws at him.

The Wanderer asks who made the sword so sharp and hard that it could fell such a strong enemy? Siegfried replies that he forged it himself, since the blacksmith could not. Otherwise he might still have been swordless. The Wanderer then asks who made the tough pieces out of which the boy forged the sword? Siegfried replies that he wished he knew. He was only aware that the pieces would be of no use to him if he hadn't forged the sword anew. The Wanderer bursts out laughing and says that that's his opinion too.

Siegfried asks why he is laughing at him, this inquisitive old man. He tells him to stop it and not keep him chattering there. If he can point out the way to him then he should do so. If he can't, then he should hold his tongue.

The Wanderer tells him to have patience. If he looks old to the boy, then he should treat him with respect. Siegfried thinks that's a joke. All his life, an old man has been forever standing in his way. Now he's got rid of him. If this stranger keeps blocking his way, then he'd better watch out that he doesn't go the same way as Mime. What does he look like then? Why does he wear such a big hat, and why does it droop over his face like that? The stranger replies that this is the Wanderer's custom when he goes against the wind.

Siegfried observes that under the hat, one eye is missing. Someone's knocked it out, no doubt because he insisted on blocking the way! The stranger should be off now or he might easily lose the other eye as well. The Wanderer replies that he sees that although the boy knows nothing, he does know how to look after himself. The old man says that with the eye that he is missing, the boy is himself looking at the one that is left. Siegfried replies that the stranger is good for a laugh but that he can't go on chatting this way. He wants to be shown the path, and then the old man should be off. He can't think of any other use for him, so he should speak, or else Siegfried will send him packing.

The Wanderer says under his breath that if the impudent youngster had recognised him, he would spare him such insults. Being so fond of him, he is upset by such threats. Although he has always loved people with such a sunny disposition, they have also had cause to fear his rage. But the boy is dear to him, a paragon of heroism. He should not arouse Wotan's anger today – it could destroy them both.

Siegfried asks if the annoying fellow is holding his tongue? He should move out of the way, for Siegfried knows the path that leads to the sleeping woman. He had been told as much by the bird that had just flown away. The Wanderer bursts out angrily that it had flown away for its own salvation. It had recognised the lord of the ravens and would suffer if they caught it. The path that it showed must not be taken!

Siegfried steps back, astonished but defiant. So, he is forbidden is he? Who is this who wants to stop him? The Wanderer replies that Siegfried should fear the guardian of the rock. The sleeping girl was imprisoned by the Wanderer's power. Whoever wakes her, whoever wins her, makes him powerless forever. A sea of fire flows round the woman. Bright flames lick the rock. Whoever wants her as his bride will be fighting the burning blaze. He points to the summit with his spear and asks if the boy sees the light? The glare is increasing, the fire is rising, clouds of smoke and flaring flames roll and scorch and crackle down the mountain. A sea of light surrounds his head like a halo. He'll be mauled and devoured by ravenous flames. The reckless boy should go back.

Siegfried says that the braggart should go back himself. There, where the blaze burns, he'll go to Brünnhilde. As he sets off, the Wanderer bars his way and says that if he does not fear the fire, then his spear must block the boy's path. His hand still holds this lordly sceptre. The sword the boy is brandishing was once shattered on this shaft. For a second time then, it will break on the eternal spear. He stretches out his spear and Siegfried draws his sword, believing that he has found his father's enemy. How glorious is the revenge that is granted him. This enemy should brandish his spear and his sword will smash it to pieces.

With a single blow, Siegfried severs the Wanderer's spear. A flash of lightning springs from it and darts up the rock to the summit where the glow begins to blaze with increasing brightness. The flash is accompanied by a clap of thunder that quickly dies away. The fragments of the spear land at the feet of the Wanderer who quietly picks them up. He gives way and tells the boy to continue. He is unable to stop him. He then vanishes in total darkness.

Siegfried asks if the coward has run off, now that his spear has been broken. He then sees the sea of flame gradually grow brighter, as it blazes down the mountain. Ah, what a marvellous fire, he thinks. How brightly it shines. The way stands radiant and open. He'll bathe in the flames, and in the fire find his bride. Now he can win a loving companion.

Siegfried raises his horn to his lips and plunges into the sea of fire which sweeps down from the heights. He is soon lost from sight apparently moving towards the summit. The firelight reaches its brightest and then begins to fade, gradually disolving into finer and finer mist, lit up as if by the red light of dawn. The upper part of the mist floats away, revealing the bright blue sky in daylight. The scene is set exactly as at the end of *Die Walküre*. Under the broad fir lies Brünnhilde fast asleep, fully armed, her helmet on her head and her long shield on top of her.

Siegfried reaches the summit and gazes about him in astonishment for some time. He sees something lying in the shadow of the trees. It is a horse, fast asleep. Then as he walks slowly forward, he stops in amazement, noticing some way off, the form of Brünnhilde. Something is shining – it is gleaming metalwork. He wonders if he is still dazzled by the fire. He walks towards her and notices the shining armour, wondering if he should take hold of it.

He lifts the shield and sees Brünnhilde's form, although her face is covered by her helmet. He thinks it is a man in armour and is impressed by his form. The noble head is confined by the helmet. The sleeper would be more comfortable without this headgear, he thinks. Siegfried carefully undoes the helmet and removes it. Then, long tresses of hair tumble out and Siegfried starts back, fascinated by the beauty of this sight. It reminds him of shining clouds, hovering on the waves of the bright sea of heaven. The gleaming sun laughs as it streams through the cloudy waves.

He bends lower over the sleeping form, whose breast heaves with gentle breathing. Perhaps he should remove the tight breastplate? He tries with great care to loosen the breastplate, and then takes his sword to cut the iron rings. With gentle care, he cuts through the chain-mail on both sides of the armour. Then he lifts off the breastplate and greaves to reveal Brünnhilde, dressed in a soft female garment. He jumps up terrified and amazed. This is not a man! He gazes at the sleeping form with great excitement. A magic fire is consuming his heart; burning anxiety seizes his eyes. He feels weak and dizzy.

In utmost desperation, Siegfried wonders who he can turn to for help. 'Mother, mother' he cries, 'think of me!' He falls, almost fainting, on Brünnhilde's bosom and then raises himself with a sigh. How will he wake the girl and make her eyes open? And when her eyes do open, won't he be blinded by the sight? Is he rash enough to dare? Could he bear the brightness? He is dizzy and reeling and swaying about. A painful longing burns his senses, his hand trembles on a pounding heart. Why is he so cowardly? Is this fear? 'O mother, mother, your brave child!' A sleeping woman has taught him to be afraid! How does he stop this fear? How shall he pluck up courage? If he himself is to wake up, then he must awaken the girl.

Her bud-like lips quiver sweetly. Their gentle trembling attracts him, even in his fear. Ah, her breath is so lovely and warm and fragrant. He urges this blessed woman to wake up. She cannot hear him. Then he must suck the life from those sweet lips, even if he should die in the attempt. He falls like a dying man onto the sleeping form and, with his eyes closed, presses his lips to hers.

Brünnhilde opens her eyes. Siegfried jumps up and stands gazing at her. She raises herself slowly into a sitting position. She raises her arms and greets the sun, and then the light, and then the radiant day. She has long been asleep and has been wakened. Who is the hero who has woken her?

Siegfried is deeply moved by what he sees and by the sound of her voice. He says that he had struggled through the fire that blazed around the rock. He had removed her tight helmet. His name is Siegfried, and he woke her.

Brünnhilde greets the gods and then the world and then the shining earth. Her sleep is now over. She is awake and can see that it is Siegfried who has woken her.

Siegfried, in delight, blesses his mother who bore him and the earth that fed him. They had enabled him to see those radiant eyes that bring him joy.

Brünnhilde with equal emotion, blesses the mother who bore him and the earth that fed him. His alone were the eyes fit to see her. He alone could waken her. Siegfried, the wonderful hero who woke her to life with his conquering light. If only he – the joy of the world – knew how long she had loved him. He was in all her thoughts and all her cares. She fed him tenderly before he was conceived, and before his birth her shield had protected him. For all that long time, she had loved Siegfried.

He then asks softly and shyly if his mother didn't die after all? Was she whom he loved, only asleep?

Brünnhilde smiles and stretches out her hand to this dear child. His mother will not come back but he and she are one if he is happy to love her. What he doesn't know, she knows for him. Yet she is made wise only because she loves him. She has always loved Siegfried – the conquering light – for she alone knew Wotan's idea, an idea that she could never name, one that she did not think about but only felt. She fought for it, struggled and did battle. For it she disobeyed him and was punished, confined by his sentence because she didn't think of it but only felt it. That idea – can Siegfried guess it? – was only her love for him!

Siegfried remarks on the miraculous sound of her glorious voice, even though he finds it hard to understand. He can see clearly the light of her eyes, the touch of her breath feels warm, her voice is sweet to hear, but he does not understand her words. He cannot grasp what is so strange to him because all his senses see and feel only her. She has bound him with anxiety; she is the only one who has taught him fear. She has bound him in strong fetters. He doesn't want her to stifle his courage.

Brünnhilde looks towards the firs. She sees Grane, her blessed horse. How pleased he is to graze after being asleep like her. Siegfried has woken him too.

Siegfried says that he can't take his eyes of her fascinating lips. With a passionate thirst, his lips are burning to caress her eyes. Brünnhilde gestures towards her weapons, seeing the shield that used to shelter heroes, the helmet that covered her head. They no longer shelter or cover her. Siegfried says that a glorious girl has pierced him to the heart. His head is wounded by a woman's work and he came there without shield or helmet.

Brünnhilde remarks sadly that she can see her breastplate's shining steel. A sharp sword has split it in two. With it were removed the defences of her maiden's body. She is left without protection or shelter, unarmed – a miserable woman.

Siegfried says he came to her through blazing fire. No breastplate or chainmail covered his body, and now the fire has taken hold of his heart. His blood boils in a blaze of passion. A scorching fire is lit up inside him. The fire that encircles Brünnhilde's rock now burns in his breast. He asks her to extinguish the blaze, to silence the crackling fire. He embraces her passionately. She jumps up in terror and pushes him away with all her strength. Not even the gods had come so close to her – the heroes had humbled themselves before her maidenhead. She was chaste when she left Valhalla. Oh, how shameful and disgraceful is her plight. She is wounded by the man who woke her. He broke her breastplate and helmet – she is Brünnhilde no longer.

Siegfried replies that, for him, she is still the dreaming girl. Brünnhilde's sleep has not ended. She must awaken and be his wife. Brünnhilde is shocked, her senses are confused, her knowledge is stifled. Must her wisdom vanish?

Siegfried asks her: didn't she tell him that all her wisdom came by the light of her love for him? She replies that melancholy darkness clouds her sight, her eyes grow dim, their light has gone out. For her it is like night. Out of mist and misery comes a turbulent mixture of fear and confusion. Horror emerges and looms over her head.

Violently, she covers her face with her hands. Siegfried gently removes her hands and says it was night that frightened her enchanted eyes. When the fetters fall, so will her gloomy fear. She must drive out the darkness and see that the day is bright with sunshine. Brünnhilde, in great apprehension, says that the day illuminates her shame as brightly as the sun. Does Siegfried see how frightened she is?

A lovely thought then enters Brünnhilde's mind, and she looks gently at Siegfried. She always was and is enveloped in the bliss of sweet longing, always caring for him. Siegfried, splendid man, is the treasure of the world. He makes the earth live – a laughing hero. He must go and leave her alone. He shouldn't come to her, overwhelming her passionately. He mustn't force her with a power that might break her. He mustn't destroy his sweetheart. Did he ever see his reflection in a clear stream? Did it make him glad? If he disturbed the surface, he would have caused ripples in the stream and lost sight of that reflection. So, he must not touch her or make her unhappy. Then, ever afterwards her eyes will smile happily on the cheerful hero. Siegfried, the radiant boy, must love what is him and leave alone what is her. He should not destroy what is his.

Siegfried replies that he loves her. If only she could love him! He no longer has himself. If only he had her! A marvellous waterfall flows before his eyes. It is all that his senses can absorb – that wonderful streaming flood. If it disturbs his reflection, then he is burning for his fiery passion to be cooled in its waters. Just as he is, he will jump into the stream. If only its waves would blissfully swallow him, his longing would be lost in the tide. Brünnhilde must awaken, laugh and be alive to the sweetest of joys, and be his.

Brünnhilde says that she has always been Siegfried's. He replies passionately that if she has always been his, then she should be now. She says that she will be his forever and ever. He asks that what she would be, she should be at this moment. If his arms clasp her and hold her tight, if his breast pounds passionately next to hers, if their eyes catch fire, if the breath of one consumes the other – eye to eye, lips to lips – then she would be to him what she was and will be. Then he would cease to worry whether Brünnhilde is his.

He embraces her and she asks if she is his, for divine peace floods in waves inside her. Purest light blazes in the fire. The wisdom of heaven streams away from her, for the joy of love has chased it away. Is she his now – can't Siegfried see her? As her eyes devoured him, wasn't he blinded? As her arms embrace him, doesn't she set him alight? As her blood stream surges towards him, doesn't he feel a wild fire? Isn't Siegfried afraid? Isn't he afraid of this wild, passionate woman? She embraces him fervently.

Siegfried, both frightened and delighted, replies that as their blood streams set one another alight, as their blazing eyes scorch one another, as their arms embrace in passion, so he regains the boldness of his heart. And the fear? Ah, the fear that he never learned, the fear that she had only just taught him. He fancies that he has foolishly quite forgotten it.

Brünnhilde laughs aloud in the utmost joy of love. He is a child-like hero, this wonderful boy, the foolish guardian of glorious deeds. She has to laugh because she loves him. She would go blind laughing. Let them laugh and die, and laugh as they are buried. Farewell, Valhalla's glorious world! Collapse into the dust, proud fortress. Farewell, glorious pomp of the gods. End in ecstasy, immortals. Norns, break your runic rope! Let twilight of the gods

– *Götterdämmerung* – draw near. Let the night of annihilation and mists descend. Brünnhilde is bathed in Siegfried's starlight; he is hers eternally – always hers – her inheritance, her own, one and all, radiant love and laughing death!

For his part, Siegfried says that his beloved has awoken to him. Brünnhilde is alive, Brünnhilde is laughing. He greets the day that shimmers around them, he greets the sun that shines upon them, he greets the light that drives away night, he greets the world in which Brünnhilde lives. She is awake, alive, and smiles on him. Brünnhilde's starlight falls gloriously on him; she is his forever – always his – his inheritance, his own, one and all, radiant love and laughing death!

Brünnhilde falls into Siegfried's arms.

TWILIGHT OF THE GODS

Dramatis Personae

FIRST NORN	contralto
SECOND NORN	mezzo-soprano
THIRD NORN	soprano
BRÜNNHILDE	soprano
SIEGFRIED	tenor
GUNTHER	baritone
HAGEN	bass
GUTRUNE	soprano
WALTRAUTE	mezzo-soprano
ALBERICH	bass-baritone
WOGLINDE	soprano
WELLGUNDE	soprano
FLOSSHILDE	mezzo-soprano
VASSALS	
WOMEN	

Prologue

The scene shows the Valkyrie rock as at the end of *Siegfried*. It is night. Firelight glows at the back from further down the mountain. The First Norn asks what light is glowing there? The Second Norn wonders if it is daybreak already? The Third Norn says that Loge's armies blaze with fire around the rock. It is still night. Why don't they spin and sing?

The Second Norn says that if they're going to spin and sing, where should they fix the rope? The First Norn unties a golden rope from around her and fastens it with one end to a branch of the fir. For better or for worse, she says, as she winds the rope and sings. She used to weave at the world ash tree when, large and strong, its trunk put forth vegetation, a forest of noble branches. In its cool shade, gushed a spring. It whispered wisdom as its

THE RING TEXT IN PROSE

waters flowed. Her song then was sacred. A valiant god came to drink at the spring. He forfeited one of his eyes as payment forever. From the world ash, Wotan then broke off a branch. Using all his strength, he cut a spear shaft from the trunk. In the course of time, the wound blighted the forest. The faded leaves dropped; the tree withered and died. Sad and dry was the fountain. Sad at heart was her song. So if today she weaves no longer by the world ash, a fir must suffice to tether the rope.

As she throws the rope to her sister and tells her to sing, she asks if she knows what happened then? The Second Norn passes the rope around a rock projecting at the mouth of the cave. She says that the terms of binding treaties were recorded by Wotan in runes on the shaft of the spear. He wielded the spear as guardian of the world. A bold hero broke the spear in battle. The sacred testament of treaties fell in pieces. Then Wotan sent the heroes of Valhalla to the world ash. They chopped to pieces its withered branches and trunk. The ash tree fell and the spring dried up forever. Today she anchors the rope to the jagged rock. She throws an end to her sister and asks if she knows what is to come?

The Third Norn catches the rope and throws its loose end behind her. She says that the fortress built by the giants still stands. Wotan sits there in the hall with the gods and heroes as his sacred companions. Chopped logs are heaped up around the hall in a huge pile. They were once the world ash. When the wood catches fire and burns brightly and terribly, the flames will seize on the splendid hall and consume it. Then the twilight of the eternal gods will fade forever. If the others want to know more, they should pass the rope again. Once more from the north she would throw it to them. She throws the rope to the Second Norn, who passes it to the First, who unties the rope from the branch and fastens it to another one.

The Second Norn urges her sister to spin and sing. The First Norn, looking around, asks if the day is dawning, or is it firelight?

Her eyes are dim and deceive her. She does not remember clearly the sacred days of old, when Loge sprang up in bright flames. Do the others know what happened to him? The Second Norn says that Wotan tamed him with his magic spear. He helped the god with advice; he gnawed and nibbled at the runes on the spear to gain his freedom. Then with the spear's forceful point, Wotan commanded him to burn around Brünnhilde's rock. Does her sister know what will happen to him?

The Third Norn says that Wotan will one day thrust the broken spear's sharp splinters deep into his breast. A consuming flame will flare up on them. The god will hurl it at the remnants of the world ash, piled together. The Second Norn says that if the others wish to know when that will be, then they should pass the rope again.

The First Norn notes that night is fading and she can no longer see. She can't find the strands of the rope any more. The twine is tangled; a blurred vision troubles and confuses her mind. She asks what had happened to Alberich, who had once stolen the Rhinegold. The Second Norn says that the sharp edge of the rock is cutting into the rope. There is no more tension in its strands and its twine is tangled. She sees the Nibelung's ring loom up out of distress and hatred. An avenging curse is gnawing through her plaited strands. Do the others know what will come of it?

The Third Norn says that the rope is too slack; it doesn't reach her. If she must direct the loose end to the north, it has to be pulled tighter. She tugs hard at the rope. It breaks, and the three Norns start up in terror. They grasp the pieces of the broken rope and with them, tie their bodies to one another. Together, they lament that their eternal knowledge is finished; the world will learn nothing more from their wisdom. They descend to their mother, and vanish.

Day dawns. The morning sky grows increasingly pink. The firelight below continues to glow faintly. Siegfried and Brünnhilde emerge from their cave. He is fully armed and she is leading her horse on the bridle. Brünnhilde tells Siegfried, her beloved hero, that she knows he longs for other adventures. How little she would love him if she didn't let him go? Only one concern makes her hesitate – he was so poorly rewarded for winning her. What she has learned from the gods she has given him – sacred charms in great quantity – but her strength and heritage were taken by the hero to whom she now submits. Drained of knowledge but full of longing, rich in love but deprived of strength, he must not despise the poor creature who begrudges him nothing but has nothing more to give.

Siegfried replies that this wonderful woman has given him more than he knows how to keep. She should not scold him if her teaching has left him ignorant. Of one piece of knowledge he is fully aware – that Brünnhilde lives for him! One lesson he has learned easily is to think about Brünnhilde.

She says that if he wants to give her love, he should think only of himself; think of his adventures, think of the raging fire through which he fearlessly walked, though it burned around the rock ('to win Brünnhilde', he interjects). She says that he should think of the woman under the shield, that he found fast asleep, whose enclosing helmet he broke open ('to wake Brünnhilde', he adds). She says that he should think of the vows that made them one, the trust they give to one another, the love that keeps them alive. Brünnhilde will always burn like a sacred flame in his breast.

Siegfried says that he must leave her there in the solemn care of the fire. He takes Alberich's ring from his finger and gives it to her saying that, in exchange for her teaching, he'll give her the ring that encircles the virtue of all his deeds. He'd slain a savage dragon that had long and angrily guarded it. Now she must guard its power as the sacred pledge of his constancy.

Brünnhilde puts on the ring and says that she will delight in it as her only property. In exchange for the ring, she gives him her horse. He used to travel boldly with her through the sky and, along with her, he had lost his powerful heritage. No more will he fly through the clouds in thunder and lightning, but wherever Siegfried takes him – even through the fire – Grane will fearlessly follow because he will obey the hero. She tells Siegfried to look after Grane well, for he will listen to what he says. He should often give him greetings from Brünnhilde.

Siegfried says that he will go on performing deeds inspired sole-ly by Brünnhilde. She chooses his battles, and his victories will honour her. On her horse's back, protected by her shield, he no longer considers himself to be Siegfried but only Brünnhilde's arm.

Brünnhilde says that she wishes she might be his soul. Siegfried replies that his courage is kindled by her. Then, she says, he must be both Siegfried and Brünnhilde. He says that wherever he is, there shall they both be. She suggests that her rocky home might not be empty after all, and Siegfried says that since they are one, it will contain them both.

Brünnhilde, with great emotion, calls on the sacred gods – majestic beings – to feast their eyes on this blessed pair. Parted, who could separate them; separated, they will never part. Siegfried salutes Brünnhilde as his shining star and resplendent love, and she calls him triumphant light and resplendent life.

Rapturously, they take their leave of each other.

Siegfried and the horse are lost from sight as they begin their descent. Brünnhilde remains standing alone and watches Siegfried's descent. His horn-call is heard in the valley below.

Act I

The hall of the Gibichungs by the Rhine. Gunther and Gutrune are sitting on tall chairs to one side. A table with drinks is in front of them. Hagen sits on the opposite side of the table.

Gunther asks Hagen whether his name is honoured along the

Rhine. Is Gunther worthy of Gibich's fame? Hagen says he is envious of Gunther's title but their mother, Grimhilde, taught him to respect it. Gunther says that he envies Hagen, who has no cause to be jealous. Although he inherited position, Hagen alone was given wisdom. The rivalry of half-brothers was never better resolved. He is simply praising Hagen's judgment when he inquires about his reputation.

Hagen replies that he must then criticise his own judgment, for Gunther's reputation still leaves something to be desired. He knows of some prized possessions that the Gibichung does not yet have. Gunther replies that if his half-brother keeps them secret, then he too will criticise him.

Hagen says that Gibich's children are in their prime and maturity but Gunther is unmarried and Gutrune has no husband. Gunther asks whom he suggests they should marry in order to improve their reputation. Hagen says that he knows of a woman, the most splendid of all. Her home is high on a rock and fire blazes around her dwelling. Only by going through the fire could a man be Brünnhilde's suitor.

Gunther asks if he would be brave enough. Hagen replies that there is only one – a stronger man – who qualifies. Gunther asks who is this boldest of men? Hagen replies that he is Siegfried, offspring of the Volsungs. He is the strongest of heroes. Siegmund and Sieglinde, a pair of twins, driven by love, bore this noble son. He grew up sturdily in the forest. Hagen would choose him for Gutrune's husband.

Gutrune asks what had Siegfried done that warrants the description of most glorious of heroes. Hagen says that, at the Cave of Envy, the Nibelung treasure was guarded by a monstrous dragon. Siegfried closed its fearsome jaws. He killed it with his victorious sword. It was this exceptional deed that secured his fame as a hero.

Gunther says that he's heard of the Nibelung treasure and

thinks that it is greatly to be desired. Hagen says that the man who knew how to use it would have the world in his power. Gunther asks if Siegfried won it in the fight? Hagen replies that the Nibelungs are his slaves. Gunther asks if he is the only one who can win Brünnhilde? Hagen says that the fire will yield to no other.

Gunther rises impatiently and asks why Hagen stirs up doubts and quarrels? Why should his hopes be raised for something he could never have? Hagen suggests that if Siegfried could obtain the bride for Gunther, then wouldn't that give him Brünnhilde? Gunther wonders who could persuade the happy man to win a bride for someone else? Hagen says he would soon be persuaded if Gutrune had conquered him first.

Gutrune thinks Hagen must be joking. How could she conquer Siegfried? If he is the most glorious hero in the world, the loveliest women on earth would have long since satisfied him. Hagen leans secretively towards Gutrune and reminds her of a drink kept in the cabinet. He had obtained it, and she should trust him. It would bind in love the hero that she longs for. If Siegfried were to come in now and taste that spicy drink, he would forget entirely about any woman he had seen before Gutrune – even the idea that any woman had come near him. He asks what the others think of his plan?

Gunther praises their mother Grimhilde, for giving them Hagen as a brother. Gutrune says she wishes she could see Siegfried, and Gunther asks how he might be found. A horn is heard in the distance and Hagen listens. He turns to Gunther and says that, when Siegfried is looking for adventure, the whole world is like an enclosed forest. In the course of his restless hunt, he may well come to Gibich shores on the Rhine. Gunther says he would be glad to welcome him.

Again a horn is heard, coming closer. Gunther notes that it is coming from the Rhine. Hagen goes down to the riverbank and gazes down stream. He reports that a hero and a horse are approaching in a boat. It is his horn-call that they hear. With easy strokes, as if it were no effort at all, he is driving the boat quickly against the current. The massive strength propelling the oar can only belong to the man who slew the dragon. It is surely Siegfried and no one else.

Gunther fears he might be rowing past, and Hagen calls across the stream through cupped hands, asking where the hero is bound.

Siegfried replies from the river, that he is looking for Gibich's sturdy son. Hagen invites him to the hall and suggests that he tie up his boat. He then welcomes Siegfried, who asks which is Gibich's son. Gunther replies that he is the man he's looking for. Siegfried says he has heard of Gunther's fame far down the Rhine. He should fight with him or be his friend. Gunther says that they should forget all about fighting – Siegfried is welcome.

Siegfried looks around and asks where he should tether his horse. Hagen replies that he will find a stall for it. Siegfried notes that Hagen had called him by his name. Had he seen him before? Hagen replies that he had recognised him simply by his strength. Siegfried asks him to take good care of Grane; he would never hold a nobler horse.

Gunther extends to Siegfried the happiness of his father's house. Wherever he walks, whatever he sees, he should treat it as his own. Gunther's inheritance is his – his land, his people. He is his, body and soul. Siegfried replies that he has no lands or people to offer – no paternal house or grounds. He inherited only his own body and, while he lives, he wastes it away. All he owns is a sword, forged by himself. Let the sword support his oath. He offers it – with himself – as Gunther's ally.

Hagen asks about the Nibelung treasure. Rumour has it that Siegfried is the master of that? Siegfried replies that he had almost forgotten the treasure; that's how little it means to him. He left it lying in a cave where a dragon used to guard it. Hagen asks if he took anything away. Siegfried points to the metalwork hanging from his belt. He doesn't know what it's for. Hagen recognises it as the Tarnhelm, the most skilful piece of the Nibelung's work. When worn on the head, it will change the wearer into any shape. If you hanker for some distant spot, it will take you there in a twinkling. Had Siegfried taken anything else from the treasure?

'A ring', says Siegfried. Hagen asks if he has kept it safe. Siegfried replies that a marvellous woman is keeping it. Hagen realises at once that he means Brünnhilde. Gunther says that Siegfried need not give him anything. For his part, he would be giving Siegfried only a trifle if he exchanged all his possessions for the Tarnhelm. Out of friendship he freely serves him.

Gutrune comes from her room, holding a filled drinking horn. She takes it to Siegfried and welcomes him as a guest in Gibich's house, whose daughter offers him this drink. Siegfried takes the drinking horn and holds it aloft. He says to himself that if he forgot everything that he had been taught, one lesson he would never forget. This drink is offered to Brünnhilde, his true love.

He takes a long drink and returns the horn to Gutrune who lowers her eyes in embarrassment and confusion.

Siegfried fixes his gaze upon the woman, with increasing desire. He says that, as if by lightning, she had burned his sight. Why does she lower her eyes in front of him? Gutrune, blushing, lifts her eyes to meet his. He calls her the loveliest woman and says that she should close her eyes, since their beams are burning his heart. He feels rivers of flame scorching and consuming his blood.

Siegfried asks Gunther for his sister's name and is told that she is called Gutrune. He wonders if he can read good omens (gute Runen) in her eyes. He takes Gutrune by the hand and says that he offered to serve her brother who could not bring himself to accept. Would she take him seriously if he offered himself to her in marriage?

Gutrune involuntarily catches Hagen's eye. She bows her head modestly and leaves the room. Siegfried, closely watched by the others, follows her with his eyes as if bewitched.

Siegfried asks if Gunther has a wife, and Gunther replies that he is not married yet and is unlikely to find the one he has his heart set on. He has no means of winning her. Siegfried asks if there is anything Gunther could not have if Siegfried helped him?

Gunther explains that her home is high on a rock. Siegfried is astonished and repeats: '... her home is high on a rock?' Gunther adds that a fire blazes round her dwelling, and again Siegfried repeats: '... a fire blazes round her dwelling?' Gunther says that only by going through the fire (Siegfried, makes strenuous efforts to retain a memory) can a man be Brünnhilde's suitor. It is now clear from Siegfried's expression that Brünnhilde's name means nothing to him.

Gunther says that he can never climb the rock, for the fire will never die down for him. Siegfried replies that he is not afraid of fire. He will win the woman for Gunther, for he is Gunther's man and his courage is for him if Siegfried can have Gutrune as his wife. Gunther says he would gladly give him Gutrune, to which Siegfried replies that he will bring Brünnhilde. Gunther asks how she would be tricked. Siegfried explains that he'll do it by the magic of the Tarnhelm and will disguise himself as Gunther. Gunther then suggests that they swear an oath, and Siegfried replies that it should be an oath of blood-brotherhood.

Hagen fills a drinking horn with new wine and holds it out to Siegfried and Gunther who prick their arms with their swords and hold them for a short time over the mouth of the drinking horn. They each place two fingers on the horn that Hagen holds between them.

Siegfried says that life is burgeoning through the refreshing blood he has dropped into this drink. Gunther adds that their blood, boldly mixed in brotherly love, will flourish in the drink.

They drink loyalty to one another and proclaim that their bond will grow happily and free on this day of blood-brotherhood.

Gunther says that if a brother breaks his oath ... Siegfried adds that if a friend betrays his trust ... both swear that the drops that today have been solemnly drunk, will flow in streams as atonement to a friend.

Gunther drinks and hands the horn to Siegfried and thus, each accepts the oath.

Siegfried holds out the empty horn to Hagen, who cuts it in two with his sword. Gunther and Siegfried clasp hands.

Siegfried asks Hagen why he didn't take part in the oath. Hagen responds that his blood would spoil the drink; it doesn't flow pure and noble like Siegfried's. It is obstinate and cold and lies stagnant inside him. It won't even redden his cheeks. That's why he steers clear of hot-blooded promises.

Gunther tells Siegfried to leave the unhappy fellow alone. Siegfried suggests that they be off on their journey; his boat will take them quickly to the rock. He tells Gunther that he must spend one night by the riverbank, with the boat. Then he will be able to bring home his wife. Gunther asks if he wants to rest first but Siegfried replies that he's in a hurry to return here. Gunther tells Hagen to guard the hall.

Gutrune appears and asks where the other two are hurrying. Hagen says they are sailing off to court Brünnhilde. Gutrune is surprised, and Hagen tells her that Siegfried is in a hurry to have Gutrune for his wife. This prospect makes her very excited and she returns to her room.

Alone and motionless, Hagen leans against the doorpost of the hall. There he sits on watch, he says, guarding the house, defending the hall against enemies. For Gibich's son, the wind is blowing and he has gone courting. His tiller is guided by a strong hero who will face danger for him. His own bride he will bring back to the Rhine, but for Hagen he'll bring the ring. These sons of freedom, happy companions, sail away cheerfully. Though they think him inferior, they'll eventually serve him – the Nibelung's son.

The curtain falls, and when it rises again we see the summit of the rock, as in the prologue. Brünnhilde is gazing at Siegfried's ring in silent thought. Overwhelmed with happy memories she covers the ring with kisses. Distant thunder is heard. She looks up and listens and then looks down at the ring again. A flash of lightning. Again she listens and peers into the distance.

She notes a familiar, distant sound. A winged horse is coming here, travelling stormily through the clouds to the rock. Who is seeking her out in her solitude? From far away comes Waltraute's voice, calling her sister, asking if she is asleep or awake. Brünnhilde recognises her voice and anticipates happy news. She calls to her, directing her to this familiar place. She urges her to dismount and let her horse rest. Excitedly she asks if Waltraute is so brave that, fearlessly, she can bring greetings to Brünnhilde.

Waltraute replies that it is only for Brünnhilde's sake that she has hurried here. Her sister asks if she has dared, for Brünnhilde's sake, to break Battle Father's orders. She asks if Wotan's enmity has faded. When she had disobeyed the god and protected Siegmund by her action, she knew that she still fulfilled his wishes. She knows too that his anger has abated, for he put her here to sleep, imprisoned on this rock – left to a passing man who would find her and wake her. Yet he granted her anxious plea. He surrounded the rock with a scorching fire that barred the way of cowards. Her sentence had brought her happiness when the most marvellous hero won her for his wife. Today she is beaming and laughing in his love.

Brünnhilde asks if her fate had enticed Waltraute; did she want to see for herself her delight, and share what had happened to her? Vehemently, Waltraute asks why she would want to share the hysteria that has seized Brünnhilde. Something else had moved her, in fear, to break Wotan's command.

Brünnhilde asks if anxiety and fear hold her dear sister captive? Has Wotan not regretted his sternness? Is she afraid of his vengeful rage? Waltraute replies that if she could still fear his rage, she would have nothing else to fear. Brünnhilde is astounded and doesn't understand.

Waltraute tells her to control her excitement and listen carefully. Her fear drives her back to Valhalla just as, from Valhalla, it had driven her here. Shocked, Brünnhilde asks what is happening with the immortal gods.

Again, Waltraute tells her to listen clearly to what she tells her. Since Wotan had farewelled Brünnhilde, he has no longer sent the Valkyries into battle. Randomly and chaotically, they had ridden anxiously to war. The brave heroes in Valhalla were ignored by War Father. All alone on his horse, and without rest, he roved around the world as the Wanderer. Not long ago he had come home, holding the fragments of his spear that had been shattered by a hero. Without explanation, the noble ones of Valhalla were sent by him to the forest to cut down the world ash. The logs from the tree he had piled up into an enormous heap around the hall of the blessed. He sent for the council of the gods and took his seat on the throne. He told them to sit, in their fear, at his side. The heroes filled the hall in a great circle. And so he sits on his majestic throne, speaking not a word, silent and grave, with the remains of his spear grasped in his hand. He will not touch Holda's apples. Astonishment and fear overwhelm the motionless gods. His two ravens he has sent off. If ever they return with good news then, for one last time in eternity, the god will smile. The Valkyries lie, clasping his knees. He remains blind to their weeping glances. They are consumed with fear and unending anxiety. Waltraute had clung to his breast, weeping, and then his eyes softened and he thought of Brünnhilde. He sighed deeply and closed his eyes and, as if he were dreaming, he whispered the words: 'If she would give back the ring to the Rhinedaughters in the depths, the gods and the world would be saved from the weight of the curse.'

Waltraute continues that she had thought about this and had stolen out from his side through the silent ranks. Secretly and hurriedly she mounted her horse and rode in haste to Brünnhilde. She beseeches her sister to carry out the deed – to have the courage to do it and put an end to this eternal misery.

Quietly, Brünnhilde says that Waltraute is relating such dreams of anxiety. She, Brünnhilde, is separated in her folly from the gods in their cloudy heaven. She doesn't understand what she is being told. Waltraute's story seems confused and meaningless to her. Flickering fires glow in her sister's tired eyes. What does her pale-cheeked sister want of her? Waltraute anxiously and hurriedly points to the ring on Brünnhilde's hand and urges her, for Wotan's sake, to throw it away.

Brünnhilde reacts in astonishment. Waltraute implores her to give the ring back to the Rhinedaughters. Brünnhilde says she must be mad to think that she will give the ring – Siegfried's pledge of love – to the Rhinedaughters.

Waltraute asks her to listen to her fears, since the sorrows of the world are certainly caused by the ring. Brünnhilde should throw it away – away in the water. To end Valhalla's misery, she must throw the accursed ring in the river.

Brünnhilde asks if she knows what the ring means to her. How can such an unfeeling girl understand? The ring means more to her than the joys of Valhalla, more than the glory of the gods. One glance at its bright gold, one gleam from its majestic brightness, means more to her than all the gods and their everlasting happiness. From it, Siegfried's love shines on her like paradise. Siegfried's love! If she could just explain that joy. This is what the ring means to her. Waltraute should go back to the gods and their secret assembly; she should tell them about her ring. Brünnhilde will never give it up. They won't take love from her, even if the radiant splendour of Valhalla itself collapses in ruins.

Waltraute asks if this is her loyalty – to abandon her sister in lovelessness and mourning.

Brünnhilde tells her to fly away on her horse. She won't take the ring from her.

Waltraute can only exclaim in despair that her sister is doomed and Valhalla's gods are doomed. She hurries away.

A thundercloud in a storm soon rises out of the forest. Brünnhilde watches the brightly flashing cloud as it disappears in the distance. For her, clouds and lightning, carried on the wind, should be off and not come her way again.

Evening has fallen. From below, the firelight begins to shine more brightly. Brünnhilde looks calmly out over the landscape, noting the evening twilight filling the sky and the guardian fire, shining more brightly.

The firelight comes nearer and tongues of flame dart up over the edge of the rock. She wonders why the defensive wave of flame darts so angrily. The fiery tide is rolling up to the summit of the rock. A horn-call is heard in the distance. Brünnhilde listens and jumps up ecstatically. Siegfried has returned! He's playing her his call. She must meet him and fall into the arms of her god!

In the greatest excitement she runs to the edge of the cliff. Flames rise up. Siegfried jumps up out of them onto a high rock. At this the flames fall back at once and flare only in the valley. Brünnhilde shrinks back in terror and looks with speechless astonishment at Siegfried. He is disguised as Gunther. The Tarnhelm is on his head, covering the top half of his face leaving only his eyes visible.

A shocked Brünnhilde cries out that she is betrayed. Who has forced his way to her?

Siegfried looks at Brünnhilde and says in a deep voice: *Brünnhilde! A suitor has come who did not fear your fire. Now I have won you for my wife. You must follow me.*

Trembling violently, Brünnhilde asks who is this man who can match a champion? Siegfried replies that he is a hero who will tame her if she resists.

Seized with fear, Brünnhilde says that a demon has taken control of the rock. A bird of prey has flown down to devour her. Who is this frightening man? Is he human, or does he come from Hell's hosts of night?

Siegfried replies that he is a Gibichung, and Gunther is the name of the hero whom she must follow.

Brünnhilde, breaking out in despair, cries that Wotan is an angry, cruel god. Now she sees the meaning of her punishment. He has banished her to mockery and wretchedness. Siegfried comes closer to her and says that night is falling. In her cave she must be married to him. Brünnhilde threatens him with Siegfried's ring, commanding him to stand back for this is a symbol to fear. He cannot force her into disgrace as long as the ring protects her.

Siegfried says that by conjugal right, the ring must be given to Gunther. With this ring she will be married to him.

Brünnhilde calls him a robber, a villainous thief, and tells him to get back. He wouldn't dare to come near her; the ring makes her stronger than steel and he shall never take it from her. Siegfried replies that she can now teach him how to take it from her.

He hurls himself at her. They struggle. Brünnhilde escapes and turns round to defend herself. Again, Sigfried seizes her. He grips her by the hand and removes the ring from her finger. Brünnhilde gives a piercing cry and, as if crushed, falls into his arms. Her eyes unconsciously meet Siegfried's. He lets her limp body sink onto the stone in front of the cave.

Now she is his, says Siegfried. Brünnhilde, Gunther's bride, must give him the use of her chamber. Exhausted, she asks herself how such a wretched woman could prevent it. As she goes into the cave, Siegfried draws his sword and, in his own voice, invokes *Notung* to bear witness that he woos honourably. Keeping him true to his brother, the sword will separate him from his bride.

Act II

The shore in front of the Gibichung hall. It is night. Hagen sits leaning against one of the columns, fast asleep, with his spear on his arm. The moon suddenly comes out and illuminates Hagen and his immediate surroundings. Alberich is now visible, crouching in front, his arms supported on Hagen's knees.

Softly, Alberich asks if Hagen, his son, is sleeping. Does he sleep and not hear him who has been betrayed by rest and sleep? Hagen, motionless and evidently still asleep, although his eyes are open, replies that he hears the crafty dwarf. What does he have to say to his sleep?

Alberich tells him to remember the power he controls if he is as brave as the mother who bore him. Hagen replies that if his mother gave him courage, he is not inclined to thank her for yielding to Alberich's trickery. Aged before his years, sallow and pale, Hagen hates happy people; he is never glad.

Alberich tells his son to hate happy people. Alberich is joyless and burdened with sorrow, so Hagen will love him as he should. If he is strong, bold and cunning, those whom they fight in nocturnal battles will know the distress that comes from hate. Wotan the treacherous robber, the one who stole his ring, was defeated by his own offspring. He lost his power and authority to the Volsung and, with all the company of gods, fearfully anticipates his downfall. Alberich is no longer afraid of him. He must fall with the rest.

Alberich asks again if his son is asleep? Hagen asks who will inherit the power of the immortals? His father replies: 'I, and you!' Together they will inherit the world if he is not mistaken about Hagen's loyalty – if he shares his father's misery and rage. Wotan's spear was shattered by the Volsung who killed Fafner the dragon in battle and innocently claimed the ring. He created his own authority. Both Valhalla and Nibelheim bow before him. That fearless hero even neutralised Alberich's curse, for he has no idea of the ring's value. He makes no use of its power. He is burning away his life, laughing in the fires of love. The solution is to destroy him. Is Hagen, his son, listening?

Hagen replies that the hero is now on his way to destruction by serving him. Alberich insists that they must get the golden ring. A clever woman lives for the Volsung's love. If she ever advised him to go to the Rhinedaughters (who once beguiled Alberich in the watery depths) and give back the ring, the gold would be lost and no cunning would ever get it back. So Hagen must not delay; he must work to get the ring. He was bred for this purpose, to stand firm fighting heroes. Admittedly, he was not strong enough to confront the dragon – that was only granted to the Volsung – but Hagen was raised for fierce hatred. Now he'll avenge Alberich, win the ring and subject Wotan and the Volsung to derision. Hagen must swear that he will do this.

Hagen replies that he will have the ring. His father should rest and wait. Once again, Alberich asks him to swear that he will do it. The son replies that he has sworn it for himself; his father should stop fretting. Alberich reminds Hagen – son and beloved hero – to be faithful. Slowly, Alberich disappears from sight.

Hagen, who has remained unchanged in his place, gazes motionless at the Rhine, over which dawn light is beginning to spread. Gradually, the river glows more and more brightly with dawn colours. Hagen gives a start as Siegfried appears suddenly from behind a bush by the riverbank. He is in his own form, though the Tarnhelm is still on his head. He removes it as he walks forward.

Siegfried greets Hagen, who has begun to stir, and asks if he saw him coming. Hagen welcomes the speedy hero and asks where he has hurried from. Siegfried replies that he has come from Brünnhilde's rock. The breath he had used to hail Hagen had been inhaled there, so fast was his journey. The other two are following more slowly by boat.

Hagen asks if he overcame Brünnhilde, but Siegfried in turn

asks if Gutrune is awake. Hagen calls into the hall for Gutrune and tells her that Siegfried is here, why is she lingering indoors? Siegfried says he will tell them both how he overpowered Brünnhilde. Gutrune comes out of the hall and Siegfried asks her for a welcome. He has good news for her. She invokes Freia to welcome him in the name of all women. Siegfried asks her to be generous and kind to him, for he is happy. Today he has won her as his wife.

Gutrune asks if Brünnhilde is following with her brother. Siegfried replies that the woman was easily made Gunther's. Why didn't the fire burn him, wonders Gutrune. It wouldn't have hurt him says Siegfried but he, Siegfried, had gone through the flames instead because he wanted to win Gutrune. She asks if the fire spared him, to which Siegfried replies that he enjoyed the roaring blaze. Gutrune asks if Brünnhilde mistook him for Gunther. Siegfried replies that he resembled him to the last hair. The Tarnhelm did it, as Hagen had thoughtfully suggested. Hagen acknowledges that he gave good advice.

Gutrune asks if Siegfried mastered the bold woman, to which he replies that she capitulated to Gunther's strength. 'And was she married to you?' asks Gutrune. Siegfried says that Brünnhilde submitted to her husband for her whole wedding night. Gutrune notes that it was Siegfried who stood in for her husband. Siegfried stayed with Gutrune, he says. 'Wasn't Brünnhilde beside you?' asks Gutrune. Siegfried replies that between east and west is north. Brünnhilde was so near and so far.

Gutrune asks how Gunther acquired Brünnhilde from Siegfried. The hero replies that, at dawn, she followed him through the fire's dying flames, down the misty rock to the valley. When they reached the shore, Gunther changed places with him and, using the Tarnhelm, Siegfried quickly wished himself here. Now a strong breeze is blowing the lovers up the Rhine. She should get ready now to receive them. Gutrune confides that she is frightened of Siegfried – he is such a strong man.

Hagen reports that he sees a sail in the distance. Siegfried suggests that some thanks for the messenger wouldn't go amiss. Gutrune proposes a grand welcome for Brünnhilde, to make her glad and happy to live here. She asks Hagen to call out the men for the wedding at Gibich's court. The women will be delighted. She'll call them to the feast – they'll gladly attend her in her happiness. She asks Siegfried if the fearsome hero would like to rest. He replies that helping her is all the rest he needs.

Hagen summons the men of Gibich. He tells them to stir themselves – danger's at hand! He calls them and the whole country to arms. He tells them to bring good weapons, strong weapons, sharpened for battle. There is a crisis! Crisis and danger!

The men ask why the signal is being sounded. Why are forces being called out? They've come armed. They've come with weapons. What's the crisis? What enemy is coming? Who's attacking them? Is Gunther in danger? They've come armed with sharp weapons.

Hagen tells them not to delay in arming themselves. They must give Gunther a warm reception – he's taken a wife!

The men ask if danger is threatening Gunther – is an enemy following him? Hagen replies that he's bringing home a proudly independent wife.

Is her family in pursuit with a hostile force, the men ask. Hagen says no one's following Gunther, he's a solitary traveller. The men ask if he overcame the danger, did he win the battle? Hagen says the dragon-killer overcame the danger; Siegfried the hero saw to Gunther's safety.

The men ask how can his forces help him? Hagen tells them to slaughter sturdy bulls. The altar should run with their blood for Wotan.

They ask what he wants them to do then. He says they should kill a boar for Froh, and a full-grown goat for Donner. But sheep must be killed for Fricka so that she'll bless the marriage.

Amusement spreads amongst the men as they ask what they should do after they've killed these animals? He tells them to take their drinking horns and let their dear wives fetch mead and wine and fill them cheerfully.

The men ask how they should behave when the drinking horns are in their hands. Hagen tells them to keep drinking until drunkenness tames them, in honour of all the gods who must grant a good marriage.

They burst out in peals of laughter. Good luck and health will prevail along the Rhine if fierce Hagen can be so cheerful. The hawthorn (Hage-Dorn) doesn't prick any more; he's been promoted to proclaimer of weddings!

Hagen joins the men. After a while he tells them they've laughed enough. They must give Gunther's bride a welcome. Here comes Gunther with Brünnhilde. The men must be kind to their mistress and loyal in their support. If she is wronged, they must be quick to avenge her.

The men greet and welcome Gunther and his bride.

Gunther presents Brünnhilde to his men. She follows him – pale and with downcast eyes. He describes her as the most noble of women, brought up the Rhine to his people. Nobody ever won a more noble wife. She has been given to the Gibichungs by the grace of the gods, and now his race will attain the height of its fame. The men revel in this good fortune for the Gibichungs.

Gunther greets the hero Siegfried and his own beloved sister. He says he is happy to see her at the side of the man who won her as wife. There are two happy couples looking so radiant: Brünnhilde and Gunther, Gutrune and Siegfried.

Brünnhilde looks up in astonishment and sees Siegfried. She remains looking at him in amazement. Gunther lets go of her hand when she pulls away, and looks bewildered at Brünnhilde's behaviour. The men and women wonder what is wrong with her. Has she become deranged?

Siegfried calmly takes a few steps towards Brünnhilde and asks why she looks upset. She can only stammer: 'Siegfried – here? Gutrune?' Siegfried explains that Gutrune is Gunther's gentle sister, married to him, as Brünnhilde is married to Gunther.

Brünnhilde retorts that he is a liar in saying that she is married to Gunther. She staggers and seems likely to faint. Siegfried holds her up. Her eyes grow dim – she can't understand why Siegfried doesn't recognise her. Siegfried remarks to Gunther that his wife is unwell. Gunther tells her to pull herself together – here stands her bridegroom.

Brünnhilde sees the ring on Siegfried's outstretched finger and reacts terribly, pointing to the ring on his hand and repeating his name. The men and women wonder what she means. Hagen moves among the men, telling them to note carefully what the woman is complaining about.

Brünnhilde tries to pull herself together and says that she saw a ring on Siegfried's hand. It doesn't belong to him. It was snatched from her by another man – she points to Gunther. She asks how Siegfried was able to get the ring from him.

Siegfried looks carefully at the ring on his finger and says that he won the ring, but not from Gunther. Brünnhilde turns to Gunther and insists that he took the ring from her when he wedded her. He should demand what is his and ask for the return of this pledge. Gunther, in great confusion, replies that he didn't give Siegfried the ring – but does Brünnhilde recognise it? She asks where he had hidden the ring that he seized from her. Gunther, deeply embarrassed, remains silent.

Brünnhilde bursts out in anger that it was this man (pointing to Siegfried) who snatched the ring from her. Siegfried is a despicable thief.

Everyone looks at Siegfried, who is lost in his own thoughts as he contemplates the ring. He says that no woman gave him the ring, nor was it from a woman that he first obtained it. He recognises it perfectly. It was the prize he had won from his fight at the Cave of Envy, when he slew a monstrous dragon.

Hagen steps between them and asks Brünnhilde if she truly recognises the ring. If it is the one she gave Gunther, then it belongs to him, and Siegfried obtained it by a trick. He must pay for such disloyalty.

Brünnhilde, in grief, cries that there has been appalling deceit – a treachery that demands unparalleled revenge! 'Treachery? To whom?' asks Gutrune, and the men and women echo her question.

Brünnhilde invokes the sacred gods, heavenly rulers. Was this part of their plan? Did they want her to suffer as no one has ever suffered? Did they plan a disgrace for her such as no one has ever borne? Then they must help her in revenge without equal, kindle in her an anger that never abates. They should make Brünnhilde break her heart if that will also destroy the man who betrayed her.

Gunther implores his wife to control herself but she calls him a traitor, and drives him away. He has betrayed himself. She announces that she is not married to Gunther but to the other man. The astonished men and women cannot believe that she means Siegfried, Gutrune's husband. Brünnhilde says that he was the one who had drawn love and desire from her.

Siegfried asks if this is how she values her self-respect. Must he accuse of lying, the tongue that does her such a disservice? The others can judge whether he broke faith. He swore blood-brotherhood with Gunther and *Notung*, his worthy sword, guarded that oath of loyalty. Its blade separated him from this wretched woman.

Brünnhilde replies that he is devious and lying and is falsely calling his sword to witness. She knows its sharpness well and she also knows the sheath in which it lay so peacefully against the wall – *Notung*, the true friend when its master was wed to his beloved.

The men and women wonder whether Siegfried had broken faith. Had he sullied Gunther's honour?

Gunther tells Siegfried that he will be disgraced and dealt with shamefully if Siegfried does not contradict her.

Gutrune asks Siegfried if he had been disloyal. Could he contemplate cheating? He should prove that this woman accuses him falsely.

The men tell him to clear himself if he is in the right, and silence her accusations. He should swear an oath.

Siegfried replies that if he were to silence her accusations and swear an oath, who would dare to offer his weapon for it?

Hagen offers the point of his spear, to defend the oath with honour.

The men form a circle round Siegfried and Hagen. Hagen holds out his spear and Siegfred puts two fingers of his right hand on the blade. He addresses the spear as shining spear, holy weapon, and calls on it to endorse his binding oath. He makes the oath on the spear point. Where sharpness can pierce him let it pierce him, where death may strike him let it strike him if the woman accuses him justly – if he broke faith with his brother.

In a rage, Brünnhilde bursts into the circle, tears Siegfried's hand away from the spear and places her own on its point. She calls on the shining spear, holy weapon, to endorse her binding oath. She makes her oath on the spear point, dedicating it to striking him down. She blesses its sharpness that will pierce him, for this man breaks every vow and has perjured himself.

The men call on Donner to help them, to pour down his storms and silence this monstrous disgrace.

Siegfried tells Gunther to be careful with his wife. She is a shameful, disgraceful liar. She is a wild mountain woman who needs time and rest. That may calm her wild rage. Some mischievous plot has focussed her rage on them all. The men should go home and forget squabbling women. It is a relief to make a cowardly retreat when tongues wage war. He tells Gunther that he is annoyed with himself that his deception on the rock was imperfect. He can but conclude that the Tarnhelm only half disguised him. Nevertheless, he says that angry women are soon calmed down and Gunther's wife will soon be grateful that she had been won for him.

He tells the men to be cheerful and follow him in to the banquet. He asks the women to enjoy the wedding and lend a hand. They should delight in laughter. In the hall and in the fields he will be cheerful in front of them all today. If they celebrate love, his happy heart must make them happy too.

Relaxed and confident, Siegfried takes Gutrune by the arm and leads her into the hall. The men and women follow his example. The stage is empty except for Brünnhilde, Gunther and Hagen. Gunther, deeply ashamed and confused, sits down at one side and hides his face.

Brünnhilde gazes sadly at Siegfried and Gutrune for some time and then asks herself what mischievous cunning is hidden here; what sorcerer's plan has stirred things up. Where will she find the wisdom to deal with this mystery? Where are her spells to undo this riddle? Everything is misery and disaster. She has passed all her knowledge to him. He holds her powerfully in his clutches and clasps his prey. Although she laments in disgrace, he is rich now and cheerfully abandons her. Who can offer her a sword with which to cut these shackles?

Hagen comes right up to Brünnhilde and tells her to trust him. She is a cheated woman and he will take vengeance on the betrayer. 'On whom?' asks Brünnhilde. 'On Siegfried who betrayed you', comes the reply. Brünnhilde laughs bitterly. One look from his flashing eyes – as fell on her, from his deceiving shape on the rock – would turn Hagen's greatest courage to fear.

Hagen asks whether, even so, he should withhold his spear from this perjurer? Brünnhilde says that oaths and perjury are not worth bothering about. Hagen should look for something stronger on which to sharpen his spear if he is to defeat that champion. He replies that, of course, he knows Siegfried's conquering strength that makes him hard to kill in battle. Brünnhilde must give him expert advice on how to overcome the hero.

Brünnhilde laments her thankless, shameless reward. There is no skill known to her that has not protected his body. Unknowingly, he was subdued by the magic that now protects him from wounds. Hagen asks if there is no weapon that can hurt him? 'Not in battle' she replies. But if he is struck in the back … She knew he would never turn it to an enemy, run away and bare his back, and so there she withheld her spells. There, Hagen decides, his spear will strike. He turns to Gunther, urging him to stand up. Here stands his brave wife – why is a noble Gibichung wallowing in misery?

Gunther is overwhelmed by a sense of his disgrace and shame. He is doomed and the most wretched of all men. Hagen says he cannot deny that Gunther is disgraced.

Brünnhilde calls Gunther a coward and a false companion. He had hidden himself behind the hero who would pay the price of fame for him. His family had sunk to the very bottom when it sired such a coward.

Beside himself with despair, Gunther says that he cheated and was cheated; betrayed and is betrayed. His bones should be crushed and his heart broken. He implores Hagen to help him, help his honour, and help the mother who had borne them both.

Hagen replies that no brain can help him; neither can any hand. Their only hope is – Siegfried's death.

Gripped with fear, Gunther repeats: 'Siegfried's death'.

Hagen says that this alone will compensate for Gunther's disgrace. Gunther recalls that they had sworn blood-brotherhood together, and Hagen says that the breaking of that oath must be atoned in blood. 'Did he break the oath?' asks Gunther. 'Yes' replies Hagen, 'when he cheated you'. 'Did he cheat me?' asks Gunther.

Brünnhilde responds that Siegfried had cheated him and they had all cheated her. If she had what was owed to her, all the blood in the world wouldn't wipe out their guilt. But this one death will suffice for everything. Siegfried shall die to atone for himself and for the others.

Hagen tells Gunther that Siegfried shall die to save him. Gunther will have enormous power if he obtains the ring, and death alone will enable him to take it. Gunther doesn't understand. Brünnhilde's ring? Hagen explains that it is the Nibelung's ring. With a heavy sigh, Gunther agrees that Siegfried must meet his end. Hagen assures them that his death will benefit them all.

Gunther then remembers Gutrune, to whom he had given Siegfried. If they punish her husband like this, how would they justify themselves to her? Brünnhilde springs up with rage. What did her wisdom tell her? What good were her runes? In her helpless misery she now understands that Gutrune is the sorcerer who enticed her husband away. May terror strike her!

Hagen tells Gunther that since Siegfried's death will make Gutrune sad, the deed should be hidden from her. They will set off tomorrow on a hunting party. The noble man will hurry ahead and a boar will kill him. Gunther and Brünnhilde agree – Siegfried shall fall! He will pay for the disgrace brought on them. He has betrayed the oath of loyalty and he will atone with his blood. All-guiding, avenging god! Sharer of promises, guardian of oaths – Wotan – look down on them. Tell the divine hosts to listen to this oath of vengeance.

Hagen too declares that the radiant hero shall die. The treasure is Hagen's – it must belong to him – and so the ring shall be torn from Siegfried. The elf-father, fallen prince, Guardian of Night! Lord of the Nibelungs – Alberich – should listen, and once again command the Nibelung hosts to obey him as master of the ring!

As Gunther turns towards the hall with Brünnhilde, they are confronted by a bridal procession coming out. Siegfried and the men blow the wedding-call on their horns. The women invite Brünnhilde to join them and Gutrune beckons her with a friendly smile. When Brünnhilde tries to move away Hagen stands in her path and Gunther once again takes her hand. As the procession moves towards the heights, the curtain falls.

Act III

A wild woodland and rocky valley through which the Rhine flows. The three Rhinedaughters surface and are seen swimming in circles.

Woglinde, Wellgunde and Flosshilde cease their swimming and observe that Dame Sun pours down her beams of light. Night now lies in the depths. Once they were bright when, safe and majestic, their father's gold glistened there. Rhinegold, shining gold, how brightly it gleamed then – the noble star of the deep.

They resume their singing until there is a distant horn call. They listen and then splash delightedly about in the water. They ask Dame Sun to send them a hero who'll give them back the gold. If he lets them have it, they'll no longer envy the sun's bright eyes. Rhinegold – bright gold – how happily it would gleam then, the liberated star of the deep.

Siegfried's horn is heard. The Rhinedaughters welcome his coming and make their plan. They dive down quickly as Siegfried appears on the cliff. He says that some goblin had led him astray and he's lost the path. He calls to the scoundrel to tell him in which mountain he had hidden his quarry. The three Rhinedaughters surface again and call Siegfried's name. They ask what he's grumbling about. What elf is he cross with? Has some sprite been teasing him?

Siegfried asks them if they have enticed his missing shaggy companion into their midst. If he were their sweetheart Siegfried would gladly leave him to them. The Rhinedaughters laugh loudly.

Woglinde asks Siegfried what he would give them if they revealed his quarry. He replies that he hasn't caught a thing, so they could name their price. Wellgunde notes that a golden ring is glinting on his finger. All three ask him to give it to them. He replies that he had slain a monstrous dragon for this ring. Must he now exchange it for a wretched bearskin?

The Rheindaughters accuse him of being mean and stingy when he's out shopping. They tell him he should be generous to women. Siegfried says that if he wastes his possessions on them his wife would surely scold him. She must be strict then? Does she beat him? Perhaps the hero already feels her hand! They roar with laughter.

Siegfried tells them to go on laughing; he'll leave them miserable. Even if they crave the ring, he'll never give it to them. The Rhinedaughters think him so handsome, so strong, so desirable! It's a pity he's so stingy! They laugh and dive down again.

Siegfried climbs down towards the water's edge and wonders how he can put up with their grudging compliments. Should he let himself be so insulted? If they came back they could have the ring. He calls out to them to come quickly and he'll give them the ring. He takes it off his finger and holds it aloft.

The three Rhinedaughters surface again. They look serious and solemn. They tell the hero to keep the ring and look after it well until he knows the peril of having it. Then he'll be pleased to let them free him from its curse.

Siegfried calmly puts the ring back on his finger and tells them to reveal what they know. They say that they know of an evil in store for him. He keeps the ring at his peril. It was fashioned from the gold of the Rhine. The one who cleverly forged it and shamefully lost it had put a curse on it that forever brings death to anyone who wears it. Just as Siegfried killed the dragon, so he will be killed too – this day in fact. They can tell him that much if he doesn't give the ring to them, to hide deep down in the Rhine. Only the stream can purge the curse!

Siegfried tells them they are cunning women and should leave him alone! He wasn't persuaded by their flattery and their threats impress him even less.

The Rhinedaughters say that they are speaking the truth. He should beware of the curse that is entwined each night by the Norns, who weave the rope of primeval law. Siegfried tells them that his sword severed a spear and will sever the Norns' primeval law and its unending rope if they weave wild curses into it. It's true he was once warned of a curse by a dragon who had been unable to teach him to fear it. Ownership of the world he had won with the ring. He'd give it up gladly for the gift of love; he'd give it to the Rhinedaughters if they would let him make love to them. But by threatening his life and limb – though worth less than a finger to him – they wouldn't get the ring. As for life and limb, he throws these away as easily as he throws a clod of earth behind him. He picks up a clod of earth from the ground, holds it above his head and tosses it behind him.

The Rhinedaughters decide to leave this fool. The hero thinks himself wise and strong although he behaves like a captive and a blind man. He swore oaths and does not keep them. He knows mysteries and pays no heed to them. A glorious possession was granted to him and he doesn't even realise that he threw it away. He wants to keep only the ring – the ring that condemns him to death. They bid Siegfried farewell and tell him that a splendid woman will today become his heir. She will give them a better hearing. They'll go to her. And with that, they swim leisurely out of sight.

Siegfried tells himself that in the water, as on land, he's learned what women are like. When their flattery doesn't have the desired effect, they'll resort to threats. Anyone who boldly defies them is met by abuse. And yet – if it weren't for Gutrune's trust in him, he could easily have seduced one of those desirable women.

He gazes after them. The Rhinedaughters are heard from far away. From up above, hunting horns sound. They come closer and closer.

Hagen's voice is heard and Siegfried answers him. The men also call from the forest. Hagen appears with Gunther behind him. Hagen sees Siegfried and says that at last they had discovered where he'd got to. Siegfried tells them to come down. It's airy and cool by the river. Hagen decides they should rest there and prepare their meal. He tells them to put down the day's bag and bring out the wineskins. Siegfried had scared the game away, so they'll have to make do with stories of his hunting successes.

Siegfried laughs and says he is ill prepared for a meal and will have to beg some of their food. 'You killed nothing?' asks Hagen. Siegfried replies that he went hunting for forest game but found only waterfowl instead. If he'd been properly warned in advance, three wild waterbirds would have been in his bag. There, by the Rhine, they had told him he would be murdered today. Hagen says that it would indeed be a poor hunt if a hunter with no catch were to be killed by his lurking prey.

Siegfried says that he's thirsty. Hagen has a drinking horn filled and offers it to him. He says he has heard that Siegfried understands the language of birdsong. Is that true?

Siegfried replies that it has been a long time since he paid attention to their twittering. He takes the drinking horn and turns to Gunther. After drinking, he offers the horn to Gunther, telling him to drink – his brother offers it to him. Gunther looks thoughtfully and gloomily into the horn and says that the liquid is thin and pale; Siegfried's blood is all that he sees in it. Siegfried laughs and says that he'll mix it then with Gunther's. He pours Gunther's drink into his own horn so that it overflows. He remarks that the mixture has spilled over as refreshment for Mother Earth.

Gunther says that the hero is much too happy. Siegfried asks Hagen if Brünnhilde is giving trouble, to which Hagen replies that he wished Gunther understood her as well as Siegfried understands birdsong. Siegfried replies that since he has heard the song of women he has quite forgotten the song of birds. 'But you did understand them once?' asks Hagen.

Siegfried turns in lively fashion to Gunther, the miserable man, asking if it would cheer him up to hear some stories of his boyhood. Gunther replies that he would, and Hagen urges Siegfried to commence.

Siegfried speaks of Mime, a bad-tempered dwarf. Hatred had driven him to raise Siegfried to be strong enough to kill for him a dragon that lazily guarded a treasure in the forest. He taught the boy smithing and metal smelting, but the one job the craftsman couldn't do had to be done by the bold apprentice. The fragments of a broken sword had to be worked anew into a sword. It was his father's weapon and he forged it afresh. He made *Notung* as hard as nails. The dwarf judged it fit for battle. He took the boy into the forest and there he killed Fafner the dragon. Then something strange happened. The dragon's blood burned his fingers and he put them to his mouth to cool. His tongue had hardly touched them when the birds started to sing and he immediately understood them. One sat on a branch and sang: '*Hei, Siegfried now owns the Nibelung treasure. He'll find it in the cave. If he wants to take the Tarnhelm it will help him work wonders. And if he can get the ring, that will make him master of the world*'.

Hagen interrupts to ask if he took away the ring and Tarnhelm. One of the men wants to know if he heard the bird again. Siegfried says that he picked up the ring and Tarnhelm and then listened again to that wonderful warbler. It sat in the trees and sang: '*Siegfried now has the helm and the ring. He mustn't trust Mime who is treacherous. He only wants to steal the treasure and is slyly lurking, waiting for Siegfried whose life he is after. Oh, Siegfried mustn't trust Mime'.*

Hagen interrupts again to ask if this was good advice. Another of the men asks if he settled scores with Mime. Siegfried says that Mime came to him with a poisonous drink. Fearful and stammering, he gave the game away. *Notung* dispatched the wretch!

Hagen laughs coarsely and says that what he couldn't forge, Mime could still taste! Some of the men ask what the bird said next. Hagen meanwhile has a drinking horn filled and squeezes the juice of a herb into it. He tells the hero to have a drink first from his horn; he has mixed it well for him and it will awaken his memory properly. He won't forget what's past. He hands the horn to Siegfried who looks thoughtfully into it and then drinks slowly.

Siegfried continues that he gazed again at the treetops in sorrow, and listened. There sat the bird, singing that: *'Siegfried had killed the evil dwarf and could now be told of the most marvellous woman. She is asleep high on a rock and a fire burns around her home. If he can walk through the fire and wake the bride, then Brünnhilde would be his'.*

Hagen asks if he took the bird's advice. As Gunther listens with growing amazement, Siegfried says that he set off without delay, until he reached the fiery rock. He walked through the flames and, rewarded, found a marvellous woman asleep, clothed in shining armour. He took the helmet off this glorious maiden and awoke her with a daring kiss. Oh! how he seemed to be burning as he was enfolded in the beautiful Brünnhilde's arms.

Gunther jumps to his feet, shocked by what he hears.

Two ravens fly up from a bush, circle over Siegfried's head and fly off towards the Rhine. Hagen asks Siegfried if he understands the cry of the ravens. As Siegfried jumps up and looks, he turns his back towards Hagen. 'Vengeance, they cry to me!' exclaims Hagen and plunges his spear into Siegfried's back.

Gunther, too late, pushes Hagen away. Siegfried lifts up his shield with both hands to smash down on Hagen. His strength fails him; his shield falls behind him and, with a crash, he falls back on top of it.

Four men, trying vainly to restrain Hagen, ask desperately what he's doing. Others ask what has he done! Hagen, pointing to the body prostrate on the ground, replies that he has punished perjury. He turns calmly aside and walks alone out of sight over the cliff. He is seen going slowly away through the twilight that began to fall when the ravens appeared.

Gunther bends sorrowfully over Siegfried's form while the men stand sympathetically round the dying man.

Siegfried, assisted by two men, sits up and opens his eyes radiantly. He greets Brünnhilde – holy bride – asking her to awake. Who had put her back to sleep? Who has bound her in this fearful slumber? Her awakener came and he kissed her awake, and when the bride's bonds were broken, Brünnhilde's joy smiled on him. Ah, those eyes, opened forever! Ah, that wonderful breath! Leaving is sweet, trembling blissful. Brünnhilde offers him her greeting!

He falls back and dies.

Night has fallen. At a sign from Gunther the men lift Siegfried's body onto his shield and slowly carry it in solemn procession away over the rocky heights. Gunther follows behind the corpse. The moon breaks through the clouds and illuminates the funeral procession with increasing brightness as it reaches the summit. Mists rise from the Rhine and gradually fill the whole stage. The funeral procession passes out of sight, and during the orchestral interlude the stage is completely veiled. The mists eventually disperse and gradually reveal the Gibichung palace as in Act I.

The moonlight is reflected on the Rhine. Gutrune comes out of her chamber and into the hall. She asks if that was his horn she heard. No, he still hasn't come home. Nightmares have disturbed her sleep. His horse neighed wildly. Brünnhilde's laughter had woken her. Who was the woman she saw walking to the river-bank? She is afraid of Brünnhilde but wonders if she is inside. Gutrune listens at the door and calls softly: 'Brünnhild! Brünnhild! Are you awake?' She opens the door timidly and looks into the inner room. The room is empty, so it must have been Brünnhilde whom she saw walking to the Rhine. She shudders and listens to some distant sound. Was that his horn? No, it is all deserted. If only Siegfried would come soon. She starts to go back to her chamber but hearing Hagen's voice, she pauses and stands motionless for some time, gripped with fear.

Hagen's voice comes nearer. He calls on everyone to wake up and bring bright torches; they are bringing home the spoils of the hunt! Light from glowing torches is seen outside. Hagen enters the hall. He calls to Gutrune to rise and welcome Siegfried. The mighty hero is coming home!

In great fear, Gutrune asks what's happened. She had not heard Siegfried's horn. Men and women in great confusion, with lights and flaming torches, join the men returning with Siegfried's body. Gunther is amongst them. Hagen replies that the hero is pale and can't blow his horn now. He can't go off hunting or to battle, and he can't pay court to lovely women.

With mounting horror, Gutrune asks what it is they are bring-ing. The procession halts in the centre of the hall, where the men put the corpse on a hastily erected dais. Hagen says that they have a wild boar's victim – Siegfried, Gutrune's dead husband! She shrieks and collapses onto the corpse amidst general shock and grief. Gunther attends his sister, who has fainted. He implores her to open her eyes and speak to him.

Gutrune rouses herself and confronts again the horror of Siegfried's death. She pushes Gunther violently away from her, calling him faithless brother and accusing him of murdering her husband. 'They've killed Siegfried' she cries.

Gunther tells her to direct her lament not to him but to

Hagen. He is the cursed boar who gored this noble man! Hagen asks if she is angry with him. Gutrune curses him, wishing him fear and bad luck forever!

Hagen then steps forward with terrible defiance, admitting that he had killed Siegfried. He, Hagen had struck him dead! He was stabbed with the spear on which he had perjured himself. He was Hagen's rightful victim and he has now claimed him. For this act he now demands the ring!

Gunther tells him to stand back. What had fallen to him, Hagen would never take.

Hagen calls on the men to support his action. Gunther asks if this shameless son of an elf would touch Gutrune's legacy. Hagen draws his sword and says that it is an elf's legacy and he will take it. He falls upon Gunther and they fight. The men try to separate them but Gunther is struck dead.

Hagen lunges for the ring and seizes Siegfried's hand, which raises itself menacingly. Gutrune and the women shrink back in terror.

From the background, Brünnhilde walks forward, firmly and solemnly. She tells them to cease the wailing and woeful clamour. They had all betrayed the woman who has come for her vengeance – his wife. She has heard children whining for their mothers when milk has been spilled, but not a lament befitting the noblest of heroes.

Gutrune confronts her, saying that Brünnhilde is soured by jealousy. She had brought this tragedy on them – she had turned the men against him. Woe that she had ever come near this house.

Brünnhilde replies that this poor wretch should be silent. She had never been his true wife – merely his whore. Brünnhilde is his lawful wife. Siegfried swore eternal loyalty to her long before he set eyes on Gutrune.

Breaking down in utter despair, Gutrune damns Hagen for suggesting the drug that took away her husband. Ah, what misery. Now she realises that Brünnhilde was the beloved that the drink made him forget. She turns timidly from Siegfried and bends over Gunther's body and remains there motionless until the end. Hagen stands defiantly leaning on his spear and shield, sunk in deep thought.

Brünnhilde, alone in the centre, gazes at Siegfried's face for a long time, at first profoundly shocked and then with almost overwhelming despair. Then, in solemn exaltation, she turns to the men and women. She instructs them to pile up stout logs on the banks of the Rhine. The fire on which the noble body of this great hero burns shall blaze high and bright. She asks for her horse, which shall follow the warrior with her. The hero's sacred honour is to be shared; her own body craves it.

The younger men erect an enormous pyre in front of the hall beside the Rhine. Women adorn it with rugs on which they scatter spices and flowers. Again, Brünnhilde is lost in contemplation of the dead man's face. Her own face gradually becomes transfigured with tenderness and she describes how his radiance shines on her like pure sunlight. He was most pure and he betrayed her; he cheated his wife but was loyal to his friend, and from his own beloved – his only love – he kept apart with his sword. No truer man than he ever swore an oath; no more loyal man than he ever made a bargain. No more honest man ever fell in love. And yet, all his oaths, all his bargains, his truest love, he betrayed as no one ever did. Do the others know why this was?

Brünnhilde calls on the solemn guardian of oaths on high to turn his glance to her welling sorrow and recognise his eternal guilt. The majestic god must hear her complaint. By the hero's bravest action, which the god desired, he was involved in the ruinous curse. She had to be betrayed by this pure one in order to become wise. Does she know now the needs of the god? Everything is known to her, everything has become clear. She can hear the flapping wings of his ravens. She sends them home with news, feared and desired.

She signals to the men to carry Siegfried's body to the pyre, and at the same time removes the ring from Siegfried's finger and gazes at it. She says that the god should be at peace now. Her legacy she has accepted for herself. Accursed ring, terrible ring! She seizes its gold and now gives it away. She thanks the wise sisters of the depths – the Rhine's swimming daughters – for their good advice. What they desire she will give them. They should claim it themselves from her ashes. The fire that burns her will cleanse the curse form the ring. Those in the water will dissolve it and carefully preserve the bright gold that was vilely stolen from them.

Brünnhilde puts on the ring, and then turns to the pyre on which Siegfried's corpse is lying. She snatches a torch from one of the men and bids the ravens to fly home! They should tell their master what they heard by the Rhine. They'll travel past Brünnhilde's rock, where the fire is still blazing. They should send Loge to Valhalla, for the end of the gods is now approaching. Thus she throws the torch at Valhalla's proud fortress.

She hurls the torch onto the pile of logs, which quickly bursts into flame. Two ravens fly up from the rock on the shore and disappear into the background.

Brünnhilde sees her horse, Grane, which two young men bring to her. She runs to him, quickly removes his bridle and speaks lovingly to him. Does he know where she will take him? His master lies there, shining in the fire – Siegfried her glorious hero. Is Grane neighing eagerly to follow his friend? Is he drawn towards him by the laughing flames? Her breast burns too. Bright fire has seized her heart. She is longing to embrace him, to be clasped by him, and united in infinite love. *Heiajoho! Grane! Greet your master. Siegfried! Siegfried! See! Blissfully, your wife greets you!*

Brünnhilde has mounted her horse and leaps, with a single bound, into the burning pyre. Immediately, the flames flare up high so that they fill the square in front of the hall, which seems to ignite as well. The men and women press to the foreground in terror.

When the whole stage appears to be filled with flames, the fire-light suddenly dies down and soon, only a cloud of smoke is left, drifting towards the back where it lies on the horizon as a bank of cloud. At the same time, the Rhine overflows its banks and floods over the fire. The three Rhinedaughters swim to the surface and appear above the pyre. Hagen who, ever since the episode with the ring, has been watching Brünnhilde's behaviour with growing concern, is seized with the greatest fear when he sees the Rhine-daughters. Quickly, he throws aside his spear, shield and helmet and rushes wildly into the water, crying 'Get back from the ring!' Woglinde and Wellgunde twine their arms around his neck and, swimming backwards, draw him into the depths.

Flosshilde, swimming in front of the others, jubilantly holds up the ring. Through the cloudbank on the horizon, a red glow breaks out with increasing brightness. By its light, the Rhine-daughters are seen happily playing with the ring and swimming in circles on the calm surface of the Rhine, which is gradually returning to its bed. From the ruins of the collapsed hall, the men and women, with great anxiety, watch the growing firelight in the heavens. When, at last, it attains maximum brightness, the hall of Valhalla is seen, with the gods and heroes assembled, just as Waltraute had described them in Act I. Bright flames set alight the hall of the gods. When the gods are completely hidden by the flames, the curtain falls.

THEMATIC EXAMPLES FROM

The Ring

———————◆———————

Many books have been written about the musical fabric of *Der Ring des Nibelungen*, and no over-view would be complete without some musical examples. However, the following is not intended as a comprehensive guide to leitmotifs and their relationships. Such guides are readily available elsewhere. Rather, it illustrates some of the characteristic themes of the work.

With a few exceptions, Wagner never gave his themes names, nor did he attempt to produce a thematic road map for the *Ring* traveller. Indeed, it is hardly practicable, during the course of a performance, to try to pick out and name various motifs as they appear, evolve and disappear in the musical stream. We register them intuitively and absorb them instinctively. Music, after all, speaks chiefly to our emotions. As Wagner himself wrote: 'The artist addresses himself to Feeling, and not to Understanding. If he is answered in terms of Understanding, then it is quite clear that he has not been understood.'

Wagner was one of the great masters of melody. He regarded himself (with justification) as the most significant melodist since Mozart, and he never ceased to admire the melodic genius of Bellini. It was in his 1837 essay, *Bellini*, that he made the famous appeal to his countrymen: 'song, song, and yet again song, you Germans!'

All of the constituent operas of *The Ring* contain wonderful examples of Wagner the melodist. Some are just a few notes long, while others are extended phrases. Some take the form of elaborate melodic figurations, expressive of the natural world. As *The Ring* narrative unfolds, and actions, thoughts and feelings begin to impinge upon one another, so the themes also interact. By the time we reach *Götterdämmerung*, the extraordinarily complex and compressed musical texture is used to convey interlocking relationships, motivations and recollections with great dramatic force. But even then, at the heart of it all, is melody.

Many of the seminal melodic themes are to be found, appropriately enough, in *Das Rheingold*.

Example 1 Nature, growing from the single 'cell' with which the Prelude begins.

Example 2 The same melody after acquiring figurations that suggest the flowing waters of the Rhine.

Example 3 The carefree lullaby of the Rhinedaughters

Example 4 The glowing Rhinegold.

Example 5 The Rhinedaughters' simple delight in the gold.

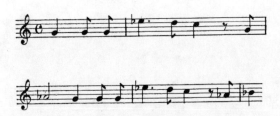

Example 6 The foreswearing of love.

Example 7 Valhalla

Example 8 The Tarnhelm.

Example 9 Alberich's curse.

Example 10 The melody associated with Erda.

Example 11 The sword.

In *Die Walküre*, key melodic themes include:

Example *12* The tragic Siegmund.

Example *13* Sieglinde's pity.

Example *14* The sadness of the Volsungs.

Example *15* The Volsung race.

Example *16* Siegmund's Spring song.

Example 17 The Valkyries.

Example 18 Annunciation of Siegmund's death (latter part).

Example 19 Annunciation of Siegfried's birth.

Example 20 Glorification of Brünnhilde.

Example 21 Slumber.

In *Siegfried*, notable melodic themes include:

Example 22   Scheming (especially associated with Mime).

Example 23   Siegfried's horn-call.

Example 24   Mime's whining 'Starling' song.

Example 25   The Wanderer.

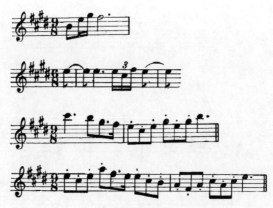

Example 26   The Woodbird (four aspects).

Example 27 Getting of wisdom.

Example 28 Brünnhilde and Siegfried's love (joy).

Example 29 Peace.

Example 30 Brünnhilde and Siegfried's love (ecstasy).

Melodic themes in *Götterdämmerung* include:

Example 31 Brünnhilde.

Example 32 Hagen.

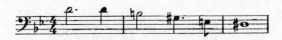

Example 33 Atonement.

Example 34 Rhinedaughters warning Siegfried.

Themes that are descriptive or dramatic rather than melodic.

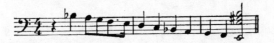

Example 35 Authority, spear, agreement.

Example 36 Giants.

Example 37 Loge, fire, trickery.

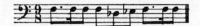

Example 38 Smithying.

Example 39 Dragon.

Example 40 Storm.

Example 41 Hunding.

Example 42 Forest murmurs.

Example 43 Weaving of fate, Norns.

Example 44 Draught of forgetfulness.

Example 45 Funeral music.

Examples of compound melodic themes from *Götterdämmerung.*

Example 46 The ring, Alberich's destructive ambition and Hagen, compressed
into a single phrase (Act I, transition Scenes 2–3).

Example 47 The sword, agreement and Hagen (Act I, end of Scene 3).

FURTHER READING

This list is intended for the reader who would like to identify general material on Wagner and The Ring which is likely to be available in book shops and libraries. Many of these books contain detailed bibliographies from which particular forays may be made into the enormous resources of Wagner scholarship.

Barth, H., Mack, D. and Voss, E. (eds) *Wagner, A Documentary Study*, Thames and Hudson, 1975.

Cooke, D., *I Saw the World End*, Oxford, 1997.

Cord, W.O., *An Introduction to Richard Wagner's Der Ring des Nibelungen*, Ohio University Press, 1995.

Culshaw, J., *Reflections on Wagner's Ring*, Secker and Warburg, 1976.

Darcy, W., *Wagner's 'Das Rheingold'*, Clarendon Press, Oxford, 1993.

Donnington, R., *Wagner's 'Ring' and its Symbols*, Faber and Faber, 1963.

Evans, M., *Wagner and Aeschylus, The Ring and the Oresteia*, Faber and Faber, 1982.

Fricke, R., *Wagner in Rehearsal 1875–1876. The Diaries of Richard Fricke*, trans. George Fricke, Pendragon Press, 1998.

Gutman, R., *Richard Wagner, The Man, His Mind and His Music*, Secker and Warburg, 1968.

Magee, B., *Aspects of Wagner*, Oxford, 1988.

Magee, B. *Wagner and Philosophy*, Penguin Press, London, 2000. Published in the USA as *The Tristan Chord*, Metropolitan Books, New York, 2001.

Millington, B. ed. *The Wagner Compendium*, Thames and Hudson, 1992.

Newman, E., *The Life of Richard Wagner*, 4 Vols. London 1933–1947.

Newman, E., *Wagner as Man and Artist*, London 1914,

Newman, E., *Wagner Nights*, Putnam 1949.

Sabor, R., *The Real Wagner*, Andre Deutsch, 1987.

Sabor, R., *Richard Wagner 'Der Ring des Nibelungen'* and separate volumes on each of the four dramas, Phaidon, 1997.

Spencer, S. and Millington, B. (eds and trans.) *Selected Letters of Richard Wagner*, London, 1987.

Spotts, F., *Bayreuth, A History of the Wagner Festival*, Yale, 1994.

Tanner, M. *Wagner*, Flamingo, 1997.

Taylor, R., *Richard Wagner, His Life, Art and Thought*, Paul Elek, London, 1979.

Wagner, Cosima: *The Diaries 1869–1883*, 2 Vols. ed. M.Gregor-Dellin and D. Mack (Munich 1976-7); Eng. trans. G. Skelton, New York 1978–80.

Wagner, Richard, *My Life*, ed. M. Gregor-Dellin (Munich) trans. A. Gray, ed. M. Whittall, Cambridge, 1983.

INDEX

Wakefield Press is an independent publishing and
distribution company based in Adelaide, South Australia.
We love good stories and publish beautiful books.
To see our full range of titles, please visit our website at
www.wakefieldpress.com.au.

Wakefield Press thanks Fox Creek Wines
and Arts South Australia for their support.